Women in Academia:
Gender and Academic Freedom in Africa

Women in Academia:
Gender and Academic Freedom in Africa

Edited by Ebrima Sall

The State of Academic Freedom in Africa Series

COUNCIL FOR THE DEVELOPMENT OF SOCIAL SCIENCE RESEARCH IN AFRICA

Women in Academia: Gender and Academic Freedom in Africa

First published in 2000 by CODESRIA
© Council for the Development of Social Science Research in Africa 2000
Avenue Cheikh Anta Diop Angle Canal IV BP 3304, Dakar, Senegal

ISBN 2-86978-078-8
Cover : detail of a painting by Ousmane Dago
Production consultant: Lliane Phillips
Distributor: CODESRIA and African Books Collective, 27 Park End Street
Oxford OX1 1HU, UK
Printed by Russell Press, Nottingham, UK.

CODESRIA would like to express its gratitude to the Swedish Agency for
International Development Cooperation Agency (SIDA/SAREC), the Interna-
tional Development Research Centre (IDRC), the Ford Foundation, the
MacArthur Foundation, the Carnegie Corporation, the Norwegian Ministry of
Foreign Affairs, the Danish Agency for International Development (DANI-
DA) the French Ministry of Cooperation, the United Nations Development
Programme (UNDP), the Netherlands Ministry of Foreign Affairs, the Rocke-
feller Foundation, and the Government of Senegal for their support of its
research, training and publications programmes.

Contents

Notes on Contributors

Mohamadou Abdoul is a Mauritanian researcher. He holds a doctorate in history and is currently project coordinator for an NGO based in Dakar, Senegal. His areas of research cover questions on politics, urbanity and the media in contemporary Africa.

Olutoyin Mejiuni Fashina, PhD, is Lecturer in the Department of Continuing Education, Obafemi Awolowo University, Ile-Ife, Nigeria. She has been involved with research on Women's education, mass media and training and development opportunities for workers. She is co-founder of an NGO in Nigeria working towards ways of assisting sexually abused children and women.

Penda Mbow teaches History at the Université Cheikh Anta Diop, Dakar, Senegal. She is an activist on women's rights issues in Senegal and its relation to Islamic studies.

Joe Oloka-Onyango is a Senior Lecturer, Faculty of Law at Makerere University, and a Senior Research Fellow of the Centre for Basic Research (CBR) in Kampala. He has taught at a variety of institutions in the United States including the Universities of Florida, Minnesota and Harvard Law School. He has published extensively in journals as varied as *Human Rights Quarterly, Africa Development*, and the *California Western International Law Journal*. He is the associate editor of the *East African Journal of Peace and Human Rights*.

Norbert Ouendji is a journalist and correspondent for the independent Camerounian weekly *Le Messager*.

Isabel Apawo Phiri is Senior Lecturer in the department of Theology and Religious Studies, Chancellor College, University of Malawi. She is based at Department of Theology and Religion, University of Namibia.

Ebrima Sall coordinates the Academic Freedom and Child and Youth Studies Programmes for CODESRIA. He holds a PhD in sociology from the University of Paris I, Sorbonne France.

Helmi Sharawy is the Director of the Arab Research Centre in Cairo, Egypt. He was former president of the African Association of Political Science (AAPS).

Sylvia Tamale holds law degrees from Makerere University and Harvard Law School and is a Lecturer-in-Law at Makerere. Currently pursuing PhD studies in Sociology and Feminist Studies at the University of Minnesota, her most recent publications cover the areas of gender and the law, women in politics and race relations.

Saida Yahya-Othman teaches in the Department of Foreign Languages and Linguistics at the University of Dar es Salaam. She is presently the Associate Dean (academic) in the Faculty of Arts and Social Sciences. Her research interests include language politics, critical discourse analysis, particularly questions of language and power, pragmatics (including the relationship between language and gender), and the mainstreaming of gender in academic institutions. She has published on language policies in Tanzania, and Kiswahili pragmatics.

Introduction: Engendering Academic Freedom in Africa

Ebrima Sall

The first volume of *The State of Academic Freedom in Africa* series was published in 1996. As the inaugural volume, it presented an overview of the situation in Africa. The twelve chapters in that volume present country case studies and a discussion on the legal framework for the actual defence of academic freedom in Africa. With this book, we begin a series of thematic and sectoral studies that are meant to highlight specific aspects of academic life and issues related to academic freedom, human rights, and intellectual citizenship.

The main purposes of publishing these reports and books are to contribute to our understanding of changes in the research environment, itself dependent on the broad socio-political, economic and cultural environments, and to deepen our understanding of the complexities not only of intellectual freedom, but also of the general struggles for democracy and citizenship of a new type. Understanding the ways in which the gender relations in our societies and the gendered nature of academia impact on the freedom of academics, particularly female academics, as well as on the freedom and autonomy of academia itself appeared to us to be a good starting point for a series of thematic volumes.

The struggle for academic freedom is in many ways a struggle for 'citizenship' involving members of the academic community (particularly young scholars, students, women, junior faculty, adjunct professors, academics from ethnic, religious and other kinds of minorities, etc.), individually and collectively, engaged in the struggle for rights and democracy within the academy as well as in the broad polities within which the academy is located. This struggle could actually involve academics at any level of the teaching or administrative hierarchy, given that restrictions to academic freedom are quite often based on ideological, political or other grounds. It is also the struggle of the academic community as a whole for freedom and for the autonomy of its institutions (Diouf & Mamdani 1994; Busia 1996; Jega 1994; Okoye & Yau 1999).

These struggles are part and parcel of the much broader struggles for human rights, freedom and democracy. Indeed, as noted by Mkandawire in the preface to the first volume in this series, the academy is one among the many sites of the struggle for democracy (Mkandawire 1996). However, like other sites and social locations, the academy is also traversed by contradictions of a class, gender, ideological and other nature. Virtually every kind of contradiction that exists in our societies finds its expression within the academy as well. The papers presented in this volume show the extent to which the struggle for the freedom to study, teach, research or otherwise work in academia is as much a struggle taking place within academia itself, as it is a struggle against various kinds of forces located outside of academia.

At the Kampala Symposium on Intellectual Freedom and Social Responsibility, four key categories of actors were identified as those whose actions may expand or restrict academic freedom: the state, civil society, donors and the academics themselves. None of these categories of actors is characterised by a single, or a coherent, clear-cut, once-and-for-all strategy or approach to academia. On the contrary, each has multiple ways of relating with the academy, or with some of its constituents, based on a variety of factors ranging from structural factors (such as the division of labour), to the attitudes of the other actors such as the Sate and civil society, and their relations with the same academy.

Besides these four, clearly identifiable actors there are structures and major global processes that also have a tremendous impact on the freedom of research. Gender is one of these determinants of social relations within the academy, although gender relations are also over-determined by other factors. Discrimination exists between male and female teachers and students. Gender is also a factor in the relations between female students and male teachers, between the university administration and female teachers and students, and in the relations that the latter have with, and in how government officials perceive them, and civil society. So is it in the nature of school and university curricula, career prospects and the general academic environment.

What is true of gender relations is also true of class and other kinds of social relations. Both have an impact on current and former members, or 'would be' members of the academic community, i.e. those confronted with the very problem of access to the academy, to start with.

Access

Access to higher education institutions is still a major issue for an extremely large number of people in Africa and elsewhere. For women, it is a particularly critical issue. Apart from the institutions that are reserved specifically for women (such as Ahfad University, Sudan), the latter are still a minority in higher education institutions in Africa, both as students and as faculty. Women are also under-represented in the upper echelons of the academic hierarchy (senior lecturers, professors), and in senior administrative positions within the academy (deans, heads of department, vice-chancellors). This has already been noted in some of the contributions in Volume One of the State of Academic Freedom in Africa. A UNESCO/BREDA publication focusing on women in higher education in Africa puts the issue in the following words:

Women are, as a general rule, under-represented in higher education (as

students, teachers, researchers, senior level administrators, and managers).
This under-representation is seen as a reflection of the marginalisation of
women and girls at other levels and forms of education (UNESCO/BREDA
1995:vi).
The under-representation of women in higher education and research is well
illustrated in some of the studies in this volume. In the chapter on Tanzania,
Yahya-Othman[1] shows how the problems of access to tertiary institutions and
other gender related restrictions to academic freedom are actually rooted in the
lower levels of the schooling system. This means that the real issue is not only
one of access per se. Access theory generally focuses on the how, why or why
not of access to institutions whose lack of 'neutrality' (e.g. gender neutrality)
is significant to the extent that it makes access difficult or easy:
Access consists of actions about eligibility, priority and administrative
encounters, how these are handled, how they are avoided, what it means
from the point of view of applicants, or organisational connection, and what
it means from the point of view of institutional performance, and of action
through institutional levels (Schaffer, 1975:13).[2]
Although the discussion from which the above citation was taken was on public administration, it does have some general relevance. As has been argued by
Ken Post (1989:4), 'access, thus, is [also] the question of what social classes
or other social groups – are able to find a direct voice in the policy process'
(Post 1989:4;).[3]
'Access' is defined by some as the 'freedom or ability to obtain or make use
of' (Merriam-Webster 1993—cited in Ribot 1998:310). 'The term access is
closely related to the term property, which MacPherson (1978:3) characterises
as a 'right in the sense of an enforceable claim to some use or benefit of something' (Ribot 1998:310). As has been rightly pointed out by Ribot (1998: 310),
having a right to something does not necessarily imply having the ability to
actually 'obtain or make use of it:
'The term 'right' implies an acknowledged claim that society supports
(whether through law, custom or convention) (...) right is a prescriptive concept. Ability is a descriptive term. Property is de jure. Access includes the de
jure and the de facto or extra-legal. Extra-legal mechanisms, structures and
relations governing resource use (or institutions) include: social identity (or
status, based on gender, age or nobility; see Berry 1993); social relations (as in
friendship, family, lineage, historical ties among individuals and groups, often
based on social identity; coercion and trickery (i.e. misinformation, threats of
violence¹); material wealth; or physical circumstance (e.g. location). Access is
not just gained via singular legal or extra-legal mechanisms. Powerful actors
harness multiple mechanisms to produce structural complementarities that are
also part of the ability to benefit...' (Ribot 1998: 310-311).

This has important policy implications. Institutional reform in such a perspective cannot therefore be seen solely in terms of ways of facilitating access for relatively 'marginalised' groups or, conversely, restricting access for certain categories of people. Often, the assumption is that the playing field is even or 'levelled', and all players have equal opportunities once they enter the field. The problem, though, is that, as has already been noted, the field is uneven. There is, of course, a link between the nature of the field and the easiness or difficulty with which it can be accessed. For instance, where the 'equitable chances of success' for girls and women (UNESCO/BREDA 1995), do not exist – and they rarely do – efforts, like most current efforts at increasing the participation of women in higher education, are geared towards increasing both access and chances of success for women. The unevenness of the playing field, however, needs to be addressed as an issue in itself, which may well mean having to question the very institutions of access as well as the whole political economy governing access. 'An access analysis is empirical: it is concerned with who has the 'ability to obtain or make use of' benefits [in this case from higher education and research]. It does not presume any set of rights, structures, processes, and so forth, that confer this ability; instead it derives them from observed practice' (Ribot 1998: 312).

The whole human rights ethos of our age makes 'access' to education, including higher education, and research a right—which it is. 'Access' to educational institutions is, indeed, a right. Feminist, democratic and human rights struggles have led to the recognition of this right to education. Yet, there is a need for specific human rights instruments to facilitate the elimination of all obstacles to the freedom of research and specific measures to facilitate the participation of women in higher education. However, as the chapters in this volume show, there is also a need for us to go beyond access and question the class, gender and other kinds of dynamics in academia.

A Paradigm Shift

This volume on *'Women in Academia'* is coming out in a post-Beijing era.[4] Hence it is far from being a manifestation of a return to the 'women-in-something' or 'women-and-something' paradigms (Bruyn 1995:12; Imam & Mama 1993). For CODESRIA, women's studies are seen as an important subject area needing to be institutionalised and 'mainstreamed' (Mama 1996, Nzomo 1998). Yet the emphasis is on 'gender', rather than on women per se. That is the emphasis is less on the biological attributes than on the social character of manhood and womanhood, the production of each of which goes on in the context of the social relations between the two genres. As has been rightly pointed out by Maria de Bruyn: 'the term "gender" can be defined as socially-ascribed meanings given to the categories man and woman' (Bruyn 1995: 12).

'Gender connotes the social and historical constructions of masculine and feminine roles, behaviours, attributes, ideologies, etc. which refer to some notion of biological sex' (Imam 1997:2). 'Engendering African social sciences', as Imam rightly points out:

... is not a simple development of knowledge, but is also necessarily and simultaneously profoundly a political struggle over power and resources. This is not unique to gender analysis. Every theoretical and methodological framework of knowledge production has implicit values and assumptions about the nature of society and will be resisted by those who do not have the same position (Imam 1997:2; also see Imam & Mama 1994).

Gender struggles are therefore not only about access or about 'mainstreaming' gender (in education, development, etc.), but also about engendering whole socio-political and economic processes and institutions, i.e. about 'changing the course of the stream' as well:

The concept of mainstreaming women's issues in development planning has been around since the 1980s. The key questions, though, are who is to be brought into whose mainstream, why, and in what ways should the mainstream be modified by this process? Most analyses of gender and development focus on the fact that the mainstream is controlled by men, not that is unfair both because it affects women and because women's contributions to the mainstream are under-recognised. Women should therefore be brought into the mainstream both because this would be fair (equity) and because development will be helped as a result (efficiency). Far less attention is paid to the ways in which this male-dominated mainstream ought to be changed by the processes of promoting greater gender equity in development (Thin 1995: 29).

It is important for women to have the opportunities and the possibilities, and to actually be university students, teachers, researchers and administrators. It is equally important for the academic institutions, the laws governing the latter, course contents, career prospects, relations between academics and between the latter and the state, civil society and donors become as 'gender-neutral' as possible. In the patriarchal societies where the African academic institutions are located, that would however take quite a struggle to achieve; but it is precisely that struggle that the feminist movement, as well as the rights and democracy movements in general are all involved in. That struggle is also at the heart of CODESRIA's efforts to 'engender' the social sciences (*CODESRIA Bulletin* 1991; Imam & Mama 1994; Mama 1997; Imam, Mama & Sow 1997; Hamza & Sall 1997).

CODESRIA's attempts to promote gender sensitive social science research and research outputs date back to the very early years of the Council. For some time, the 'women and...' and 'women in...' approaches were predominant among researchers in CODESRIA networks, as they were predominant within the UN system and elsewhere. In 1991, participants in an international workshop organised by CODESRIA decided to move away from such approaches towards a more scientifically pertinent and politically acceptable one: that of engendering the social sciences. This means considering social processes (which include development processes) as gendered processes involving men and women whose relations may or may not be relations of equality but are definitely both a product of, and a factor in these processes. Hence the idea of 'engendering development', 'engendering democracy'[5] engendering the CODESRIA work environment itself, and so forth (*CODESRIA Bulletin* 1991; Imam & Mama 1994; Philips 1991; Mama 1997; Imam, Mama & Sow, 1997; Hamza & Sall 1997). This was a major paradigm shift which certain feminist movements and gender aware scholars had already carried out, but which the 1991 CODESRIA Symposium brought out to the open.[6]

The launching of the CODESRIA Gender Institute in 1994 and a Gender Task Force set up by the CODESRIA Executive Committee in 1996 were other milestones in this process. Important as these efforts were, the Gender Task Force felt that a lot more could be done to increase the participation of women in the research networks and in other CODESRIA activities. There are still relatively few women co-ordinators of National and Multinational Working Groups, or Directors of the Governance Institute (which still attracts more male scholars than female scholars), and so forth. Outputs (publications) need to reflect an increase in the participation of women in the networks and, generally speaking, greater gender sensitivity particularly among male scholars and in male-authored papers. Similarly, it was recommended that effort be made to increase the participation of women and gender sensitivity in the governing bodies of CODESRIA (General Assembly and Executive Committee) and at senior levels in the staffing of the Secretariat.

Our Own Instruments of Struggle

In their contribution to this volume, Onyango and Tamale draw our attention to our very instruments of governance and of struggle for academic freedom, rights and democracy. They show how the Kampala and Dar Es Salaam Declarations on Intellectual Freedom, which were intended to be the 'standard-bearers' of the African academic community, need to reflect greater gender sensitivity! This actually echoes what feminist critiques of human rights instruments have been saying.[7] The participation of women in the drafting of declarations, charters, treaties, laws and decrees would certainly help in raising the level of gender sensitivity of these documents. So is it at the level of actual implementation.

The mandate of the CODESRIA Gender Task Force was to advise on ways of moving on with the 'total' engendering of society and its institutions, and of our ways of looking at social processes.[8] The Task Force, not surprisingly, advised on how to engender the social sciences in Africa, specifically CODESRIA activities, as well as the CODESRIA governing bodies and work environment. The issue is however not simply one of 'political' will, or rather, the lack of it. As mentioned above, CODESRIA's Governance Institute still attracts more male scholars than female scholars, whereas the situation is the exact opposite with the Gender Institute. Of course, it would be quite absurd for anyone to talk about 'male' or 'female' research or discussion themes, etc. There are historical and sociological explanations for these tendencies, which exist at various levels of the academy (choice of disciplines and courses, etc), as shown in the chapters in this volume. For instance, in her contribution on female academics in Nigeria (chapter 7), Olutoyin Meijiuni Fashina shows how research on women is not considered as 'serious' research. She cites the case of a 'concerned' male scholar advising a female colleague of his who had just 'been promoted to a senior lecturership based on the researches she carried out mainly on women's issues now to work hard at 'more serious issues and forget about all those things about women', for her subsequent promotions'. Women's studies and gender studies are also too often seen as areas for female scholars only. The relatively few male scholars who specialise in gender issues run the risk of not being taken seriously by their colleagues.[9]

The CODESRIA Task Force did show that there are ways of impacting on the trends, some form of 'affirmative action' being just one of them although, as some have rightly pointed out, one of the problems with affirmative action is that it rarely questions the instruments of access.

The Chapters

In the first chapter, Tamale and Oloka-Onyango present an overview of the situation of women in academia, and the issues involved in the intellectual struggle to attain gender parity.[10] Women academics carry a dual burden: in addition to their academic pursuits, they also have to meet traditional obligations, such as 'childbearing and rearing, cooking, domestic household chores or their supervision'. Supportive male partners are hard to come by. Society's responses to cases of sexual abuse involving female academics sometimes consist of blaming the victims. The crimes therefore remain unpunished.[11] Both feminist theory, largely of western origins, and the instruments (such as the Kampala and Dar Es Salaam Declarations) being used in the struggle for academic freedom are subjected to a critical analysis. The authors call for 'a comprehensive, all-embracing gender-sensitive normative framework in which concerns of gender and academic freedom are clearly spelt out'. In addition to appropriate legal instruments, there is a need for an all-round, all-embracing democratisation of society, right down to the level of the family.

Yahya-Othman in her chapter on Tanzania also emphasises the need to link the struggles for academic freedom and gender equality to the struggles for democracy and the respect of human rights and the rights of the people.[12] She shows how student politics have evolved from being progressive and socially conscious in the sixties and seventies, to being petty bourgeois today. Once the formidable problems of access to higher education have been overcome, the biggest threats to the female student's freedom on campus come from male students. Student tabloids, for instance, have been among the most disrespectful of the liberty of female students and teachers. Yahya-Othman point is even better illustrated by the proliferation of campus cults in universities in Africa today. These cults have seriously restricted academic freedom and have also promoted, through their ideologies, a celebration of masculinity in ways that degrade women. However, the root causes of gender and class limitations to academic freedom, specifically the freedom of female academics, she argues, are in the broader society and its institutions. The implementation of structural adjustment policies and growing 'commoditization' has contributed to making matters worse.

Isabel Apawo Phiri discusses her personal experience of harassment from groups of students for having simply presented a paper titled, precisely, 'Violence against women in educational institutions: the case of sexual harassment and rape on Chancellor College campus'.[13] The paper was presented at a Conference on University Research and Development, held in Malawi, her home country. The reaction of the authorities (including at the highest level, the President of Malawi) was however quite encouraging.

In her chapter on Senegal, Mbow also recounts a personal experience that is somewhat similar to that of Apawo-Phiri.[14] In her case, discussing HIV and AIDS at a conference and daring to challenge certain religious-based practices (such as temporary marriages) made her the subject of attacks from some extremist religious groups. Here too, the responses of the authorities were quite encouraging. Mbow also discusses the almost total absence of women's studies from the curriculum of the University (in this case Cheikh Anta Diop University of Dakar). This is an issue that Mama also discusses at length in her state of the art review of women's studies and studies of women in Africa (Mama 1996; also see Mama 1997).

Helmi Sharawy examines the 'Social Dimensions of Intellectual and Academic Freedom in Egypt', where the religious factor is also extremely important. Sharawy shows how complex the situation is.[15] For instance, one of the key institutions playing a major role in regulating the space for intellectual freedom is, precisely, an academic institution, and one of the oldest in the world, for that matter: Al Azhar University, Cairo.

In chapter six, Abdoul discusses the crises of the university in Mauritania, as well as the struggles of academics and the media to overcome the crises of intellectual freedom and expand the space for democracy.[16]

Fashina's contribution to this volume is of a slightly different nature, compared to the other chapters.[17] Discussing the situation of academics and female academics in Nigeria, she emphasises the importance of the perceptions that academics have of their own situation and struggles, and highlights the views of both male and female academics on academic freedom. According to her, many female academics attach equal importance to being successful academics, and to 'being able to have a baby and taking good care of it'. Fashina also pinpoints one of the key issues that are at the heart of the problematic of gender and academic freedom, and that is how gender issues themselves are seen as issues that are not issues for 'serious' research.

In the final chapter on Cameroon, Norbert Ouendji discusses the racketeering going on in academia – women academics, especially the female students, being among the principal victims – as well as what he calls 'ethnic demands' on the university.[18] Ouendji also examines the situation of women writers, who have to find time to write while having to 'spend a great deal of time caring for others'.

In short, changes within our societies are already showing how subtle some of the issues connected with gender and academic freedom have become. This volume helps in bringing out some of the key issues in the struggle for academic freedom and gender equity in academia, and in the society.

References

African Rights 1994, Crimes Without Punishment: Sexual Harassment and Violence Against female students in Schools and Universities in Africa. London: African Rights (Discussion paper No 4; July).

Berry, S. 1993, *No Condition is Permanent: The Social Dynamics of Agrarian Change in Sub-Saharan Africa.* Madison, University of Wisconsin Press.

Bruyn, Maria de 1995, 'A Gender-based Approach to Advancing Women's Social Status and Position'. In KIT, *Advancing Women's Status: Women, Society & Development. Women and Men Together?* Amsterdam, KIT: 11-22.

Busia, N. 1996, 'Towards a Legal Framework for the Protection of Academic Freedom. Perspectives of the African Human Rights System'. In CODESRIA, *The State of Academic Freedom in Africa* 1995: 13-44.

CODESRIA Bulletin 1991, Special Issue on: 'Engendering Social Science', Report of an International Workshop organised by CODESRIA.

CODESRIA 1996, *The State of Academic Freedom in Africa* 1995. Dakar: CODESRIA.

Ibrahim, J. 1991, L'acces a l'Etat: classes sociales, elites, factions; une etude du 'National Party of Nigeria'. Unpublished PhD Dissertation, Bordeaux: Institut d'Etudes Politiques, Universite de Bordeaux I.

Jega, A. 1994, *Nigerian Academics under Military Rule*: Stockholm, University of Stockholm, Department of Political Science, Report no 3: 1994:3

Diouf, M. & Mamdani, M.(eds.), 1994, *Academic Freedom in Africa*. Dakar: CODESRIA

Mkandawire, T. 1996, 'Preface', in CODESRIA, *The State of Academic Freedom in Africa* 1995.

Mkandawire, T. 1997, 'The Social Sciences in Africa: Breaking Local Barriers and Negotiating International Presence. The Bashorun M.K.O. Abiola Distinguished Lecture Presented to the 1996 African Studies Association Annual Meeting'. In *African Studies Review*, Vol. 40, No.2 (Sept. 1997): 15-36.

Imam, A. 1997, 'Engendering Social Sciences: An Introductory Note'; in Imam, Mama & Sow (eds.), *Engendering African Social Sciences*; Dakar: CODESRIA.

Imam, A. & Mama, A. 1994, 'The Role of Academic in Expanding and Limiting Academic Freedom'; in Diouf & Mamdani, M., *Academic Freedom in Africa*; Dakar: CODESRIA

Imam, A., Mama, A. & Sow, F. 1997, *Engendering African Social Sciences*. Dakar: CODESRIA.

MacPherson, C.B. (ed.) 1978, *Property: Mainstream and Critical Positions*. Toronto: University of Toronto Press.

Mama, A. 1996, Women's Studies and the Studies of Women in Africa during the 1990s. Dakar: CODESRIA (Working paper Series 5/96).

Mama, A. 1997, 'Postscript: Moving from Analysis to Practice?' in Imam, Mama & Sow, *Engendering African Social Sciences*. Dakar, CODESRIA.

Nzomo, M. 1998, 'Gender Studies'; paper for CODESRIA-Graduate School of Humanities (University of Witswatersrand)-HSRC symposium on Globalisation and the Social Sciences in Africa; Johannesburg, September.

Okoye, F. & Yau, Y.Z. 1999, *Years of Darkness: Academic Freedom in Nigeria 1993-1998.* Kaduna, Human Rights Monitor.

Philips, A. *Engendering Democracy*; Cambridge: Polity Press & Pittsburgh: Pennsylvania State University Press.

Ribot, J. 1998, 'Theorizing Access: Forest Profits along Senegal's Charcoal Commodity Chain'; in *Development and Change* Vol. 29 (1998), 307-341

Royal Tropical Institute (KIT) 1995, *Advancing Women's Status: Women, Society &*

Development. Women and Men Together? Amsterdam, KIT, Critical Reviews and Annotated Bibliographies Series.

Thin, N. 1995, 'A Critical Review of Women's Status and Rights'; in KIT, *Advancing Women's Status: Women, Society & Development. Women and Men Together?* Amsterdam, KIT.

UNESCO/BREDA 1995, *Women in Higher Education in Africa.* Dakar: UNESCO/BREDA

Notes

1. Yahya-Othman, S., 'Tanzania: Engendering Academic Freedom' (pp. 24-46)
2. Cited in Ibrahim 1991:43. See Ibrahim's review of some of the literature on access, in Ibrahim 1991:41-49.
3. Cited in Ibrahim 1991: 44.
4. The World Conference on Women was held in Beijing in September 1995.
5. For a good essay on the gendered nature of politics, democracy, the demarcation between 'public' and 'private' spheres, etc, see Ann Philips book: *Engendering Democracy;* 1991.
6. I am grateful to Dr. Maria Nzomo for drawing my attention to the fact that the paradigm shift might have actually predated the 1991 symposium, given that some feminist movements had already begun to call for the engendering of democracy well before 1991.
7. The Universal Declaration of Human Rights has itself been critiqued from this point of view, and some feminist movements have actually proposed gender-sensitive, re-written versions of the Universal Declaration.
8. At the 9th General Assembly of CODESRIA (held in Dakar on 14-18 December 1998), it was recommended that the Gender Task Force be upgraded into a standing sub-committee of the Executive Committee.
9. At a meeting of the CODESRIA Gender Task Force in 1997, some task force members cited cases of male scholars in gender studies being asked whether it was because they had lost their 'manhood' that they chose to be in that field.
10. '"Bitches" at the Academy : Gender and Academic Freedom in Africa' (pp. 1-23).
11. See African Rights, 1994: Crimes Without Punishment: Sexual Harassment and Violence Against Female Students in Schools and Universities in Africa, Discussion Paper No. 4, July.
12. Yahya-Othman: 'Tanzania: Engendering Academic Freedom'; (pp. 24-46).
13. Apawo Phiri, I., 'Gender and Academic Freedom in Malawi' (pp. 47-62).
14. Mbow, P..: 'Academic Freedom and the Gender Issue: A Report From Senegal' (pp64-78).
15. Sharawy, H. : 'Social Dimensions of Intellectual and Academic Freedom in Egypt' (pp. 79-104).
16. Abdoul, M. : 'The Challenges of Scientific Research in Mauritania' (pp. 105-120).
17. Fashina, O.M. : ' Academic Freedom and Female Academics in Nigeria' (pp. 121-127)
18. Ouendji, N. : 'Academic Freedom and the Position of Women in Cameroon' (pp.154)

1. 'Bitches' at the Academy: Gender and Academic Freedom in Africa

Sylvia Tamale and J. Oloka-Onyango

Who Are These "Bitches"?

The title of this chapter is derived from an anonymous letter to one of the authors. Addressed to: 'You Bitch!', and castigating her for being a bad role model, the letter was clearly a response to several recent critiques of gender-insensitive articles in the local media: 'We don't need your views in the press or on the (sic!) radio,' the nameless author wrote. The letter demanded that the author 'keep whatever nonsense you have in your head to yourself.' Such a dispatch reflects the stark reality of gender struggles that continue to pervade the intellectual arena, even in a relatively gender-progressive society, such as Uganda has recently become (Boyd, 1991; Harries, 1994; Tamale, 1996). Although the language of the protagonists within the staid walls of academia may be somewhat more civil, the antagonism towards issues relating to gender parity and feminism still abounds.

Feminism, women-sensitive agendas and the struggle for gender-equality continue to meet a great deal of resistance and resentment from both within and outside academic life.[1] It is reflected in issues as specific as the choice and structure of a particular curriculum (Phiri, 1994),[2] in the underfunding of gender-related research (Imam and Mama, 1994; Iweriebor, 1990) and in the issue of affirmative action in faculty hiring (Mbilinyi and Mbughuni, 1991). It extends to the question of academic promotions and the overall administration of the university (Hamad, 1995: 77). In an institution traditionally led and controlled by men — as academic life has and continues to be — it is of little surprise that such matters remain of paramount importance. Indeed, when combined with the globalized crisis presently afflicting African universities,[3] it is clear that the situation can only get worse. The strictures also relate to what can and cannot be said about gender relations, the place of women and men in the articulation of these viewpoints, and the response of both academia and society at large to the intellectual struggle to attain gender parity. By prefacing the discussion of the topic in this fashion, we seek to illustrate the problems of theory and praxis involved in dealing with the issue of gender and academic freedom in the contemporary African university.[4]

As a topic of intellectual discourse, the subject of academic freedom in Africa has attracted much recent attention (cf. Diouf and Mamdani, 1994). However, few examinations of this important subject have incorporated a gender analysis of the phenomenon (Sow, 1994: 6).[5] A critical investigation of gender and academic freedom will reveal the relations of power, resources and personalities among men and women at the academy: To what extent can women freely exercise their academic skills in a context that emerges from sociocultural, political and religious systems which shape gender roles that subordinate women to men? How can women be deemed really free actors when academic life is itself riddled with prejudices that derive from the exercise of power in an institution that is traditionally authoritarian and isolationist?[6] Finally, have African academics moved out of the shadow of the colonial influences of their formative years – influences that have dictated a divorce between academic life and society, between politics and practice, between theory and praxis? Many of the answers to these questions will illustrate the extent to which progress in the area is real or ephemeral.

We likewise need to be cautious about uncritically projecting the concept of gender, which has mainly developed in Western feminist theory, onto African culture and politics. This is because the nuances of gender relations manifest variable factors in different societies, informing gender discourse in distinct contexts. In particular, the dialectic relationship between gender, class, colonialism and decolonization is pertinent for an analysis of gender in the African context (Okeyo, 1981; AAWORD, 1982). While the university, as we know it, is a product of Western educational and institutional developments, its transplantation to the African context — as with the English Common Law — has produced an amalgam of the specific sociocultural conditions into which it was transplanted and the colonial dictates by which the system was informed. As we have stated elsewhere, in discerning to what extent the 'personal' constitutes the 'political' in an analysis of the question of gender, it is essential to always remember that, 'what in Africa appears to be a local political act is compounded by the frustrations and tensions set in motion by global forces' (Oloka-Onyango and Tamale, 1995: 702). At the same time, we must be sensitive to the continuing influences of global hegemony (particularly in the field of information) over present African reality. Just as modernization theory in the late 1950s was hatched in American social science faculties and exported to their African counterparts to disastrous effect, the Women-in-Development (WID) phenomenon was conceived by the international financial institutions (IFIs) and rammed down the throats of loan-recipient governments and pliant educational institutions. Needless to say, it has left a dubious legacy that has proved wanting in achieving 'the desired result of gender equity' (Etta, 1994: 58).

This chapter considers the nature and character of formal structures of higher education in which both the myths and realities of gender parity and academic freedom in the African context are initially played out. It takes a broad overview of the topic attempting to illustrate the historical, sociocultural, political, economic, geopolitical and legal dimensions of the issue. Drawing mainly from theoretical and empirical studies in the area as well as the lived experience of both authors, the study considers both historical and contemporary dimensions of gender struggles and academic freedom.

Gender and Academic Freedom
The Historical Context
'Academic freedom' has been defined as 'the freedom of members of the academic community, individually or collectively, in the pursuit, development and transmission of knowledge, through research, study, discussion, documentation, production, creation, teaching, lecturing and writing.'[7] While the general perception of institutions of learning is that they are designed to propagate knowledge and stimulate inquiry, it is not always the case that those institutions are themselves free of serious structural and ideological impediments to achieving those objectives. As Anthony Arblaster has pointed out in an early study of academic freedom in the British context:

> *Academic freedom and academic democracy go hand in hand. For the principal, though not the only, threats to freedom in education derive from the authoritarian structures of educational institutions. A society which constantly advertises itself as free and democratic manages to tolerate an extraordinary degree of authoritarianism within almost all its major institutions. This contradiction between pretensions and practice is unlikely to last indefinitely. Sooner or later a choice will have to be made between greater freedom and democracy, or less. (Arblaster, 1973: 1).*

Consequently, academic freedom is positioned both between the state and educational institutions, as well as within the latter. The concept of academic freedom itself has not been free of gender bias particularly since women have not only been discriminated against in access to institutions of learning, but also with regard to what they can study and research. The basis of such an insidious demarcation is deeply rooted in the colonial history of our continent.

Women in Africa (as is the case the world over) generally entered academia later than their male counterparts. A systematic and deliberate colonial policy ensured that African women were excluded from the various 'ivory towers' that dotted the continent. Not only did missionary education disproportionately extend educational opportunities to males, but men's education was also accorded higher priority than that of women (Staudt, 1981). A variety of factors, including the emphasis on domestic chores, generalized conditions of poverty and the overarching influence of patriarchy, combined to make access and entrance to academic institutions for women a mirage for much of the colonial period.[9] Women were a rare commodity in the annals of academia, and were Africa's true 'drawers of water, and hewers of wood.'

As if to confirm that academic life was not free of the gender-biases of the outside world, when women did obtain access, it was merely to secure a more sophisticated, and simultaneously delocalized, version of their original domesticated and subordinate status. The educated housewife was viewed by the colonizers as a potential consumer who could motivate her husband's productivity:

> *She must be educated to want a better home, better furnishings, better food, better water supplies, etc. and if she wants them she will want them for her children. In short, the sustained effort from the male will only come when the woman is educated to the stage when her wants are never satisfied.* (Roddan, 1958, quoted in Staudt, 1989:78)

In the same vein, a 1935 Commission on Higher Education in East Africa, chaired by the British peer Earl de la Warr, was paternalistic in the extreme (Oloka-Onyango, 1992: 50-51). In catering to 'the needs of the women' who would become the beneficiaries of the education on offer at the prestigious Makerere College, the Commission emphasized that women should be educated for 'home making' (Lugumba and Ssekamwa, 201-202). Such would obviously include Westernized versions of elite education — sewing, home economics and hygiene, domestic management, nursing and midwifery.[10] Neither the technical subjects — engineering, general, medical and animal sciences, or agriculture — nor the 'esoteric' arts subjects, were opened up to gender parity.[11] It was a classic instance of the transfer of perceptions and realities outside the classroom concerning the appropriate role of women in the family and rooted in male interpretations of 'culture.'[12] At the same time, it was also riddled with the desire to maintain male domination of the labour market, biological determinism, and gender-based divisions (cf. Hyde, 1993: 108).

Women, Education and Gender Discrimination

Obviously, the broad context of academic freedom for women is directly dependent upon the extent to which the conditions of their access to institutions of learning have become generalized and free of sex-based discrimination. In the words of Odaga and Heneveld:

> *Perhaps the most daunting challenge is that of promoting female education. This must be a central concern in efforts to improve learning achievements, school effectiveness, teacher motivation, education management, and issues of resource mobilization and reallocation of expenditure. Such initiatives provide an important opportunity for creating an enabling environment where girls and other disadvantaged groups can participate fully* (Odaga and Heneveld, 1995: 1).

Needless to say, the context in which such objectives are to be realized must be viewed against the background of freedom of expression generally. When former Ugandan president Idi Amin banned the Department of Political Science and the teaching of the subject at Makerere in the early 1970s, the move coincided with a massive assault against democratic rights in general and freedom of expression in particular. In a situation where the state not only monopolizes the available avenues for expression through the print and broadcast media, but also unduly influences school and university curricula and the appointment of university administrators, it is inevitable that women in particular, and gender issues in general, will be adversely affected.

Freedom of expression and the right to education are simply two sides of the same coin, with academic freedom intrinsic to both. The right to education is especially important if the former is to be exercisable in any consistent and liberative fashion. Thus, the stark illiteracy and under-education of African women clearly affects their ability to articulate and express their interests in a wide variety of fields, ranging from politics to the economy. As Rebecca Cook has pointed out, realization of the right to education serves the goal of individual and reproductive health (Cook, 1995: 267). Access to contraception, knowledge about different mechanisms of child-spacing, health and welfare invariably mean that women are operating in a more liberated and aware context. Denied these benefits women in Africa face the blunt end of the oppressive element in the system.

But while female education in general has been on the rise in Africa, in some instances 'out of the few who are admitted in the university again fewer do complete their course.' (Kakwenzire, 1996: 299).[13] This is essentially because women academics carry a dual burden that directly affects their freedom to operate and articulate issues in the academy. This burden is that women must pursue both their academic interests while meeting traditional obligations, for which they get little or no help from their male partners and spouses (even when those are academics!). So a woman academic is concerned with child-bearing and rearing, cooking, and domestic household chores or their supervision (Tamale, 1996: 319, 320). The male partner rarely participates in these duties. But when women and men academics' output and competence are compared with each other, this is not taken into account. In general, terms for maternity leave and other related benefits and conditions of leave and employment are no better in academic life than they are in the traditional civil service.

At the other end of the spectrum, male university practitioners are loath to include a gender dimension to their analyses. This is not only the case with outright gender bigots, but even among scholars who believe that they teach 'progressive' subjects.[14] As Imam and Mama point out:

> *The example of gender and women's studies is an alarming case where there is automatic, voluntary and even active self-censorship. The clear willingness of most social scientists in Africa to omit, ignore and deny the evidence that there is no such thing as 'gender neutral' science is worth exploring. Conformism is not even perceived as collusion with the dominant patriarchal order, despite the evidence that it produces biased and inaccurate data and contributes to the subordination and oppression of women* (Imam and Mama, 1994: 96).

At the same time, women academics are confronted by the sexual prejudices that abound among their male counterparts and the lack of a suitable framework within which they can articulate their concerns. To compound it all, within the context of IMF and World Bank Structural Adjustment Programmes (SAPs), women academics carry an increased total burden of work as they attempt to make ends meet in a context of decreased access to social services (cf. Kuenyhia, 1994: 434-435). Against such a background, it is important to examine the gender contradictions women academics face in greater detail.

Sex, Power and Academic Freedom: the Gender Contradictions
The forces of patriarchy which pervade the majority of African societies skew the balance of rights to academic freedom in favour of the male gender, vividly illustrating, in the words of Fatou Sow, that 'human rights are not gender neutral' (Sow, 1994: 7). This is partly illustrated by the fact that the architects of all the existing documents on academic freedom in Africa — including the Dar and Kampala Declarations — were almost exclusively men. It also explains why the declarations were more directly preoccupied with the state (another patriarchal institution) than they were with the more gender-related aspects of the concept of academic freedom. The declarations duplicate the international legal and human rights instruments and the highly sexist discourse about the 'generations' of human rights. Male (mainly Western) intellectuals who support the generational paradigm have given pride of place to civil and political rights because this is the arena within which men dominate to the broad exclusion of women. The so-called second generation of rights — health, shelter, education and social services in general — adversely affect women in greater proportion than they do men (cf. Chinkin and Wright, 1993; Oloka-Onyango, 1995). Is it of any surprise that when we get to the so-called third generation — rights to peace, a clean and pollution-free environment and the right to development — the jurisprudes in the area are completely at sea? Without the appreciation that the roots of patriarchal oppression lie in the smallest unit of societal organization, the family, attention on the state alone

can only achieve limited reform.

While making a significant contribution to the jurisprudence and politics of academic freedom on the continent (Shivji, 1994), none of the African declarations addresses the root causes of inequities within academia based on the underlying division of labour by gender. They also omit a consideration of the overarching patriarchal order existing in most African states. Such a bias furthermore explains their inadequate attention to specific gender inequalities such as sexual harassment and gender violence,[15] the latter of which is believed to have no place in academic life, and is generally regarded as a 'domestic' matter. When the basic principles of academic freedom are juxtaposed with the principles of patriarchy, the contradictions between the two are glaring. Below, we examine some of the basic principles of the Dar and Kampala Declarations[16] which have most relevance to the issue of gender and we examine some of the salient features of academic freedom, analyzing their efficacy vis a vis gender contradictions in African societies.

Access to education shall be equal and equitable[17]
There is a considerable disparity between men's and women's access to education. Sixty-four per cent of women in sub-Saharan Africa are illiterate compared to 40 per cent of the male population (UNESCO, 1990). As one proceeds up the educational hierarchy, these gender disparities grow in magnitude – the higher the level of education, the greater the gender disparity (Ballara, 1991). A cursory glance at the gender ratios of students and academic staff in African institutions of higher learning reveals the stark imbalance that favours men against women. For example, in Chad and the Central African Republic, women make up less than 10 per cent of the student population of tertiary institutions (Hyde, 1993: 100). At Khartoum University in the Sudan, the ratios of women to men academics in Political Science, Sociology, and Law are 1:15, 3:18 and 1:12, respectively (Hamad, 1995: 77). Such inequitable proportions are not accidental. Instead, they reflect deep-rooted social and cultural norms which infiltrate the educational system right from the elementary level (see Mbilinyi and Mbughuni, 1991).

When one examines the class origins of the few women who make it to African universities either as students or faculty, one finds that the percentage with a peasant background is minuscule (Eisemon, et al. 1993: 39).[18] This is true despite the fact that over 80 per cent of the population in sub-Saharan Africa is made up of the peasantry. In the absence of state-supported primary and secondary schools in the greater part of the continent, few peasant children make it to university. Thus, even within the purview of gender relations, the dynamics of inequality in African societies bestows privilege to a minority class of women. This implies that the disparities between the sexes with regard to accessibility to education invariably mesh with class distinctions within the different sexes. It is thus important to pay attention to the interrelationship of class and gender when addressing issues of academic freedom. In sum, the problem of disparities between the sexes is exacerbated for women by the fact that they constitute the majority of the economically impoverished class on the continent.

The legacy of unequal access to education primarily stems from obstacles resulting from the gendered division of labour. The traditional production and reproduction roles performed by most African women including domestic work, childrearing and agricultural and cultural activities, virtually leaves them with no time for educational pursuits. These obstacles are compounded by patriarchal structures of power which not only place greater value on boys' education than that of girls, but also discriminates against women in all spheres of social life. The same factors dictate women's submissiveness to male authority. Religion also plays a part in reinforcing gender disparities in education. As Ballara observes: 'Some religious traditions may restrict women's activities to domestic tasks, stressing their role as mothers, which limits their access to education' (Ballara, 1991:11). This implies a much more comprehensive approach to the issue of gender parity, and a concerted assault against the barriers that stand in its way. Etta is right on the mark when she argues:

Improving the status of women will therefore require a reorientation of development and development efforts, a redefinition of key concepts such as education and empowerment, and gender development planning to improve the range and quality of integrated gender responsive operations. A conceptual approach to gender issues in education is of immediate necessity to improve the gender sensitivity of educational provision and analysis and to offer an acceptable or common approach for addressing gender issues in education (Etta, 1994: 60).

Obviously this is a long drawn-out struggle, but the essential elements thereof need to be put in place immediately. Such struggle must include a more intensive scrutiny of the phenomenon of schooling itself. In the absence of such a process, the issue of discrimination will continue to remain a significant impediment to the betterment of the condition of women. A review must incorporate both the microscopic elements of gender discrimination that emanate from within the family as well as the macroscopic factors that pervade society, the state and its structures and institutions.

Education shall prepare a person to strive for and participate fully in the emancipation of the human being and society from oppression and subjugation [19]

The educational environment in African schools from the elementary level upwards — as is the case elsewhere in the world — is designed to ensure the maintenance of the status quo. In other words, the educational system in the main represents the institutionalization of patriarchal consciousness and values.[20] As Sheila Ruth observes:

In functioning both as trainer for participation in the wider society and as a reflection of that society, the schools transmit to their students the rather traditional views on sexual identity, and very early they convey, create, and reinforce in females and males the segregated conceptual systems of the sexes (Ruth, 1980: 382).

Whether transmitted directly (for example, by encouraging girls to take 'soft' subjects such as home economics, stenography and literature, and pushing boys in the direction of the 'hard' ones like science, business management and engineering), or subliminally (such as the gender distribution of the administrative hierarchy in the typical school or university which reflects masculine power), such messages hardly prepare the girl child to strive for the emancipation of her oppressed sisters (cf. Iweriebor, 1990: 18-21). For patriarchy to do otherwise would spell doom to its very existence.

Certain Western feminist scholars like Rhoda Howard have put forward the argument that it is more important for African women to study the humanities, social sciences and law because, she claims, for such subjects their 'primary objective of study is gender relations' (Howard, 1995: 310). In this way, she believes that women will be empowered to emancipate themselves from male hegemony and be liberated. However, such an argument is predicated on two faulty presumptions. First, that in African universities the teaching of the disciplines she favours is at all sensitive to gender issues, or even bothers to integrate them into their curricula. Second, it ignores the fact that even in supposedly advanced contexts such as the USA where women's studies departments abound, there has not been a fundamental restructuring of gender relations broadly. This means, therefore, that there is a need for a more fundamental restructuring of the curricula which instead of de-emphasizing one discipline at the expense of another, seeks their integration and an inter-disciplinary approach.

Furthermore, and most fundamentally for our purposes, the question of gender equality must be a critical component of intellectual discourse and study at African universities. The solution Howard offers to this problem — the creation of more scholarship opportunities for African women to pursue courses of instruction on 'certain social issues key to the abolition of patriarchy — such as violence against women' is a thinly-disguised attempt at modern-day proselitization.

This latter point relates to the whole question of the position of donors in relation to the quest for academic freedom. While Article 17 of the Kampala Declaration stipulates that 'states shall continuously ensure adequate funding for research institutions and higher education,' the present reality of SAPs and misprioritization in Africa means that the state is in serious breach of this provision. As a consequence, the international donor community has stepped in to fill the gap. Although neither the Dar nor Kampala declarations make reference to donors in their analyses, nevertheless the issue is of paramount importance. This was manifest in the Kampala symposium at which the latter declaration was promulgated. In the report of the conference, note was taken of the fact that:

... on the one hand the financial and material support extended by donors, who were generally considered to be of high moral standing, aided African grantees in universities and other institutions to protect themselves against the repression of the state. On the other hand, such protection comes with substantial power, leading to both intentional and unintentional constraints on research into the social sciences (Oloka-Onyango, 1994: 344).

The report was particularly concerned about the 'often obtrusive and undemocratic methods of work employed by donors, including the rejection of peer appraisal, sitting-in on the deliberations of scientific committees of African research organizations and dictating not only the form but the content of research undertaken (ibid: 344).' There is little doubt that the area of research into gender is one of the current favourites of the donor community — a veritable 'flavour of the month.' This raises serious questions about the extent to which women and gender-sensitive academics in the African context are able to design and execute a truly liberative agenda in this arena. While this criticism is true of almost all areas of intellectual discipline that are being researched in Africa today, it is of special prominence in the context of gender and women studies. Of particular concern is the onslaught instituted by the IFIs, with the World Bank leading the way in this respect (Oloka-Onyango and Tamale, 1995: 728-730).

In what we have elsewhere described as 'Third Stage Colonialism,' the World Bank has mapped out a gender strategy that places the issues of research into women and the economy, law, politics and culture, at the centre of its concerns and agenda for the African continent. Aside from the fact that the Bank focuses on the effects of gender inequality (for example, WID), rather than its root causes, it also amounts to a case of giving with one hand what is taken away with the other. Through its Structural Adjustment Programmes, the World Bank emasculates women scholars and intellectuals of much of their autonomous existence and economic livelihood and independence. In this way the basic tenets of their academic freedom are denied. It is thus surprising to hear the Bank charge that cost-sharing — the Bank's own brainchild — 'is especially likely to work against girl's education (Odaga and Heneveld, 1995: 15). The pretence of concern manifested by its new assault on women in this area is merely a smoke-screen over an insidious and debilitating agenda. The question must be asked: to what extent can a truly liberated research agenda on the issue of gender be developed independent of the dictates of donors?

Education shall enable a person to overcome prejudice related to gender[21]
In the arena of neutralizing the prejudices relating to gender, it is fairly obvious that there is yet a great distance to traverse. While numerous African institutions have established gender or women's studies departments, these remain outside the mainstream, confined to the particularities of their discipline. There is no attempt to marry the quest for gender-neutralization that takes place within such departments with a campus-wide assault on prejudice and domination. In essence, gender studies have become ghettoized, confined principally to women, and making only a limited impact on the overall struggle against gender bias. Furthermore, when the declarations on academic freedom address the issue of prejudice, they do so in the same fashion that is pursued in the dominant quest for racial harmony in racially-stratified societies like the United States. There, racism is defined merely as prejudice, but in fact racism comprises much more, namely, the dominance, power and hegemony of one race over another. Similarly, it is not simply gender prejudice that should be attacked and eradicated, but the power relations that underpin and foster such prejudice. Ultimately, it is in the interest of patriarchy that education is not geared towards raising the consciousness of society against gender prejudice and the power relations underpinning it. That is precisely why the 'bitches' at the academy who attempt to do this are subjected to threats and intimidation — the intellectual equivalent of the burning of a cross.

No African intellectual shall in any way be persecuted, harassed intimidated for reasons only of his or her intellectual work, opinions, gender, etc.[22]
Few people would dispute the fact that gender is an extremely significant factor in African institutions of higher learning. A woman lecturer instructing university students as well as a woman intellectual relating to her male counterparts are generally perceived through lenses tainted by their sexuality. Not only are they considered less knowledgeable than their male colleagues, but they also have to work twice as hard in order to legitimize their positions and authority. This is because the environment at institutions of higher learning is

dictated by patriarchal values and beliefs. Female intellectuals are the subject of sexual harassment,[23] exclusion from 'old boy' networks and almost never part of the hierarchy of deans, directors, departmental heads, or university administrators (Hamad, 1995: 77).

The omnibus nature of the above principle is hardly an effective statement on the issue of sexual harassment and gender violence. Extra-academic factors and the sociocultural context in a country invariably affect the possibilities for women academics to exercise their rights to academic freedom. Despite the fact that Sudan has traditionally enjoyed academic freedom of a type that is rare elsewhere on the continent, the emergence of the Omar el Bashir regime has greatly affected the expression of women's human rights to academic freedom unfettered by harassment or intimidation. Women academics are forbidden from travelling in the absence of a muhram — a close male blood relative — to act as a guardian (*Africa Watch*, 1991: 94). Women students are coerced into wearing the veil, they have been systematically dismissed from public employment, and the government has detained many women professionals (WUS, 1988: 119). The situation of women in general and of women academics in particular is compounded by the fact that a March 1991 amendment to the Penal Code relegated women to the status of second-class citizen.

Academic Freedom and the Woman Student

Paulo Friere's classic critique of the mechanics of oppression behind the walls of the classroom, *Pedagogy of the Oppressed*, laid bare the manifestly authoritarian context within which the dissemination of knowledge largely takes place. Unfortunately Friere omitted a critical consideration of an extremely important aspect of that situation, viz., the specifics of the oppression of the female student. Yet, as *African Rights* has noted, 'sexual abuse by teachers which exploits the trust of both students and parents is far more widespread than most institutions care to admit (*African Rights*, 1994: 8). That abuse ranges from sexual advances, threats of examination failure to outright rape (ibid., 8-11). Indeed, according to *African Rights*, 'the phenomenon of sexual harassment has been perceived to be so common that many women have come to regard it as "normal." ' (ibid., 21). At the same time, women students are often victimized at the expense of their male counterparts as in the instance of pregnancy (see, Etta, 1994: 73), which often results in the automatic termination and/or curtailment of her educational privileges while not necessarily the same sanction is invoked with respect to the man.

The Dar Declaration was adopted on April 19, 1990 71 days after the tragic suicide of Levina Mukasa, a first year Education student at the University of Dar es Salaam. The reason for her suicide? Sexual harassment[24]. Despite the wide publicity given to Levina's case and a general expose of the phenomenon of sexual harassment in Tanzanian institutions of higher learning by the local media, the omnibus reference to the issue of 'harassment' in the Declaration clearly failed to come to terms with the insidious nature of the issue. This omission was repeated in the later Kampala Declaration, Article 21 of which states: 'No one group of the intellectual community shall indulge in the harassment, domination or oppressive behaviour towards another group....' While recognizing that the issue of harassment is a problem, neither the Dar nor Kampala declarations are explicit in their reference to this issue as one which has clear gender-based origins and manifestations. In other words, they presume an equality in harassment and of its intent and effects between the sexes.

The Dar University wall-magazine, *Punch*, which was a key player in Levina Mukasa's fate, is a particularly poisonous form of sexual harassment. Famous for its auspicious beginnings as the magazine of radical students at the campus,[25] today *Punch* has deteriorated into an aggressive weapon directed almost exclusively against female students at the campus, where they are ridiculed and abused in the most virulent forms of language (Meena, 1994; Che-Mponda, 1990). There is no doubt that the incidence of rape too has become a particularly potent tool in the arsenal of gender-related assaults on women in the academy. Perhaps the most terrifying of incidents was the horrendous St Kizito massacre, which occurred in a Kenyan high school in mid-1991. A total of 19 girls were killed and 71 reportedly raped by their co-ed male colleagues. However, as *African Rights* pointed out, but for its scale, it was not 'an isolated event, neither in Kenya nor elsewhere on the continent' (*African Rights*, 1994: 3-4).

Following from the above experiences, our view is that there is a basic conceptual and practical problem in what Kaufman and Lindquist in a different context have referred to as 'gender-neutral' language that can be found in many international treaties attempting to address inequalities between the sexes (see Kaufman and Lindquist, 1995).

That problem is replicated in the African documents on academic freedom. The language used in these instruments assumes that with the formal acquisition of a right — in this instance the right to equal treatment and non-harassment — the problem has been solved. It omits an extremely important dimension to the question, namely that the two parties in this instance are far from equal in the first place. While, it is clear that there are women who harass men, the balance of the traffic is in the opposite direction, and yet the provision refers to both sexes. Because of the underlying imbalance in power between the sexes, any attempt to address the issue must treat the two sexes against the backdrop of the respective positions of influence and power they enjoy. It is clear that in academic life the question of sexual harassment disproportionately affects women over men. The social phenomenon of a woman harassing a man, such as that depicted in the Michael Douglas/Demi Moore scenario in the recent movie *Disclosure*, may exist but is rare, simply because men in positions of power and dominance far outnumber women. Furthermore, because of the significance of power in gender relations, combined with the cultural and institutional socialization that women have undergone, it is less likely that women who assume positions of power will manifest the same characteristics as their male counterparts. As Florence Etta has pointed out:

> *Boys are generally socialized to be inquiring, adventurous or venturesome, to subdue, conquer or at the very least understand nature while girls are expected to be obedient, malleable, traditional preservers of nature. The tragedy in the situation is that women are themselves the chief agents of this socialization which confers inequality on their kind. It is not so much the inequality as the effect of the socialization which is inimical to educational attainment and achievement* (Etta, 1994: 71).

While we disagree with the insinuation that women exclusively bear the blame for their inequality, it is quite evident that the impact of socialization has a significant influence on the ultimate evolution of gender-characteristics and relations.[26] Consequently, in relation to sexual harassment and several other issues specific to the female student, the employment of gender-neutral language simply masks and obscures the problem. It is our considered view that the use of such language serves to undermine the quest for a direct confrontation and elimination of the problem (cf. Kaufman and Lindquist, 1995: 115-116). Gender-neutral language allows for the interpretation of such clauses in the subjective social realm, where the interpretation of the right or freedom in question is subjected to the dominant cultural paradigm, which largely omits consideration of women's lived experiences. In the process of interpretation of such clauses, the dominant approach will be from the perspective of a man (ibid.).

Although the declarations on academic freedom do not have binding legal force (Busia, 1996:13), they nevertheless have served an important role in both raising the political consciousness of academics about the issue of academic freedom in Africa, as well as a caution to states that they must be sensitive to the context in which academics operate. However, the failure to develop instruments that are genuinely gender-sensitive illustrates that there is still a considerable distance to cover. In our view, the insertion of the omnibus phrase on 'harassment' in the Dar and Kampala declarations for example, is at best an expression of political correctness.

The incidents of sexual harassment we have cited above, are just a few examples of the widespread inattention to the woman student by human rights advocates in African tertiary institutions. Sexual harassment is often dismissed as an 'unAfrican' product of Western feminists mimicked by elitist African feminists. However, many female students and female faculty members at the academy can testify to several incidents where they have been victims of sexual harassment while their perpetrators are left unpunished. The prevailing point of view among males is that women like attention being drawn to their anatomical features, that they welcome unsolicited advances from their male colleagues and that in any case, every approach to a woman must in the first instance be resisted! The problem is compounded by the widespread absence of active women students' organizations to deal effectively with the issue. In addition, there is both a 'conspiracy of silence' and a dearth of sufficient mechanisms within school and university administrations designed to comprehensively address the problem. Thus most cases of sexual harassment and gender-based violence remain unreported for fear of a backlash or out of worry of being labelled or otherwise victimized (*African Rights*, 1994: 17). This implies the need to examine the legal framework which is of most relevance to this situation.

A Note on the Legal Framework
The legal regime governing women's rights in general is not wholly conducive to women academics and their expression of academic freedom. At the international level, the Convention on the Elimination of All Forms of Discrimination Against Women (CEDAW) addresses the issue of equality in education in Article 10. The article stipulates that states parties shall take appropriate measures to eliminate discrimination against women in order to ensure them equal rights with men in the field of education. In particular, states parties must take measures to ensure non-discriminatory conditions of education and access; equal standards and quality of education; the elimination of stereotyped concepts of the roles of men and women; similar opportunities to benefit from scholarships and study grants; the same opportunities of access to continuing education programs; reducing the rate of female dropping out; equal opportunities for participation in sports and physical education, and finally, for women to have access to specific scientific information to help to ensure the health and well-being of their families.

CEDAW has the highest number of states parties of any international human rights instrument but is nevertheless plagued by a variety of problems. Despite having come into force in September 1981, the idea of an individual complaints mechanism whereby individual women could present their cases to the Committee established under the Convention has only of recent come into existence. This has meant that instances of individual rights violations are not the specific concern of the Committee. Instead through the mechanism of states parties reporting to the Committee, the issue of gender-based discrimination is addressed from a progressive and collective dimension. CEDAW also has the highest number of reservations with many states predicating their observance of the rights in the instrument upon respect for local 'culture.' Such reservations have had the effect of substantially undercutting the rights that the instrument sets out to guarantee in the first instance. The Committee which has charge of the implementation of the Convention is starved for funds and it meets only once every year. Furthermore, being mainly dependent upon state reports, positive advances in the system are primarily reliant upon the goodwill of states parties to the Convention. In sum, CEDAW is a limited tool in the general struggle for the liberation of women. Elsewhere we have stated that the promulgation of CEDAW:

> *... also produced a reverse (and perhaps unintended) consequence in which the strategy and profile of the international women's human rights movement were to some extent dictated by action under CEDAW. In short, the focus on CEDAW produced a paradox by successfully highlighting, but simultaneously ghettoizing, women's human rights issues within the international legal and political arena* (Oloka-Onyango and Tamale, 1995: 716).

In the final analysis, therefore, CEDAW is quite clearly inadequate as a mechanism for the realization of the rights of women to academic freedom. Some recent advances have been made in particular respect to the promulgation of the Declaration Against Violence on Women, but since this instrument is not of binding effect, it remains to be seen whether it will dramatically add to the struggle to tackle the problem of violence against women in its various dimensions.

Viewed from a different angle, the international level is also rather remote from the lives of African academics and consequently it is necessary to look closer to home. CEDAW did not spawn a duplication at the continental level in the same way as either the international Covenants or the Convention on the Rights of the Child. Indeed, the African Charter on Human and People's Rights, which came into force the same year as CEDAW, hardly addressed the issue of women's human rights. Article 18 of the Charter is the only reference point for the rights of women in the instrument (Kois, 1996). The article covers the family, describing it as the 'natural unit and basis of society' which must be protected and assisted by the State, as the 'custodian of morals and traditional values recognized by the community.' Already, there is potential for conflict as this provision can effectively operate as a bar to the recognition and enforcement of women's human rights.

Perhaps the most important of the provisions of Article 18 is sub-paragraph 3 which stipulates that the state shall ensure the protection of the rights of the woman and the child as stipulated in international declarations and conventions. Academic controversy and discussion abounds over the general relationship between women's human rights in the African context in general and Article 18 of the African Charter in particular (see, e.g., Beyani, 1994; Oloka-Onyango and Tamale; 1995 and Kois, 1996). Whether one takes the view that the provision is a positive one that enhances respect for the rights of women and the family or in fact undermines them, the question of enforcement remains a practical issue of utmost importance in the struggle for the realization of women's human rights particularly in the arena of academic freedom. There has not been a single petition regarding the violation of women's human rights that the African Commission has considered since its inception in 1988. The first female Commissioner out of 11 was appointed in 1992 and was only joined by a second in 1995. The receptivity to and publication of women's human rights by this body thus remains very low. It is compounded by the fact that there is a general weakness in the effectiveness of the Commission, namely the fact that it is ultimately responsible to, and dependent upon, the Organization of African Unity (OAU) Assembly of Heads of State and Government. Few bodies are more undemocratic, sexist or discriminatory.

Conclusion

What does the above analysis mean? Basically that there is a lack of a comprehensive, gender-sensitive, all-embracing normative framework in which the concerns of gender and academic freedom are clearly spelt out. In the African context the essential first step must necessarily be the promulgation of a declaration or edict on gender and academic freedom to supplement and fortify the existing Dar and Kampala documents. Special attention in such an instrument would cover the essential issues of gender parity, sexual harassment, stereotypes, violence, discrimination and prejudice, among others. Secondly, there is an additional need for a continental legal mechanism building on the spirit of CEDAW and the Lima Declaration at the international level and the African Charter together with the Dar and Kampala declarations at the regional levels, which comprehensively addresses itself to the broad human rights of African women.

At the same time, the limitations of a purely legalistic approach to the problem must clearly be laid out. The problem is not a legal one per se. Rather, it is deeply rooted in a variegated web of social, economic, cultural, political and even conceptual problems. To overcome these factors, the strategies adopted must likewise be multifarious and cross-disciplinary. At the end of the day, the struggle for academic freedom for women, just as is the case with men, cannot be isolated from the broader struggle for democratic and human freedoms. As we have sought to illustrate in this chapter, the lack of academic freedom in fact has its roots in a much smaller microcosm of society — the family — the institution in which the process of learning commences. This implies, first and foremost, the democratization of the family. Of course, in the context of state structures which are inimical to the democratic evolution of either the family or the academy, the quest for gender-sensitized academic freedom remains a distant hope. The opportunity to change this condition must be seized upon by progressive, dynamic and enlightened women and men in order to move towards a democratic, engendered, and participatory social framework for African humanity.

Notes

1. While free expression is a critical component of academic freedom, the media presents an ambivalent context for gender struggles. As Ruth Meena has observed: *Women have been negatively portrayed in the media.... The mass media which is supposed to play a very instrumental role in linking the civil society and the state has been instrumental in undermining the dignity of women through negatively portraying them, or through making them invisible where visibility would have enhanced self confidence and assertive skill building. The media often fails to include the views of women in various forums, and as such the media has just managed to suppress women's democratic claims* (Meena, 1995: 4-5).

2. Isabel Phiri points to the nature of the problem in this respect: *Women experiences have been singled out as an important ingredient of a good curriculum because women comprise more than half of the population of the world. Yet for a long time our curriculum has been dominated by male perspectives. The bibliographies of many courses have shown that males have been the only thinkers. It is no wonder then that the decisions made by our graduates reflect a male bias and ignore the experiences of women.* (Phiri, 1994: 2).

3. As recently pointed out by the African Association of Political Science, this crisis has assumed a two-fold dimension: *For many lecturers the struggle for survival now takes precedence. Regrettably, also, under the wise counsel of the World Bank and the IMF governments no longer see the university as the vital agent for national development. Now the fashion is to regard university education as a luxury, expensive, and a privilege the cost of which has to be borne by those who use it. Hence the rapid decline of the university* (AAPS, 1996: 1).

4. The authors are aware that African universities are by no means homogenous institutions. The general term as used in the context of this essay symbolizes African institutions of higher learning as they are similarly and generically affected by issues of gender, class, colonialism and decolonization.

5. Gender is distinguished from sex (the anatomical and hormonal distinctions between men and women); the concept of gender refers to the learned attitudes, values, behaviours and expectations that characterize individuals as being feminine or masculine (Gonzalez-Calvo, 1993; Peterson and Runyan, 1993).

6. The lecture method in vogue at most African universities evokes the Victorian schoolmaster pontificating on a topic about which he is the 'fountain' of all knowledge. The method is peremptory, non-participatory and dictatorial (cf. Friere, 1972; Illich, 1974).

7. The Dar es Salaam Declaration on Academic Freedom and Social Responsibility of Academics, 1990.

8. Kakwenzire argues that in a situation of inadequate resources, '... parents reserve resources for educating boys in preference to girls. This is because it was and it is still believed that more economic returns and security were/are realized through educating boys and that girls education is less beneficial.' (Kakwenzire, 1996: 298).

9. Kakwenzire refers to these social roles as 'breeder-feeder-trainer.' (See Kakwenzire, 1996: 295).

10. For an interesting treatment of the rise of women in the nursing profession in the United States, see Paul Starr, who argues that, 'The movement for reform (in the nursing profession) originated, not with doctors, but among upper-class women, who had taken on the role of guardians of a new hygienic order.' (Starr, 1982: 155).

11. Of course, this is not to say that the type of colonial education for men was substantially any better in terms of its transformative potential. Mamdani has pointed out that: *The few universities set up in the colonial period were designed with a narrow focus on cost-*

effectiveness in terms of meeting the short-term needs of the colonial state and economy. Prior to World War II, this meant a near-exclusive emphasis on 'technical' education designed to train personnel for the colonial state and the small private sector. After the war, research was added as a necessary component of university education. Confronted by nationalist ferment, the colonial state discovered the practical usefulness of funding research into African societies and movements (Mamdani, 1994: 1). We may add that in any case, women were disproportionately marginalized from the ambit of even this warped form of education.

12. Florence Etta has stated that culture is the single most inclusive constraining factor in fighting the problems faced by women: *The culture of female subjugation, the religious culture, social customs, traditions, the culture of the school, or the national culture of paying lip service to the issue of gender inequity in education. Biological/genetic differences account for sex differences but cultural factors explain differential role allocation on men and women with men commanding more power that women; power to make decisions, effect them and control events. Modernisation, commericalisation, marginalisation, and the feminisation of work roles or occupations reduced the value of reproduction and work that was perceived as genuine — usually meaning those preponderantly done by women* (Etta, 1994: 70).

13. Kakwenzire's figures illustrate that over a seven-year period, the drop-out rate of women in a single class in a Ugandan primary school was 59.1%. Over a ten-year period, the enrollment of women at Makerere University has gone from 18% to 22% (Kakwenzire, 1996: 298, 299).

14. Isabel Phiri offers some explanation of this phenomenon in reflecting on why students at Chancellor College in Malawi protested against a seminar on violence against women: *One possible interpretation of the reaction of the few male students to the seminar could be that in some men's minds Human Right(s) issues exclude women. Although the whole country was eagerly anticipating the birth of genuine democracy, for some of our students this did not include academic freedom for women to hold a seminar on a topic of their choice* (Phiri, 1994:1).

15. We use the phrase 'gender violence' in a broad sense as does Nahid Toubia when she argues that such violence comprises not only a series of *commissions*, but also *omissions*, which amount to '[a] failure to recognize the existence of fundamental human rights....' (Toubia, 1994: 16-17).

16. See especially, Chapter One of the Dar Declaration, entitled, 'Education for Human Emancipation,', and Chapter One of the Kampala Declaration named, 'Fundamental Rights and Freedoms.'

17. See Principle no.2 of the Dar Declaration.

18. The question of class background was confirmed in a 1991 Makerere University survey of which a Review Team commented: *A high proportion of students, particularly those enrolled in the most selective faculties, were from professional families .... To obtain admission to Makerere, many students repeat the A level examination to boost their scores and/or have private tutoring. Few economically disadvantaged families can afford to make these provisions for their children.* (Eisemon, et al. 1993: 39)

19. See Principle no.3, Dar Declaration, and Article 22 of the Kampala Declaration.

20. Ivan Ilich makes the point more succinctly — albeit absent a gender analysis — when he states: *A society committed to the institutionalization of values identifies the production of goods and services with the demand for such. Education which makes you need the product is included in the price of the product. School is the advertising agency which makes you believe that you need society as it is. In such a society marginal value has become constantly self-transcendent* (Ilich, 1974: 113).

21. Principle no.4 of the Dar Declaration.
22. Article no.3 of the Kampala Declaration.
23. Of course, even women academics are not beyond the unwarranted sexual advances of their male students. *African Rights* quotes a former University of Liberia lecturer who stated: *Some of the boys were coming on very strongly. They knew I was single and I suppose that encouraged them. They would come into my office, leave me presents, letters etc... I put an end to it by naming them in class (African Rights,* 1994: 12).
24. For a detailed account of Levina's case see Che-Mponda C., 'Why Did Levina Kill Herself?' *Sauti Ya Siti* No. 8, January - March, 1990 at p.4.
25. Issa Shivji quotes one instance of *Punch*'s early days, when it was used as a debating-point for different views about contemporary social and political issues (Shivji, 1993: 207).
26. Socialization theory has been criticized for disregarding structural and institutional factors (see, e.g. Randall, 1987: 84; Epstein, 1988: 137-140), but in spite of its inherent weaknesses, the socialization paradigm occupies a prominent place in feminist discourse.

References

AAWORD, (1982), *The Experience of the Association of African Women for Research and Development (AAWORD),* 1/2 Development Dialogue: 101-113.

Africa Watch, (1991), *Academic Freedom and Human Rights Abuses in Africa,* London.

African Association of Political Science (AAPS), (1996), The Crisis of the University, *Newsletter of AAPS,* vol.1, no.21 (May-August).

African Rights, (1994), Crimes Without Punishment: Sexual Harassment and Violence Against Female Students in Schools and Universities in Africa, (Discussion Paper No.4; July).

Arblaster, A., (1974), *Academic Freedom,* Penguin, Harmondsworth.

Ballara, M., (1991), *Women and Illiteracy,* Zed Books, London and New Jersey.

Beyani, C., (1994) Toward a More Effective Guarantee of Women's Rights in the African Human Rights System, in R.J. Cook (ed.), *Human Rights of Women: National and International Perspectives,* University of Pennsylvania Press, Philadelphia.

Boyd, R., (1989), Empowerment of Women in Contemporary Uganda: Real or Symbolic?, 22/1 *Labour, Capital and Society.*

Busia, Jr., N.K.A., (1996), Towards a Legal Framework for the Protection of Academic Freedom: Perspectives on the African Human Rights System, in CODESRIA, *The State of Academic Freedom in Africa,* 1995, CODESRIA, Dakar.

Che-Mponda, C., (1990), Why Did Levina Kill Herself?, *Sauti ya Siti,* No.8, January - March.

Chinkin, C.M., and S. Wright (1993), The Hunger Trap: Women, Food and self-determination, 14 *Michigan Journal of International Law.*

Cook, R.J., (1994), State Accountability Under the Convention on the Elimination of All Forms of Discrimination Against Women, in Cook, op.cit.

Diouf, M., and Mamdani, M., (1994), *Academic Freedom in Africa,* CODESRIA, Dakar.

Eisemon, T.O., Sheehan, J., Eyoku, G., Van Buer, F., Welsch, D., Masutti, L., Colletta, and Roberts, L., (1993), Strengthening Uganda's Policy Environment for Investing in University Development, World Bank Working Paper WPS 1065, Washington DC.

Epstein, C., (1988), *Deceptive Distinctions: Sex, Gender and the Social Order,* Yale University Press, New Haven.

Etta, F.E., (1994), Gender Issues in Contemporary African Education, XIX/4 *Africa Development.*

Friere, P., (1972), *Pedagogy of the Oppressed*, (translated by Myra Bergman Ramos), Penguin, Harmondsworth.

Gonzalez-Calvo, J. (1993), *Gender: Multicultural Perspectives*, Kendall/Hunt Publishing Company, Dubuque.

Hamad, Sudan, in J. Daniel, N. Hartley, Y. Lador, M. Nowak and F. Vlaming, *Academic Freedom 3: Education and Human Rights*, Zed, London.

Harries, C., (1994) Daughters of Our Peoples: International Feminism Meets Ugandan Law and Custom, 25/2 *Columbia Human Rights Law Review*: 493-540.

Howard, R., (1995), Women's Rights and the Right to Development, in J. Peters and A. Wolper, (eds.), *Women's Rights, Human Rights: International Feminist Perspectives*, Routledge, New York.

Hyde, K.A.L, (1993), Sub-Saharan Africa, in E.M. King and M.A. Hill (eds.) *Women's Education in Developing Countries: Barriers, Benefits, and Policies*, Baltimore/London, Johns Hopkins.

Ilumoka, A.O., (1994), African Women's Economic, Social and Cultural Rights—Toward a Relevant Theory and Practice, in R.J. Cook, op.cit.

Imam, A., and A. Mama, (1994), The Role of Academics in Limiting and Expanding Academic Freedom, in Diouf and Mamdani, op.cit.

Iweriebor, Ifeyinwa, (1990), Restriction to Research on Gender Issues in Africa with Particular Reference of Nigeria, Presented at the Symposium on Academic Freedom, Research and the Social Responsibility of the Intellectual in Africa, Kampala, Uganda, November 26-29.

Kakwenzire, J., (1996), Preconditions for Demarginalizing Women and Youth in Ugandan Politics, in Oloka-Onyango et al., op.cit.

Kaufman, N.H., and S.A. Lindquist, (1995), Critiquing Gender-Neutral Treaty Language: The Convention on the Elimination of All Forms of Discrimination Against Women, in Peters and Wolper, op cit.

Kois., L., (1996), Article 18 of the African Charter in Human and Peoples' Rights: A Progressive Approach to Women's Human Rights, 3/1 *East African Journal of Peace and Human Rights*.

Kuenyhia, A., (1994), The Impact of Structural Adjustment Programs on Women's International Human Rights: The Example of Ghana, in R.J. Cook, op.cit.

Lugumba, S.H.E., and Ssekamwa, J.C., (1973), *A History of Education in East Africa (1900-1973)*, Longmans, Kampala.

Mamdani, M, (1994), Introduction: The Quest for Academic Freedom, in M. Diouf and M. Mamdani, op.cit.

Mbilinyi, M. and Mbughuni P. (Eds.) (1991), Education in Tanzania with a Gender Perspective, report prepared for SIDA, Dar es Salaam.

Meena, R., (1995), Politics of Transition, Women/Gender Issues in Tanzania, background paper for a workshop on Generation of Voter Education Materials, with a Gender Perspective; Dar es Salaam; June 9-10.

Odaga, A., and Heneveld, W., (1995), Girls and Schools in Sub-Saharan Africa: From Analysis to Action, World Bank Technical Paper No.298 (Africa Technical Department Series), Washington DC.

Okeyo P. A., (1981), Daughters of the Lake and Rivers: Colonization and the Land Rights of Luo Women, in M. Etienne and E. Leacock (eds.), *Women and Colonization: Anthropological Perspectives*, Praeger, New York.

Oloka-Onyango, J., (1992), The Legal Control of Tertiary Institutions in East Africa: The Case of Makerere University, XVII/4 *Africa Development*.

Oloka-Onyango, J., (1994), The Kampala Symposium on Academic Freedom and Social

Responsibility, in Diouf and Mamdani, op.cit.

Oloka-Onyango, J., (1995), Beyond the Rhetoric: Reinvigorating the Struggle for Economic and Social Rights in Africa, 26/1 *California Western International Law Journal*.

Oloka-Onyango, J, and Sylvia Tamale, (1995), 'The Personal is Political,' or Why Women's Rights are Indeed Human Rights: An African Perspective on International Feminism, 17/4 *Human Rights Quarterly*.

Oloka-Onyango, J., C.M. Peter and K. Kibwana, (1996), (eds.) *Law and the Struggle for Democracy in East Africa*, ClariPress, Nairobi.

Peterson, V.S. and Runyan A.S., (1993), *Global Gender Issues*, Westview Press, Boulder.

Phiri, I.A. (1994), Academic Freedom and a Gender Balanced Curriculum at Chancellor College, paper presented at a conference on academic freedom held at Mlangeni Holiday Resort, Malawi; October 17-20.

Phiri, I, Semu, L., Nankhuni, F., and Madise, N., (1995), Violence Against Women in Educational Institutions: The Case of Sexual Harassment and Rape on Chancellor College Campus, (paper on file with CODESRIA's Academic Freedom Programme).

Randall, V., (1987), *Women and Politics: An International Perspective* (2nd edition), Macmillan, London.

Raoul Wallenburg Institute of Human Rights and Humanitarian Law, (1992), Academic Freedom: Report from a Seminar on Academic Freedom, (Lund, Sweden, March 9-11).

Ruth, S., (1980), *Issues in Feminism: A First Course in Women's Studies*, Houghton Mifflin, Boston.

Shivji, I., (1993), *Intellectuals at the Hill: Essays and Talks, 1969-1993*, Dar es Salaam University Press, Dar es Salaam.

Shivji, I., (1994), The Jurisprudence of the Dar-es-Salaam Declaration on Academic Freedom, in Diouf and Mamdani, op.cit.

Sow, F., (1994), The Role of Gender Analysis in the Future of Social Sciences in Africa, *Codesria Bulletin*, No.2.

Starr, P., (1982), *The Social Transformation of American Medicine: The Rise of a Sovereign Profession and the Making of a Vast Industry*, Basic Books, New York.

Staudt, K., (1989), The State and Gender in Colonial Africa, in S. Charlton, J. Everett, and K. Staudt (eds.), *Women and the State in Development*, State University of New York Press, Albany.

Staudt, K., (1981), Women's Politics in Africa, 16 *Studies in Third World Societies*: 1-28.

Tamale, S., (1996) Democratization in Uganda: A Feminist Perspective, in Oloka-Onyango, et al, op.cit.

Toubia, N., (1994), Women's Reproductive and Sexual Rights, in Centre for Global Leadership, eds., *Gender Violence and Women's Human Rights in Africa*, New York.

UNESCO, (1990), Compendium of Statistics on Illiteracy, *Statistical Reports and Studies*, No. 31, Paris, UNESCO.

World University Service (WUS), (1988), *Academic Freedom: A Human Rights Report 2*, Zed Books, London.

2. Tanzania: Engendering Academic Freedom

Saida Yahya-Othman

Introduction

The issues which were at the centre of the debate on academic freedom even two decades ago have shifted both in focus and in content. Not only have academics and intellectuals been confronted with entirely new forms of challenge, oppression and violence, but they themselves have in some cases also been forced to get involved in activities which may be said to undermine the basic principles of academic freedom. The opposing sides in the fight for academic freedom are no longer clearly defined as the state and the academic community, since other agents also see academics as a threat to be subdued or even eliminated. These can be extremist groups, religious or otherwise, political parties or their supporters, and even, surprisingly, academics themselves (Imam and Mama 1994).

In recent years there have been attempts to redefine the concept of academic freedom to include not only direct and overt violations of the rights of academics, however these may be defined, or the direct oppression of academics and intellectuals. The concept also includes economic and social policies or measures which concern education, and which in some way are perceived to reduce or curtail access to education for certain groups, to make the acquisition of learning more tortuous for those groups, and to cast doubt on the academic qualifications of that group.

One such group is that of women, who have had both to struggle to confront their male colleagues and the dominant patriarchal ideology, and also to wage a war against practices which blatantly and consistently violate their academic freedom.

If academic freedom, as the Dar es Salaam Declaration states, is:

the freedom of members of the academic community, individually or collectively, in the pursuit, development, and transmission of knowledge, through research, study, discussion, documentation, production, creation, teaching, lecturing and writing,

then women are not only deprived of this freedom in the same ways as their male colleagues, but additionally, in ways that are more subtle and covert, and which may therefore have escaped scrutiny It is on these subtle, but highly disempowering, subjugating, and disadvantaging processes that I will focus. It is also the case that the state of academic freedom and its gender dimension as it exists in the tertiary institutions has its roots in the lower levels of the schooling system, apart from being influenced by the local and world sociopolitical context, so that the universities appear to be in a bind which can only be broken through the institution of specific and focused measures.

The Education System
Structure

Since independence, the Tanzanian government's efforts have been directed at the expansion of basic education, ensuring that every child obtained at least seven years of primary schooling. Under Julius Nyerere's regime, the whole thrust of 'Education for Self-reliance' was to equip children with skills and knowledge which would enable them to deal in a productive way with their environment when they left primary school at the age of about 14. Nyerere's argument was that Tanzania's resources were unlikely to expand to allow the majority of children to get access to university education, and strategic measures had therefore to be taken to ensure that the primary education that most would get would provide skills for earning a living.[1]

Thus there was rapid expansion of primary education, culminating in the introduction of Universal Primary Education (UPE) in 1977. However, secondary school places were extremely restricted. In 1983 (the year of the first graduates from UPE) there were only 19,505 secondary school places for 454,604 pupils who finished primary school. Because the government pursued a deliberate policy of expanding primary education and restricting secondary school expansion, it allowed private institutions such as religious organizations to run secondary schools. At the moment, these private secondary schools outnumber government schools (336 against 259 in 1995 (URT: 1996)). In contrast, until a few years ago, it was not possible to open a private primary school, and even now these are only allowed if they have the semblance of being 'international schools', catering for expatriate children.

The schooling system involves seven years of primary education, four of secondary, two of upper secondary, and between three and five years at university. The secondary schools are streamed into art subjects, commerce, or science. The streaming at lower secondary determines the student's specialization for the rest of his/her education.

The running of the three levels of education is distributed among three different authorities. While the Ministry of Education and Culture (MEC) is in charge of the curriculum of all levels up to high school, the primary schools are actually run by the local councils, which pay teachers' salaries and collect school fees. The secondary schools fall under the MEC, while from 1990 the tertiary institutions have been run under the new Ministry of Science, Technology and Higher Education (MSTHE). Some of these latter, notably the universities, operate as semi-autonomous institutions (parastatals), while others are controlled much more closely by their 'parent' ministries.

Access

This traditional focus by the government on primary education has meant that Tanzania has the lowest transition rate (about 52,819 in 1994 or 14.3 per cent (URT: 1996)) to secondary school in the sub-Saharan region. As the figures below indicate, the education pyramid is in consequence extremely wide at the bottom:

Table 1: Tanzania: Education Transition Rates

Level	1987	1988	1989	1990	1991
Std 1	549,099	575,888	623,537	618,104	628,005
Std 7	380,758	347,978	267,744	306,656	383,427
Form 1	32,630	36,464	42,136	47,227	48,309
Form 5	3,114	3,279	4,025	5,488	5,568
University	3,395	3,219	3,327	3,453	

Source: Computed from URT: 1993, 1996

The transition rate has in fact been dropping, from nearly 30 per cent in the early 1960s and 21 per cent in the mid-1960s, to three per cent in the mid-1980s. It is now on the rise, but as mentioned, mostly through private rather than government efforts.

While access into primary school is assumed to be universal, and was indeed so after the commencement of UPE, the recent introduction of fees has meant that some parents have had to forgo places for their children because they cannot afford the fees, even though these are quite low compared to those of other countries,.

The government insists that no child will be deprived of schooling merely because they cannot pay the fees, but in practice children are regularly turned away from schools if they appear without fees. There is of course a very wide disparity between schools in different regions, and between urban and rural schools, in the facilities available, the quality of the teachers, and the training opportunities available to teacher.

For secondary schools the situation is more acute. The Standard Seven examinations are meant to be a selection device for secondary school entrance, and because of the limited places available, many pupils are not selected although they may be academically qualified. Regional and gender quotas have been operating for many years to ensure a more equitable distribution for the disadvantaged regions and women. But clearly parents go to great efforts to ensure secondary school places for their children, and this has given rise to the explosion of private secondary schools. There is great regional differentiation in their distribution, with rich agricultural regions such as Kilimanjaro, Arusha, Mbeya and Iringa having many more private schools, some of which were started by missionaries. The quality of such schools also shows great variation, with some charging high fees and being very well-equipped, while others have only the barest essentials.

The Budget and Education

Tanzania has one of the lowest spending rates on education in the region. Only three per cent of the budget is allocated to education at present, in contrast to Botswana, Kenya and Zimbabwe, for example, where education gets 20-30 per cent of the budget.

Between 1970 (the year of the founding of the first university, the University of Dar es Salaam) and the present, the amounts spent on defence and education have been almost directly reversed. Whereas at that time the education budget was almost twice that of defence, the former underwent gradual attrition until 1978-9 when the defence budget came to double that of education. In addition, the budget allocated to the education sector decreased from about 14 per cent of government expenditure in 1970-1, to five per cent in 1986-7. In 1996/97 the defence budget was 48.2 billion shillings, while that of education is 17.1 billion shillings. The budget for the Ministry of Education and Culture alone, which covers primary and secondary education, has been decreasing from 11.7 per cent of the national budget in 1980-1 to 3.3 per cent in 1993-4, and most of this goes into paying salaries.

In this context of extremely limited resources, the competition for those resources between the various educational institutions is fierce. Educational facilities at all levels are extremely scarce, both in terms of infrastructure and materials, and in terms of human resources. Most government schools lack even the most basic facilities for teaching and learning. Desks, writing and reading materials, and teaching aids are all very scarce, with children sitting on the floor, and sharing a book between five or six. Teachers are poorly trained and poorly paid, and consequently have little motivation for carrying out their work efficiently. Parents have to pay school fees, buy their own books, as well as pay for extra tuition classes for their children. Teachers focus their teaching on getting pupils to perform well in examinations, instead of providing wider knowledge and training in critical thinking, creativity, and skills to deal with different situations. With the minimal budget allocated to primary education, it is hardly surprising that the present national outcry is the deterioration of educational standards.

The Universities

Tanzania has the lowest number entering university (total enrolment is about 5,700), in the sub-Saharan region. Of all the pupils who go to the first year of primary school, only 0.3 per cent finally enter university. With such limited access to education, competition is fierce, and the government has had to take various measures to ensure that some of the disadvantaged groups get some representation in secondary and higher education, as we will see below.

Of the three universities, only one, the University of Dar es Salaam (UDSM), is a broad-based university offering degrees on most of the conventional courses, both arts and sciences. The Sokoine University of Agriculture (SUA) grew out of a former faculty of the University of Dar es Salaam, while the Open University of Tanzania (OUT) deals with distance learning by secondary school leavers who want to get a degree on a part-time basis. Having been established only in 1992, its range of courses is still very restricted. There is now a lot of talk of starting private universities, but meanwhile the rate at which middle class families are enrolling their children in foreign universities has risen dramatically.

Academic freedom cannot be discussed without reference to autonomy and accountability. While in recent years the institutions of higher education (IsHE) have had a considerable degree of what has sometimes been called 'substantive autonomy' (the freedom of an institution to determine its own goals and programmes), they have greatly lacked in 'procedural autonomy' (the power to determine the means by which goals and programmes will be pursued). The fact that IsHE are almost totally dependent on subventions from the government seriously curtails their freedom of diversification, expansion, employment and training. For the past five years recruitment of new staff has been frozen, while at the same time the institutions face enormous pressure to diversify curricula (the exercise being euphemistically referred to as 'course restructuring') in order to meet the new challenges of a 'plural' society, and 'market forces'.[2]

The squeeze on the social services dictated by the Structural Adjustment Programmes and other programmes imposed by the IMF and the World Bank have not left education unscathed. The Tanzanian tradition of free education went up in smoke four years ago. Although in the past there had been various small sums charged under such guises as 'school buildings', these were not part of the official policy. Now, the introduction of fees at all levels, and provision of loans for university students for services other than tuition, which they are expected to repay later, has created a wider gap between the rich and the poor, as the former are not only able to take up the government places offered, but may also send their children to study in other countries. The libraries get next to no funding for books, leading to students being extremely possessive about any reading material they get hold of, and in some cases going so far as tearing pages from library books to have more time to read them at home. An environment which would encourage the production of knowledge, criticism and critical thinking, and free exchange of ideas, is thus totally lacking. The students themselves are fond of saying that they do not come to university to learn, but to get degrees, and evidence suggests that this is indeed the case (*UDASA Newsletter* no. 16).

As with the rest of the budget, the education sector depends to a large extent on aid from donor countries and agencies, and this aid is often channelled into areas which are of priority to the donors, rather than Tanzanians themselves. As a result, examples abound in the university departments of the incongruity of the high technology of computers and laser printers, side by side with an acute shortage of basic texts, stationery, and even chalk, and run-down facilities such as broken chairs, dark classrooms and stinking toilets (*UDASA Newsletter* no. 10). Recently within the same week, the Minister of Science, Technology and Higher Education inaugurated the Internet service at the University of Dar es Salaam, while the university administration announced the postponement of the new academic year for two weeks, due to the late delivery of the subvention from the government.

The academic staff are in an equal bind. Apart from a brief period in the 1970s, when Tanzanian academics were paid a salary which allowed them to devote their time to thinking and research, they have been forced to be slaves to capital. In recent years, the lack of research facilities and the erosion of salaries through the continuous devaluation of the Tanzanian shilling (17 shillings to the dollar in the 1980s, against approximately 600 shillings at present) have drastically affected the production of knowledge. In order to make ends meet, many academics have had to become dependent on consultancies commissioned by donor agencies, harness their intellectual capacities to open private practices, and undertake all manner of 'projects', often having very little to do with their areas of specialization. Their central function, of producing knowledge and pursuing the truth, has become almost incidental, and intellectual atrophy has set in,[3] with the consequence that there is more and more convergence between the students' objectives and the professors' practice.

The accountability of academics and intellectuals is becoming more and more elusive. During the late 1960s and 1970s, under Education for Self-Reliance, there was a high degree of consciousness of the link between the university and the community, the latter being not only the fountain from which the intellectuals would draw their inspiration and justification for research, but also the provider of the education of the academics as a special group using funds obtained by the rest of the society. This awareness is now dead, and in its place is the individualistic competition and desperation to achieve at all costs, in order to survive.

The 'social responsibility' aspect, as set forth in the Dar es Salaam Declaration, Chapter Two, has been further eroded. Not only are members forced by the economic conditions to commercialise the services they offer to the community, no matter how small, but they may even be 'a party to any endeavour which may work to the detriment of the people or the academic community, or compromise scientific, ethical and professional principles and standards' (Dar es Salaam Declaration). This was poignantly illustrated when a member of the academic staff acted as the lawyer for the University administration against a colleague who was facing dismissal, which was later judged to be wrongful.

Academic Freedom
Background
Following independence in 1961, all organization was conducted under a single party, and most independent organizations were banned by the government. However, students were able to organize under two umbrella organizations, a college one and a national one. The first decade of independence was fraught with conflict between students and the new bourgeois ruling elite – who the students felt were enriching themselves at the expense of the people, in effect simply replacing the colonial class with Tanzanians – without attempting to meet the aspirations of the people. The academic staff had no organization of their own, but in the period before and after the Arusha Declaration, the struggles of the two groups were very closely linked. The university left wing in particular joined forces under the banner of USARF, the University Students African Revolutionary Front, which led Marxist debate and raised students' consciousness in that debate (Peter and Mvungi: 1985). USARF came to be seen by the state as a threat to its ideology of 'Tanzanian socialism' and was banned, together with its publication Cheche. Since the independent trade union movement had earlier met the same fate, all interests were then represented as 'mass' organizations by the ruling party, TANU, with its youth movement, TANU Youth League, imposed on the students as their representative organization.

With the founding of the University of Dar es Salaam, students were organized under a body called the Dar es Salaam University Students Organization (DUSO), which fell under the jurisdiction of the university. From the time of its inception in 1970 as a full university, the UDSM was taken under the wings of the ruling party. Up to 1980, the academic staff still had no umbrella organization through which they could channel matters relating to their welfare, and under which they could organize to have an effective voice in the running of the university. As members of Tanzania's first university, the onus fell on the academic staff to wage the struggle for more democratic governance of IsHE, which would allow for effective representation, and the shifting of focus to the academic rather than administrative functions of the university. The University Act of 1970 had made no provision for such an organization, and indeed, the period from 1970 to 1980 was one of the most repressive for the staff and students of the UDSM.

During this time the government instituted very rigid manpower planning guidelines which placed restrictions on which courses students could follow at the university, and ultimately, where graduating students could go and work. Consequently, students had little control over their future.

The year 1980 ushered in the founding of the first academic staff association in Tanzania, which had to be launched under an ad hoc arrangement to get round the University Act. The University of Dar es Salaam Academic Staff Assembly (UDASA) was created as a committee of Convocation, and still operates as such, although there are now attempts to register it as an autonomous trade union organization covering all universities. UDASA has played a pivotal role in effecting more democratic practices at UDSM, and through it, at the other universities.

Violations of Academic Freedom
Between 1970 and 1980, two TANU party stalwarts in succession were appointed as Vice-Chancellors, and the party treated the university as one of its wings. In that decade, the university became a battleground, with a series of violations of academic freedom. There was close monitoring by the state party on what was taught, researched and written. Criticism was censored, and often attributed to 'foreign influence', thus denying that Tanzanian academics and students could be critical of the status quo. There were numerous incidents of the government clamping down on students, academic staff and their activities. The latter perceived their actions as being part of the struggle against undemocratic practices, bureaucratism, and the denial of people's rights.

We shall mention only a few of these critical occurrences. These took place at the same time as the publication of Mwongozo wa TANU, which articulated a policy directed at the achievement of popular democracy in Tanzania, and was taken up with great enthusiasm by workers acting against dictatorial practices in their work places. In 1971, UDSM was stormed by the Field Force Unit during the famous Akivaga crisis,[4] following which the students' leader was rusticated. Seven years later, in 1978, there were mass expulsions of students, followed by the banning of their autonomous organization, DUSO. Students had undertaken demonstrations against the government's move to massively increase the salaries and fringe benefits of political leaders, including MPs. In a protest march to the city, students were intercepted with violence by the police. Three hundred and fifty of their members were then expelled, later to be pardoned by Nyerere, the then President and Chancellor. DUSO was replaced by a national organization, MUWATA, which was imposed on the students through an organ of the state party, the CCM Youth League. The life of MUWATA was characterised by constant friction between the state and the student community, as the latter felt that their freedom to press for issues affecting them was seriously curtailed.

The biggest crisis of that decade came in 1978, triggered by the dismissal and 'retirement in the public interest' of six members of staff, who were picked for their own leftist teaching and research, as sacrificial lambs and also as an example to other academic staff on what would happen should they not toe the line. In spite of vehement and prolonged protest by the staff, the affected members had to leave the university, and all of them subsequently left the country to work in universities elsewhere. The university administration could offer no explanation for the forcible retirement of these academics (some of whom are still teaching in reputable universities), other than that 'their services were needed in other public institutions'. Accompanying these forced retirements was the refusal by the university authorities to renew the contracts of several expatriate staff, who were viewed as instilling 'foreign ideology' among the students. The departure of their fellows greatly dampened the spirits of those left behind, and they became more wary of criticising the state and its policies, which was the intended outcome. This gross violation of academic freedom took place at a time when the politics of ujamaa was in its prime, and the then President, Julius Nyerere, was heard to declare that he wanted a university which would contribute towards the search for the truth by providing constructive criticism. However, most criticism was in fact construed as destructive.

State intervention also took the form of dictating what was relevant to the national and developmental needs, by requiring that courses and research work be demonstrated to be 'relevant'. Students were also sponsored according to strict national manpower needs, to fill state posts, so that some students were forced to study courses in which they had no interest. The main goals of university education were pushed to the background.

Within East and Southern Africa, Tanzania had been viewed as an oasis of calm amidst a sea of protest, closures, and demonstrations. But the lack of democracy and the reduced funding to education has activated various incidents in all the campuses of IsHE. At SUA in Morogoro a crisis was triggered off by the introduction of double-decker beds in rooms which previously had single occupants. At the then Ardhi Institute, (now the University College of Land and Architectural Studies, UCLAS), there were frequent closures and delayed openings due to the unavailability of funds. Students had running battles with the police as they marched peacefully to present their demands to the MSTHE, which was their main sponsor. In 1989, two students who dared to question the way funds were utilised by delegates to a festival in North Korea were put in detention, interrogated at length, and roughened up.

But the greatest crisis in recent years came in 1990, when the whole country was shaken by serious unrest at UDSM, triggered by student demands for democratic reforms, accompanied by wall literature and cartoons, some of which were extremely offensive. This rattled the state hard enough for it to close down the university. It remained closed for a whole year, and since that time hardly a year goes by without some crisis. In 1992, the students again boycotted classes, as a way of underlining their demands for the government to address economic and social issues such as fair prices for farmers' crops, a living wage for academic staff, greater freedom of speech at universities, and greater discussion on the cost-sharing measures. Three lecturers at UDSM, some of whom were in the forefront in the struggle for greater democracy and improved learning and teaching environment, were transferred within 24 hours without any explanation or discussion to much more junior positions outside the university, and it was only through a protracted struggle by UDASA that they were eventually reinstated. This was followed in 1993 by the first ever strike by lecturers, in pursuance of the same goal of a living wage, and in protest at government attempts to divide the academic community by palming off various allowances to some sections of the community, instead of giving a decent wage to all.

The increased competition offered by the changed political situation is not likely to dampen the confrontational climate. For instance, the main students' sponsor, the MSTHE, has recently set conditions of sponsorship which, among other things, require students not to participate in political activity, not to present their demands physically at the Ministry and not to repeat a year. Failure to meet these conditions will mean automatic loss of their sponsorship. Students are obviously resisting these conditions, which curtail even further the few democratic gains that have been made.

The IMF and Liberalisation
The recent attempts by the management of UDSM to initiate the transformation of the university through privatisation measures are a clear manifestation of the financial pressure that IsHE are confronting. As mentioned above, spending on education has been steadily declining, and this has been a direct consequence of the implementation of policies dictated from outside, by international financial agencies. IsHE have been hit by this decline in two ways. On the one hand, the policies of the World Bank and the IMF have dictated massive cuts in the social services. On the other, these policies, together with those of other donor agencies, encourage a change of focus and direction from the IsHE to primary school and secondary school education. Aid in terms of materials, training and staff exchanges is now provided more for the lower levels, including teacher training colleges, than for the IsHE. The World Bank and the IMF have insisted on the introduction of cost-sharing measures at all levels, and for several years now students have had to pay their own way, or

get loans from the government, to cover their travel, boarding and lodging costs. With a national per capita income of US$110, the vast majority cannot expect their parents to be able to help them even in the smallest way. Right now there is a simmering crisis arising from students' resistance to signing loan forms which effectively deny them the possibility of repeating a year, as their sponsorship will be withdrawn if they are forced to do so.

From this year, 1996, UDSM has made possible the admission of private students, who have to pay between US$3,500 and $7,000 per annum for tuition alone. Clearly this is outside the income range of most Tanzanians, and those who can afford such amounts would not be thinking of sending their children to the national universities anyway, but rather to universities abroad.[5]

The shift in focus from university education has meant that IsHE are getting less and less funding every year. For instance in this academic year, UDSM had budgeted for 24.1 billion Tanzania shillings. The government allocation was 6.37 billion. However, the funds actually disbursed to the university are only a fraction of even this government allocation.

The introduction of cost sharing measures has had consequences across the board. It has reduced access to education for many, so that UPE is now only a dream. The literacy rate has dropped from 85 per cent in the 1980s to around 60 per cent.

The Gendering of Academic Freedom

As mentioned above, the concept of academic freedom in the context of the changing sociopolitical landscape in Africa has had to be rethought. It has been suggested that the problem with the concept is not so much what it includes, but rather what it does not include (Busia: 1996). Can we, for instance, exclude policies that disempower half the population of a nation; those which restrict their access to higher education; those which do not provide equal opportunities for the pursuance of any field of study; practices which make it impossible for sections of students or academics to conduct their business in peace; those which limit the amount of time that those sections can spend on their work; and so on. We can argue that all these can and should be included within the purview of academic freedom. In the consideration of academic freedom and gender, in particular, it is precisely such issues that curtail the ability of women to realise their full potential as academics. What this means is that attempts at the protection of academic freedom cannot always be placed within justiciable rights. Some of these are conditioned by cultural practices and cultural biases, which, nevertheless, are cultivated within our societies. These often cannot be changed through the legal process, or through the declaration of charters and resolutions. They can be eliminated only through the extensive education of the civil society.

Female Participation in Education

The restrictions on academic freedom for women begin very early in the educational cycle. The odds are stacked high against them right from primary school, and this comes to have serious consequences for academic freedom of women in tertiary education. Mbilinyi et al (1990) argue that equity in education, in terms of equal access, equal performance, etc., is not sufficient in ensuring that education performs the fundamental role of transforming the conditions which contribute to the societal problems which face women. But even mere equity is non-existent, as will be evident below.

Since UPE in 1977, girls' enrolment into Standard 1 has gradually increased. For instance, while it was 41 per cent in 1974, it rose to 50.1 per cent in 1986 (nearly representative of the national population, which was 51 per cent according to the 1988 census). However, the drop-out rate for girls at this level is high, for various reasons, including initiation rituals when they reach puberty, early marriage, pregnancy, and pressure from some parents who see education as irrelevant for girls. In the middle of the present squeeze on education, some parents have to choose which of their children they should send to school. Between boys and girls, the odds are usually stacked against girls (Sumra and Katunzi: 1991). Where parents treat education as an investment, they calculate that girls may have other chances (i.e. marriage) which boys would not have. Such choices are particularly relevant at secondary school level, where the fees are considerably higher, and private schooling is the more likely option.

The equal access at primary level is not sustained, however. Girls dropping out in primary schools leaves fewer of them at the end of the seven-year cycle. But girls also perform much more poorly than boys, in spite of benefiting from a quota system without which access into secondary school for them would have been even more restricted (Mbilinyi: 1990). Recent figures indicate that while the transition rate into secondary school is generally low, fewer girls than boys make the transition (URT: 1995). The explanation for this often lies in the roles that society assigns to girls in terms of housework, and the rearing of their siblings. While boys can spend after-school hours playing or doing their homework and revision, girls have less time for these activities because of the chores that are required of them after school.

Table 2: Girls' Participation in School (% of pupil total)

Level	1981	1992
Primary	47.1	49.1
Secondary	31.6	44.7
A-level	22.3	24.3

The less satisfactory performance of girls pushes more of them into finding places in private secondary schools in order to continue their education. There are consequently many more girls in these schools than boys (62 per cent against 54 per cent in 1988). Most of such schools are more badly equipped than the public schools, being started on a self-help basis, or by local communities whose access to funding is limited. Malekela (1983) and TADREG (1990) demonstrate that public schools generally perform better than private ones. The trend of inadequate performance among girls is thus sustained in the latter schools, as demonstrated in the following figures for 1986 for a selection of subjects:

Table 3: Female and Male Pass and Fail Rate

Subject	Pass (A-E)		Fail (%)	
	F	M	F	M
Kiswahili	100	99	0	0
English	54	55	3	5
Accountancy	86	72	2	12
History	74	91	3	2
Physics	25	51	36	27
Chemistry	19	29	45	37
Biology	7	17	44	33

Source: TADREG 1990

The figures above are proportional, and do not reflect the number of women and men who actually sat for those examinations. The political, socioeconomic and cultural forces which fuel the discrimination and the bias against women are also clearly manifested in the choice of subjects made by girls in secondary school. There has been a long tradition of girls avoiding the science disciplines, and opting instead for what they perceive as the 'softer' option of arts or commerce. The fear of science is instilled among girls from primary school, where it is presented as difficult and only for the 'tough', and a girl who does well in arithmetic is held up as an anomaly. Mmari (1996) notes that the representation of girls in this area is unequal in two respects. First, in absolute numbers, fewer girls than boys take science subjects. In 1995, for example, in one form, there were 2080 boys taking science as against 659 girls. Additionally, 403 boys enrolled in technical schools, but only 31 girls. The figures were reversed for the arts, where 922 girls contrasted with 403 boys. Secondly, fewer girls gain admission into university, so that even the few who specialized in science do not get the opportunity to pursue it as a career option. In 1993, for UDSM, the figures were as follows:

	Male	Female
B Sc. General	62	4
B Sc. Education	60	13
B Sc. Engineering	189	3

Source: Admissions Office, University of Dar es Salaam 1996

The fact that women avoid science and technical subjects in spite of the perceived gains that are taken to accrue from them may suggest that women lack confidence about their ability to tackle those subjects, and this confidence is further eroded by both parents and teachers. However, it has also been suggested that girls choose arts subjects deliberately as they offer much quicker and more lucrative returns for them. So gender typing is combined with practical assessment of opportunities for future jobs. All the same, even the teaching materials used in school, in both content and language, serve to imprint the gender stereotypes existing within the society. Girls and women are presented typically as teachers, nurses, secretaries and toilers in the home, while boys represent engineers, doctors and pilots. The other side of the coin is the domestic science bias, which is offered especially for girls, and aims at making them 'better wives and mothers'. Not only does this bias serve to reinforce the sexual division of labour, but it is also a subject which offers no academic or employment prospects for those who take it, since it is not offered for A-levels (Mbilinyi: 1990).

The economic measures being pursued under the guise of liberalisation and market forces, apart from the effects discussed above, also work even more strongly to the detriment of women's education. Being the main agricultural producers, women are often responsible for getting the fees for their school-going children. But the SAPs have greatly undermined women's ability to purchase farming inputs, such as fertiliser, which affects what they are able to produce. This in turn affects their ability to pay for their children's education. The same SAPs, in their insistence on cutting down funding for the social services sector, also suggest measures which would lead to girls stopping the practice of boarding in secondary school. A lot of secondary and high schools in Tanzania have provided boarding facilities in order to deal with the regional imbalance, allowing children from regions without schools to study in those better endowed. Given the poor economic condition of most Tanzanian families, most children gained some advantage in boarding schools in terms of getting better working conditions, better supervision of their studies, and fewer distractions. With the demands placed on girls in the home environment, boarding has been even more crucial for them. The drive away from boarding is thus likely to affect girls' education negatively. ·

Institutions of Higher Education

Access at the tertiary level is the most restricted. For all Tanzanians, there is a serious shortage of places. Estimates suggest that only 0.3 per cent of primary school entrants eventually enter Tanzanian universities. Even with the limited numbers that graduate from high school, many with the right qualifications are still denied opportunities for higher education. With women, the opportunities have actually been narrowing rather than expanding. In 1996, the University of Dar es Salaam had women constituting 17 per cent of its intake; SUA 25 per cent, and the Muhimbili College of Health Sciences (MUCHS) 28 per cent. The table following shows the proportion of women in IsHE in 1994/95.

Table 4: Proportion of Women in IsHE, 1994-95

	Women	Men	Percentage Women
Technical Colleges	100	1569	6
UDSM	509	2442	17
SUA	213	696	23
MUCHS	95	243	28
OUT	137	1367	9

Figures computed from URT 1995b

Whereas in 1981, 24 per cent of entrants into UDSM were women, the highest proportion since 1970, this figure had fallen to 17 per cent in 1994-5. Within different faculties in the university, the differences are quite stark, with the science and engineering faculties showing the lowest figures. Below is the proportion of women (in percentage) admitted in 1989 and 1994:

Table 5: Proportion of Women Admitted, 1981 and 1994

Year	Arts	Commerce	Engineering	Law	Science
1989	22	20	4	24	17
1994	26	18	3	22	18

Source: *Twenty-five Years: University of Dar es Salaam 1970-1995*

These figures are hardly surprising, given girls' poorer performance in science at the lower levels. The explanation lies in the lack of enough affirmative action which would introduce a greater balance between the performance of women and that of men.

This situation is not just a result of the imbalances that exist for women in the lower levels, but also the negative learning, teaching and researching environment that faces them at the universities. Among these are the recruitment practices, the training practices, and the sexual harassment, that are rampant at these institutions. I will consider each one of these in turn.

Recruitment
The student position is mirrored by that of academic staff. At the oldest university, UDSM, there are only 62 women academic staff against 539 men, the largest number (42) being lecturers and senior lecturers. There are only four women full professors out of 40 (University of Dar es Salaam: 1996). The picture is duplicated in the other institutions. SUA has 24 women out of 236, and UCLAS has 14 of 103.

Traditionally, new staff members are recruited from the pool of graduating students who show excellent performance. This has been the practice with women as well. However, as noted above, the numbers of women joining the universities has been dropping in real terms, so the number of available candidates from whom the best would be chosen is itself dwindling. The universities have now stopped recruiting staff at the level of tutorial assistant, and instead prospective staff must have at least a master's degree. Again, there are fewer women who have that qualification. In those disciplines where women perform badly because of their background in primary and secondary school, the chances of new recruits is small. Consequently, the numbers of women academics remains small, and are likely to remain so, now that the universities have frozen recruitment of all staff. Without affirmative action which would reduce the imbalance in recruitment, there is no chance that the core of women academics will be strengthened. Such action was operating with the Musoma and Lindi Resolutions of 1974, which allowed women to enter university directly, from the schools, instead of having to put in two years' work first, as was required for men. These measures allowed female enrolment to rise from 11 per cent in 1971 to 24.4 per cent in 1978.

Training Practices
In the multiple identities held by a woman academic, that of being a woman, rather than being an academic, is often put first in academic circles. This never happens with men. So women are not only addressed as the wives of so and so, although they may have their academic titles, but assumptions are often made on their behalf about what is best for them - what kind of training they need, when it should be provided, the kinds of problems they and their families are likely to encounter, and so on. Thus a woman may be bypassed for a training opportunity because her male head of department or dean thinks she

will have difficulty coping, if she has a young baby, or has just got married. The woman herself may not even be consulted on this. As a result, women who are fully trained, and who consequently have managed to reach senior positions, are relatively few.

Women who are articulate in fighting for their rights are viewed as 'frustrated' in their social and family roles. Consideration for promotion and other opportunities is often made on the basis of issues which are totally unrelated to their work. Assessment is made of the woman based on her actions outside the academic life, such as the way she dresses, her sexual life, her marital status, and so on. Such considerations are very seldom relevant for men.

As a legacy of their primary and secondary education, more women join the arts and social sciences, and law, than the sciences and engineering. But the former are precisely the areas that the donors are turning their backs on. Thus further training for women in these faculties is fraught with difficulties, and women staff have to struggle hard through their own efforts to get training. Part of academic training involves conducting research, without which members cannot build their academic careers or advance their own knowledge base. The universities themselves have hardly any funding for research. Tanzania is said to allocate only 0.2 per cent of its GNP to research, in contrast to 1.18 per cent for Singapore, 0.78 per cent for India and 0.49 per cent for Turkey, for example (URT: 1996b). Consequently, most research is conducted under donor-funded consultancies, or external research grants. The acute competition involved in these invariably favours men, who have had a headstart in establishing networks among themselves. They thus pass information to each other, recommend each other for awards and grants, and team up with each other. Women are thus able to get a foothold only if they have exceptionally brilliant proposals, or are willing to undertake the more peripheral or difficult tasks, and thus gain less recognition for their work.

Sexual Harassment/Oppression

The gendering of academic freedom is reflected in its most blatant form in the reality that the working environment for women is markedly different from that of men. In their studies, women have to face not only the usual academic competition, but also the dominant cultural ideology that bright intellectual women are an anomaly. Consequently, women's performance is judged not on the basis of their own merit, but on external agencies which are assumed to 'help' them. There have been several well-entrenched practices which have worked to undermine women's performance at universities, and we will look at some of these below.

Many women entering IsHE do so after weighing carefully the opportunities that exist for them without higher education. Particularly for the married women, further studies lay a heavy extra burden, additional to their usual productive and reproductive responsibilities. They therefore tend to take their academic work very seriously, and generally perform better than men.

Apart from such women, there are those who are intellectually bright, and women are often among the best performers in class. But this success is seldom taken on its own merit. Instead, women students are said to get good scores in exchange for favours they offer to lecturers. Bright women are thus treated with derision by their male colleagues.

The male lecturers also take advantage of this environment to harass women students, and to offer marks for sexual favours, by issuing threats of withholding of marks, extra one-to-one tuition, negotiation for marks, and so on. Cases of this sort are regularly reported by women students, and at least one such case caused the formation of a probe committee in the Faculty of Arts and Social Sciences at the University of Dar es Salaam. The committee established that there was grave misconduct on the part of two male lecturers, who had wrongly failed women students because they had rejected their sexual advances, or had allowed situations where the women were forced to bargain for their marks. Those two lecturers were subsequently dismissed from the university.

But the biggest threat to the academic freedom of women students once they are in university comes from male fellow students. Women in IsHE are not spared the dangers to their personal security both on and off campus. They are cautioned when they join to take the usual precautionary measures against sexual attacks and mugging. But apart from these, they also have to fight the paternalistic, domineering, and sexist attitudes of their mates. Women are treated as a separate class, who cannot practice the same social and academic activities as men. They are barred from some meals in the student cafeterias, dictated to about how they should dress, and a few of them even made to do housework such as cooking and washing while the men 'study' on their behalf. They are terrorised in their rooms if they refuse to take the dominant male position in student clashes with the administration. In a recent case, a large group of male students stormed the women's hall of residence, shouted threats and insults, and broke down seven doors, in efforts to force women to attend a meeting organized by the students' government. The women mobilised to condemn this event, and to build up forms of support for each other.

The oldest and most well-established force behind such activities exists at the University of Dar es Salaam, by the name of *Punch*. The genesis of *Punch* was as a form of wall literature in the 1960s, when it was used as a forum for making socially relevant critiquing of the government and the university administration. However, *Punch* gradually evolved into a control mechanism, one of whose aspects is a scandal 'sheet', in which the private lives of mostly women students and staff are discussed in the sleaziest of details.

Punch issues so-called 'ten commandments' to all freshers, and those who do not heed these or other forms of regulation, then face the prospect of the wall 'punching'. Prior warning is issued, followed by the actual punching, and the literature is placed high on the walls of the main cafeteria, where everybody can read it. Women students find this exposure extremely traumatic, and many have to have counselling following a punching. In 1990 the failure by university authorities to provide timely counselling to one first year student, Revina Mukassa, who had rebuffed sexual advances from a fellow student, and who had already received prior warning, led to her suicide. Revina Mukassa's ordeal lasted for four months, during which she was constantly abused by a group of male students, totally isolated by her female friends who feared their own possible punching, and eventually faced an attempted rape by one of her harassers. She received little help or counselling after reporting the incident, and subsequently committed suicide through an overdose. Her death shook the university community to its core. Women staff and students held a series of discussions and protests to get *Punch* eliminated, and counselling services improved. A probe team's report on the Revina case made several recommendations, relating to increased security, improved counselling services, and the banning of *Punch*. While some of these measures were taken, *Punch* could not be eliminated without instituting any measures in which the secret identities of the *Punch* group could be exposed.

Women who have been punched testify to undergoing extreme trauma, humiliation and erosion of confidence. Another serious case indirectly related to *Punch* was of a student who died shortly after graduating, having suffered from stomach ulcers which were caused by the stress she had undergone after being punched. There is no telling how many other such cases go unreported, because their victims are afraid of being punched.

Women students on university campuses also face other forms of 'sanction' when they refuse to toe the line. Women who stand their ground are 'sanctioned' by having their classmates isolating them from group activities. Those who refuse to do this to their mates are also in turn sanctioned.

In this environment, women live in constant fear of being subjected to humiliation and shame in the eyes of their peers. It takes very strong-willed women to overcome the trauma and stigma attached to being punched, and it is such women who have managed to provide guidance and support for others who have faced similar experiences. The universities are now instituting a system of peer counsellors, in which students can get support from those with whom they feel more akin, rather than some distant professional counsellor.

There are indications that sexual harassment on university campuses is on the increase, within the new environment of liberalisation, increased competition for services, cost-sharing and economic difficulties. Whereas in the sixties and seventies gender relations on campuses were amicable and even supportive, at present students are under increased tension to succeed, in the midst of greater pressure to find their own resources for studies, and extremely difficult learning conditions (including cramped and uncomfortable living quarters), and these accumulated pressures may be finding unconventional outlets for their expression.[6]

Yet, in spite of these insidious practices, and the harsh environment in which women have to study, women at universities have been performing consistently better than men, and there have been fewer women drop-outs. The explanation for this lies in part in the very confrontations that women have to continually face, not only at the universities, but in the job market, which has made them realise that they have to put much greater effort into what they do than their male counterparts. Many women come to university as mature age candidates, after their children have grown up, and for those, the level of determination and the will to achieve is very high.

Positive Measures

The discussion above should not be taken to construe that either the society or the government are not taking any action to counter the tendencies of discrimination, harassment and neglect. As mentioned above, there have always been female quotas for entrance into secondary school. These have made it possible for girls to catch up with male transition rates. Coupled with this are other selection procedures, such as those for Form 5. To qualify for selection, male students need 7 passes, while female students need only 5 (Mbilinyi 1990).

The Ministry of Education and Culture is also undertaking measures to increase the number of places for girls in secondary schools. Although this seems to take place through the increase of secondary schools generally, there are also a few schools which have been built specifically for girls.

Some of the IsHE, such as UDSM, have in recent years adopted a policy of positive discrimination, in cases such as the admission of students on reserve lists, or in the admission of extra students, where both male and female candidates are equally eligible. In such cases, women are selected rather than men. In addition, from the 1996/97 academic year, there have also been attempts in some faculties to ensure a 30 per cent women enrolment, before male candidates were considered.

But all these measures are likely to take a long time to take effect. As noted above, some of these, such as boarding schools and the quota system, are coming under increasing attack, and stand in danger of being scrapped. At the same time, the Minister of Science, Technology and Higher Education has reiterated in his 1996 budget estimates speech the government's continuing commitment to taking special measures to correct the existing imbalances (URT 1996b).

Conclusion

The paradox for the present and the future is that while the politics of pluralism (usually equated with increased democracy) are becoming dominant, they are not accompanied by greater democracy within the IsHE. The tenure of academics is seriously threatened, with members being dismissed in spite of appeals from their departments for their retention. The decisions for their dismissal are taken in committees which not only fail to offer them an opportunity to be heard, a basic tenet of democratic practice, but which often do not even have the legal powers of dismissal. The orientation of the economy towards market forces has been used as a pressure point towards the 'marketisation' of the courses, requiring staff to offer courses which presumably would offer better opportunities of employment for graduates. While this may be a desirable aim, it also poses the danger of introducing courses which are fashionable rather than knowledge creating, and also courses which create skills rather than knowledge, a function not of universities, but of technikons. Furthermore, the marketisation usually has to take the form of more courses, not simply the amendment of existing courses, and in a context where there are cutdowns on university funding, retrenchment of staff, freezing of posts, this means the placement of greater responsibilities on staff, without accompanying expansion of facilities or remuneration.

The struggle for academic freedom in Tanzania which has been briefly described above has taken place within a context of the struggle for greater democracy, decreased state bureaucracy, and the rights of people. This struggle is becoming sharper as class divisions within the society are deepened by the liberalisation measures, and there is marked deterioration in the culture of understanding and tolerance within the society generally. More specifically, a shift can be noted in student politics from progressive, socially conscious programmes to petty bourgeois, sexist, individualistic concerns, some of whose consequences are the greater oppression of women students and academics, within the general oppression by the state. Consequently, the agenda of academic freedom in Africa must bring within its purview greater awareness building and the change of attitudes within the gender dimension.

Abbreviations
MEC   Ministry of Education and Culture
MSTHE   Ministry of Science, Technology and Higher Education
MUCHS   Muhimbili College of Health Sciences
OUT   Open University of Tanzania
SUA   Sokoine University of Agriculture
UDASA   University of Dar es Salaam Academic Staff Assembly
UDSM   University of Dar es Salaam

Notes
1. It is ironic that Nyerere was upholding a position that was to be a favourite of the World Bank and the IMF later, that Africa is in need of primary education, and not higher education (Imam and Mama 1994).
2. This exercise is euphemistically referred to as 'course restructuring'.
3. See Karim Hirji's article 'Academic pursuits under the link', in *UDASA Newsletter/Forum* no. 10, February 1990.
4. Akivaga was the then President of the student organization, DUSO
5. Of 312 places offered to private candidates this year, only 12 were taken up.
6. The report of the probe team on the Revina Mukassa case stated that the living conditions at the University of Dar es Salaam are so bad that they 'brutalise' students. This is coupled by an increased incidence of sexual molestation and rape country-wide.

References
Busia Jr., Nana K. A. (1996), Towards a legal framework for the protection of academic freedom: Perspectives on the African human rights system, in CODESRIA (1996) op. cit.
CODESRIA (1996), *The State of Academic Freedom in Africa*, 1995, Dakar: CODESRIA.
Dar es Salaam Declaration on Academic Freedom and the Responsibility of Academics (1990).
Diouf, Mamadou and Mahmood Mamdani (eds.) (1994), *Academic Freedom in Africa*, Dakar: CODESRIA book series.
Imam, Ayisha and Amina Mama (1994), The role of academics in limiting and expanding academic freedom, in Diouf and Mamdani (eds.) (1994).
Kampala Declaration on Academic Freedom (1990).
Malekela, G. A. (1983), Access to secondary education in Sub-Saharan Africa: The Tanzanian experiment. Unpublished Ph D thesis, University of Chicago.
Mbilinyi, Marjorie (1990), Secondary and higher education, in Mbilinyi et al (eds.) (1990).
Mbilinyi, Marjorie, P. Mbughuni, R. Meena and P. Olekambaine (eds.)(1990), *Education in Tanzania with a Gender Perspective*, Dar es Salaam: SIDA.
Mmari, G. (1976), Implementation of the Musoma resolution, papers in education and development, no 3.
Njau, A. and T. Mruma [1995] *Gender and Development in Tanzania: Past, Present and Future*. Dar es Salaam: WRDP.
Peter, Chris and S. Mvungi (1985), The state and student struggles, in Issa Shivji (ed.) *The State and the Working People in Tanzania*, Dakar: CODESRIA.
Sumra, Suleman and Naomi Katunzi (1991) The struggle for education: School fees and girls' education in Tanzania. *WED report no. 5*, Dar es Salaam: University of Dar es Salaam.
TADREG (1990), Girls educational opportunities and performance in Tanzania. *Research Report no. 2*, Dar es Salaam.

TANU (1971), *Mwongozo wa TANU*, Dar es Salaam: Government Printer.

Tanzania Gender Networking Programme (1983), *Gender Profile of Tanzania*, Dar es Salaam: TGNP.

United Republic of Tanzania (1989, 1994, 1995, 1996) Basic Education Statistics in Tanzania (BEST), Dar es Salaam: Ministry of Education and Culture.

United Republic of Tanzania (1995b), Higher and Technical Education statistics. Dar es Salaam: Ministry of Science, Technology and Higher Education.

United Republic of Tanzania (1996b), Hotuba ya Waziri wa Sayansi, Teknolojia na Elimu ya Juu, wakati wa kuwasilisha Bungeni makadirio ya matumizi ya fedha kwa mwaka 1996/97, Dar es Salaam University Press.

University of Dar es Salaam (1996), Institutional transformation programme: Facts and figures, Dar es Salaam.

University of Dar es Salaam Academic Staff Assembly (UDASA) (1991) *UDASA Newsletter/Forum* no. 13, July 1991.

University of Dar es Salaam Academic Staff Assembly (UDASA) (1991), *UDASA Newsletter/Forum* no. 13, Supplement, July 1991.

University of Dar es Salaam Academic Staff Assembly (UDASA) (1990) *UDASA Newsletter/Forum.*, February 1990.

3. Gender and Academic Freedom in Malawi

Isabel Apawo Phiri

Introduction

When Malawi held its first conference on academic freedom in October 1994, I had the opportunity of presenting a paper entitled 'Academic Freedom and a Gender-Balanced Curriculum at Chancellor College'. In this paper I argued that not many courses in the faculties of Humanities and Social Sciences include materials that present a positive image of women, with women's experiences often excluded. This study also showed that often it is assumed that gender issues are only the concern of female lecturers. I argued that Chancellor College, like most institutions in the country, has a very small number of female lecturers who only had themselves to make an impact on gender issues. The study showed that there is a high level of faculty interest in a project on integrating women's experiences into the mainstream of learning in order to bring a gender balance to the study of humanities and social science.

It is in the interest of the development of our country that our institutions of higher learning produce students who are balanced in their outlook on gender issues. The paper was well received by colleagues, which was an encouragement to do more research and disseminate the results. However, other research showed that there is a limited academic freedom in the dissemination of information on some gender issues at the University of Malawi.

The Controversial Paper

In July 1995 I presented a paper entitled 'Violence against women in educational institutions: the case of sexual harassment and rape on Chancellor College campus', at the annual Conference on University Research and Development, held at Sun and Sand Holiday Resort in Mangochi. The paper presented findings of research conducted in June and July 1994 by Linda Semu from the Sociology Department, Flora Nankhuni from the Economics Department and Nyovani Madise from the Statistics Department and myself. These four concerned female lecturers form the Chancellor College Gender Lobby Group.

The objectives of the research were to 'determine the level of sexual harassment and incidence of rape on female students at Chancellor College campus'. In this context we wanted to find out who was responsible for harassment and rape, if the levels were increasing or decreasing, how the victims reacted and to whom they reported and also if sufficient support structures existed.[1] Questionnaires were sent to all 364 female students on Chancellor College campus. Completed questionnaires were returned by 202. All were anonymous, and no names were to be mentioned in the replies.

The results showed that 23 students (12.6 per cent) reported that they had been raped. Of these, 48 per cent had been raped by a boyfriend, 17 per cent by a friend and 6 per cent by others. Sixty-seven per cent (125/186) of respondents reported that they had been sexually harassed on campus, with 'unwelcome sexual advances' being the most frequent form mentioned (49.6 per cent). Persons mentioned were: friends (55.7 per cent), boyfriends (5 per cent), male lecturers (5 per cent). Outside the campus, male lecturers were mentioned with 28.7 per cent, strangers with 45 per cent. Outside the campus, 'to grant sexual favours' was the most frequently reported type of sexual harassment.

The survey did not produce conclusive evidence about a rise or decline in sexual harassment. Almost two-thirds (61 per cent per cent) of the students raped did not report to anyone. Out of the 39 per cent who reported, 22 per cent reported to their parents and 38 per cent to friends, none to police or the College Administration. The others seem to have reported to friends. Fear and lack of knowledge of where to report were the reasons for not doing so. On sexual harassment 64 per cent shared their experience with someone, only four per cent reported to the College Administration, or to the police. The implications we found were that students suffered problems with performance, depression, mental torture and pain. There had been one attempted suicide. As authors (supported by answers in the questionnaires) we recommended that the University should produce a policy document on sexual harassment and rape, that this policy should be effectively communicated to all concerned, that each campus should have a Gender Lobby Group composed of lecturers and students and that the University should appoint counsellors to assist victims.

The Discussion
The paper was generally accepted. There were some critical comments which included the possibility that women invited rape on themselves, that women may buy their way to the top through sex and that the definition of sexual harassment employed was too broad.

The Radio Interview
Reporters from Malawi Broadcasting Corporation (MBC), who had been invited by the Research and Publication Committee (RPC) of the University of Malawi, interviewed me and others the next morning. The interview was transmitted by MBC on a newsreel programme just after the main 12.30pm news. Of the many interviews recorded, only mine was broadcast, although the report mentioned that many papers had been presented.

The Students' Demonstration

The paper had been presented on Monday and the interview was broadcast on Tuesday. On Wednesday, students demanded airtime on MBC to make a nationwide statement to refute my report and demand that MBC broadcast an apology 'to the student body and the public for the ethnically sensitive information dissemination'[2]. The chair of the Students Union of Chancellor College (SUCC) was driven in a college vehicle to the MBC studio in Zomba and read the statement on air.[3] A large group of students staged a demonstration at the MBC studio. On their way back a sizeable group of them attacked my house by throwing heavy stones into the sitting room and the bedrooms and damaging doors, windows and the roof of the house and my car. My son (seven years old), my nephew (six years old) and my mother were in the house. From my house the students went back to the college, where they damaged my office. This occurred at about 12.30 pm. In addition to material damage, verbal damage was done. My life and those of my child, my nephew and my mother threatened, when the students said they would come back with petrol to burn the house.

At 2 pm the Principal telephoned the RPC coordinator and me at Mangochi. He informed us about the extent of the damage and about the demands of the students. He asked the coordinator to replay the taped interview and to comment. He told me to come back to Zomba immediately, but there was no transport. At the conference the tape was rerun, and the representatives of RPC stated that the tape contained what had been presented in the conference room and made a statement condemning the violence.[4] When I returned to Zomba the next day, no alternative accommodation had been arranged for me and my family, nor had any security been provided because no guards could be spared. Together with the Head of Department I visited the Principal at his home in the evening to ask for accommodation, whereupon we were granted one night at a government hostel. This is what happened. What were the reactions?

Placate the Students and Blame the Victim

This was the approach taken by the Chancellor College administration, clearly reflected in the Principal's letter to the Vice Chancellor, written the day after the attack. He wrote:

Since the students were reacting to Dr I. Phiri's radio interview which was on the air on Tuesday 18 July 1995 on the ground that her statements amounted to defamation and that the students challenge the validity of her findings, it is necessary that your office should without delay, set up a committee to carry out, inter alia, the following activities:
(a) Evaluate the questionnaire against the objectives of the survey.
(b) assess the sampling

(c) analyze the responses
(d) interpret the data
(e) compare their findings with those of Dr I. Phiri.
(f) assess to what extent the information broadcast was distorted, if at all
(g) assess the effects of the information broadcast
(h) make appropriate recommendations to your office.

Obviously I was blamed and the students were, as the letter continues, 'an aggrieved party'. There was no hint in the letter of any condemnation of the students' violence, but a clear distrust in the quality and validity of the research. There was no defence of academic freedom either. What was important was to protect the interests of the students. This was later confirmed when at the meeting of Heads and Deans at Chancellor College, the Principal informed everyone that it was difficult for him to bring to book the students who were involved in vandalizing my college house, office and personal car. However he asked for the formation of a Committee of Deans to examine the questionnaire, methodology and interpretation of the paper that I presented. He also said that I should appear before the Committee to answer charges of acting irresponsibly by giving a radio interview on a sensitive paper.

A letter was sent to me by the College Registrar informing me that I should appear before a Committee of Deans on 7 August to answer charges in connection with the radio interview. At the time I presented the conference paper, I had already applied to attend two conferences in South Africa from 1 to 12 August, and permission had already been granted by the Principal and Vice Chancellor. I wanted to retain my academic freedom to attend conferences so I suggested to the Principal that I appear before the Committee of Deans after the conferences. Neither did I want to forgo the compassionate leave that I had applied for 13 to 31 August. So I suggested I appear before the Deans after I came back. The principal reluctantly agreed and he wrote:

The meeting with the Committee of Deans will take place early September when you return. I have talked to the Chairman, who was able to talk to two other Deans. They are not happy that they cannot meet you until September.[5]

Despite the fact that the research was done by four people and, in my case, with resources from my department, the Principal demanded that I appear before the Committee of Deans alone. I became aware of this when I found out that the invitation to appear before the Deans was sent to me only. When my Department offered to appear with me at the meeting of the Committee of Deans the Principal responded in the following way:

1. *As Principal of this College, I am and have to be interested in the contents of any document that discusses the welfare of my staff or students at this College.*

2. *The paper that was presented at the Conference is not on Theology or Religion and was not co-authored by staff in the Department. Therefore, it is not a Departmental issue.*
3. *The College Administration is not going to take instructions from the Department of Theology and Religious Studies on how to manage College Affairs.*
4. *You are entitled to your opinion but please note that running away from a problem is not the same as solving a problem. Your supporting reason for the holiday that 'I need to leave the country for a while until the students have finished writing their examinations and the concerned male lecturers have cooled down' implies that you are not prepared to face reality. The students will be back next academic year and note that cooling down is not the same as forgetting or forgiving. Therefore, the sooner the differences are solved the better.[6]*

This letter obviously was meant to emphasize that I was the one to blame for all that went wrong after the presentation of the researched paper. To this I replied to the Principal in the following way:

I wish to apologise for giving you the impression that I do not recognise your authority as the Principal of Chancellor College. That thought never entered my mind. I acknowledge that as a head of the institution you have the authority to protect the welfare of this community. However, so far I am wondering why my welfare has not been your concern. I also acknowledge your power to constitute a Committee of Deans although they are also part of the aggrieved male lecturers...

As the Principal of Chancellor College, I acknowledge your authority to demand that I appear before the Committee of Deans alone... without giving you the impression that I am telling you what to do, or that I do not want to face the Committee of Deans, you may wish to note that separating the research paper from the radio interview will be very difficult and might prove to be frustrating to me and the committee of Deans... I wish to humbly inform you in advance that I will not answer questions on the research paper before the committee of Deans because I do not have the mandate to do so from the co-authors. Although the charge before me is on defamation, in my opinion, what is at stake here is doing research and disseminating information in the field of Gender. Sooner or later it will be important to establish whether lecturers who have specialized or are interested in Gender issues have academic freedom to do research and disseminate information in the University of Malawi...

I also wish to acknowledge your authority as Principal of Chancellor College to interpret my asking for a holiday from 13-31 August as 'running away from the problem', 'not being prepared to face reality', 'and thinking that people will forget and forgive'. By using this kind of judgmental language, I get the impression that I have already been found guilty without a trial... You may wish to note that it is not in my nature to run away from academic debates channelled through academic forums as long as I am not subjected to acts of violence. Hiding from danger is not the same with 'refusing to face reality' as you put it in your memo...[7]

My letter was never replied to and a new date was not proposed for the meeting with the Deans. I was left in suspense and my movements were still restricted as I did not know what was happening.

It was later learnt that the meeting with the Committee of Deans was cancelled because the MBC refused to release the tape containing my radio interview. Since the meeting was precisely based on that, then the Deans had no concrete material to pin me down with.

The Integrity of the University Depends on the Exercise of Academic Freedom

This was the position adopted by the Department of Theology and Religious Studies, to which I belong. As soon as news reached members of the department that the students had attacked my college house, personal car and college office, the department showed its solidarity by writing a memo of protest to the Chancellor College administration. Their basis for support was not just because I am a member of that department but to defend academic freedom. They expressed surprise that it did not occur to the Chancellor College Administration that they should have issued a clear statement without delay to condemn the students' unruly behaviour. They also placed responsibility for my safety and that of my family with the college administration. A demand was made to the college administration to take disciplinary action against the culprits. They further argued that 'the College ensures that academic freedom of research and expression is safeguarded and that dissent over research findings is expressed in non-violent ways'.[8]

The department also took the responsibility of making and publicizing corrections to the report that appeared in the *Daily Times* newspaper on 20 July 1995.

They made it a point to place the corrections on all notice boards on campus to show people at the university that they were reacting to wrong information. Copies of the research paper were placed in the Library, posted in the student cafeteria and in both senior and junior staff common rooms. Personal copies were sent to the chair and vice chair of the Chancellor College Student Union as well as the chair of the University Student Union.

The department went to the police to report on the damages and harassment of members of my family. When the college administration could not provide security guards on the night after the vandalism, the department hired such facilities. When no alternative accommodation was arranged after my return from the conference, it was again the department that went to the Principal's house at night to plead for my accommodation which was reluctantly provided.

The stand of the department should be understood in the context of the Principal's memo of 21 July addressed to members of staff of the Department of Theology and Religious Studies. The Principal argued that:

As you will have read in my memorandum to the Vice Chancellor and my verbal responses to your memorandum, the College Administration is doing what is possible and best under the present circumstances and by taking into account other factors which we are aware of. Thus, most of the issues you have raised are under control. However there is a limit to what the College Administration can do.

Thus what the department was doing was to fill in the gaps in the areas that the College Administration implied were outside its limits. It also decided to take full responsibility for the research paper[9], which did not please the College Administration.

When the College Administration was quiet about the whole issue in the months of September and October, on 12 October the department decided to pursue it through the Vice Chancellor.

Condemn the Violence and Catch the Perpetrators
When the Principal of Chancellor College informed the Vice Chancellor on the telephone on 19 July that students wanted to demonstrate, the Vice Chancellor's initial reaction was to 'query the wisdom of such a demonstration'. When the Vice Chancellor saw that it was a big demonstration, he again got in touch with the Principal and asked him to explain what was happening. After the damage caused by the students to my college office and my house, the Vice Chancellor was one of the first people to visit the vandalized scene and offer apologies to my mother. He was shocked to see the great damage caused and later commented that:

I fear what would have happened had Dr Phiri been at the house then... I would hate to see this college degenerate into a campus of thugs. I will do everything in my power to restore a sense of dignity, civility and responsibility to this once model institution.[10]

As a mature person who had worked in the University for 29 years, he did not support the actions of the students but instead demanded that the Principal of Chancellor College should condemn the violence and catch the culprits. It was in this vein that the Vice Chancellor refused to set up a committee to examine the research paper in question. He argued that this was a college matter which should be settled by the college.

As the opening of the new academic year was approaching, the head of the department of Theology and Religious Studies and I paid the Vice Chancellor a visit. The purpose of the visit was to inform him that since the Chancellor College Administration had not yet taken any disciplinary action against the students who attacked my college house, office and personal car, this gave me the impression that I am a legitimate target for violence and made me feel very vulnerable to go back to work. It was after this visit that the Vice Chancellor arranged that there should be a meeting to discuss the issue. The meeting was attended by the Principal, Dean of Humanities, Head of Department of Theology and Religious Studies and myself. One is left to wonder as to what could have happened if no attempt was made by the department to initiate talks before the opening of the new academic year.

'The Issue is Too Complex'

The University RPC reacted in two ways to the intimidation and violence that I experienced. The Principal gave the RPC the mandate to listen to the taped interview that I made for their comments. The Coordinator duly convened a meeting of RPC faculty representatives who were present at the conference. I was part of the meeting in my capacity as representative of the Faculty of Humanities and chair of RPC.

Fortunately the MBC reporter was still at the conference. He therefore made the tape available to the RPC Coordinator. I was consulted by the reporter before he surrendered the tape. He informed me that I had the right to say no if I did not want RPC to listen to the interview. Since I knew that what I had said during the presentation was the same with what was contained in the paper, I had nothing to hide. I therefore gave my permission to rerun the tape. When this was done, RPC agreed to release a statement to condemn the student violence and uphold academic freedom to do research and disseminate information. It was also agreed that the statement be released after the student had finished writing their end of year examinations. The examinations were to start a week after the students vandalized my property. Therefore it was hoped that the RPC statement should not be used as a scapegoat to incite more violence and therefore disturb the commencement of the examinations.

To my surprise even after the students had gone for holidays, RPC did not release the agreed statement. Therefore the issue was further deliberated at the RPC meeting of 17 September 1995. It was at this meeting that the Research Coordinator informed everyone that:

The statement had not been released because judging by the intensity and extent of the debate, it appeared that the issue was more complex than had been assumed at the ad hoc meeting in Mangochi and that the full Committee needed to give mandate to the Research Office on the suitability of releasing the statement and of action regarding the students.

Following a lengthy debate the committee agreed that the issue appeared to be very complex and RPC would find itself in a mess if it got mixed up in the debate and therefore resolved that the statement should not be released.[11]

It becomes clear here that by not condemning the action of the students in order to defend academic freedom, the RPC was implicitly sending a message to the students that it is all right to disagree in a violent way when one is not happy with results of research conducted in the University of Malawi. One may want to know as to what makes the issue to be too complex. This becomes clear with the examination of the reaction of Chancellor College staff.

Mixed Reaction from Staff
Substantial Numbers of Hostile Academic Staff
The first time I went to Chancellor College campus after the presentation of the research paper was on 8 September when I attended a research presentation by the Chancellor College Principal. This was the first time I actually experienced the intensity of hostility from a substantial section of the academic staff. Since no one actually came forward to accuse me of anything, it was difficult to pinpoint what exactly it was that offended the academic staff. However, at the meeting of Heads and Deans of Chancellor College, my issue was placed on the agenda. Three outstanding comments from the local male academic staff at the meeting were to agree with the Principal that 'I had acted irresponsibility by disseminating sensitive information on the air', that 'she brought the intimidation and violence from the students upon herself' and that 'she is only after power to become Principal of Chancellor College'.

Clear Support
The academic staff who were in support either came in person to show their support or wrote to the Vice Chancellor and the Principal of Chancellor College to condemn what had happened. Two such memos came from the Head of the Law Department and a member of the Department of Education Foundation[12]. Both letters called on the University to support academic freedom. For example, the Head of the Law Department argued that:

I would like to reiterate that unless strong measures are taken to deal with such terrorism as that displayed by those who attacked Dr Phiri's property and family, the future of academic freedom at this college remains bleak and the integrity of the University as a whole is seriously jeopardised.[13]

This group of academic staff showed that by calling the University to discipline the students concerned, it would be making a statement that academic freedom is valued at the university.

Support from Co-authors

Unfortunately when the paper was presented, two co-authors were out of the country, Nyovani was in England where she took up a job and Flora was in Zambia participating in a conference. Linda was out of Zomba in the field conducting another research project. I was therefore left alone to present the paper and bear the consequences. Nevertheless, when Linda read about the vandalism, she sent a fax to express her solidarity. Flora came back when I had gone to South Africa. During this period, the Principal of Chancellor College invited her to his office to tell her to keep away from the issue, as people were not interested in the co-authors but in the presenter of the paper.

Nyovani wrote to the Principal to argue that 'all four of us had equal responsibility of the execution and presentation of the research findings'. She further argued that:

> *Since this was academic research, conducted with the approval of the University of Malawi Research and Publications Committee and the female respondents, I find it very strange that people should express their dissent through violent action. Such behaviour is not only intimidating but crippling to the future of research at the University of Malawi.[14]*

Nyovani also queried the wisdom of inviting only one co-author to appear before the Committee of Deans as if I was the only one responsible for the paper. She also queried the action of criticising academic work in a court-like session with threats of disciplinary action afterwards. She did not see why the Principal wanted to set up a committee that was to evaluate the questionnaire against the objectives of the research, for this had already been done by the RPC. She reminded the Principal that the RPC had already seen the abstract of the paper and approved that it should be presented. She questioned the composition of the all-male Committee of Deans. She concluded by stating that the Committee of Deans had the academic freedom to examine our paper. But she opposed the idea of singling out one person to appear before this committee as if an offence had been committed. If indeed the Committee of Deans can prove that an offence has been committed, then all four co-authors should be invited to answer the charges. The Principal is yet to respond to this letter.

'Who is She to Tarnish our Image?'

According to a report written by the chair of the students union and submitted to the Principal, after my interview was broadcasted on MBC, the students began to 'sensitize' each other on the issue. As a result 'the students became so nervous and worried about what most of them called their 'image' outside the campus to their parents, guardians, relatives and mates, that tension mounted'[15]. Therefore to defend their 'image', the students met and agreed to demonstrate and 'refute the report made by Dr I. Phiri using the same mass media and [demand] that she apologizes to the student body and the public for the ethically sensitive information dissemination'.[16]

To fulfil their goal, the Executive of SUCC was consulted the Principal about what was happening. They also asked the Principal to provide them with transport to the MBC studio which he did. The report says:

> At the MBC studio, the Chairman and Vice Chairperson 'expressed the concern of the student body challenging the 67 per cent research findings as scientifically and statistically unreliable and invalid. I [chairman] concluded by demanding that Dr I Phiri should furnish us with information on how she carried out her research; the representative nature of the research sample and how she operationally defined sexual harassment and rape.

It is important to point out that these demands were made before any of the students read the research report. The majority of them did not even listen to the radio broadcast. Therefore, the demands were made in the absence of accurate information. Because of wrong information some of the demonstrators branched off to cause damage to my college house, personal car and office. However the Executive of SUCC disassociated themselves from the vandalism on the basis that they returned to campus in the same vehicle that was provided by the College Administration. The chairman of SUCC finished his report by stating that:

> The SUCC Executive however, feels incapacitated to grapple with such an issue of criminal nature because of self evident lack of proficiency. We therefore recommend to the College Administration to bring this issue to the attention of professionals in criminology to subject the matter to scrutiny.[17]

It was on this note that the students went to their homes for the long vacation.

The Public

The *Daily Times* was the first newspaper to report the issue. Its report fuelled more tension because it was also based on wrong information. The story was put on the front page and the headlines read 'Rape Survey Causes Havoc: Chancellor College Students Demonstrate' The title of the paper that I presented at the conference was said to be 'Rape and rapists at Chancellor College'. I was quoted as saying that 'there are 67 per cent rape cases on Chancellor College campus which are committed by male students and male lecturers'[18]. It is important to note that the *Daily Times* newspaper enjoys the largest circulation in the country.

Members of staff of the Department of Theology and Religious Studies phoned the *Daily Times* to protest for the wrong information. As a follow up, the *Daily Times* sent another reporter[19] to interview the Chairman of SUCC, a member of the Department of Theology and Religious Studies, another senior lecturer and two students. The report appeared in a small corner on page 1 of the Friday 21 July issue. The title was 'Student Vandalism Condemned'. The story continued on page four with a new title, 'Lecturer's property vandalized'. It also carried two photographs of my damaged vehicle and house. No apology was made for the wrong information published the previous day.

The Nation newspaper, which has established itself as a strong competitor of the *Daily Times,* did not pick up the story initially. However, it contained debates by the public on the nature of the research. Some of the writers took the side of the students to challenge the validity of the research even though they too had not read the paper. It was argued that the report was 'unrealistic and questionable'.[20] However, there were others who argued against that kind of stand. For example, one writer argued that:

If the research was seen as not to be credible, why don't the students and/or staff conduct an independent survey on the question of rape at the college. This is what academia is competent of doing: proving and disproving established and non-established theses and dogma.[21]

There were also more reports of rape and sexual harassment in different institutions. More interesting was an extensive explanation of 'When is Rape, Rape?'[22]

Of great value to me was when at the end of the year readers of *The Nation* newspaper declared me 'Woman of The Year'.[23] The front page of the newspaper carried a big portrait and the caption read 'Phiri: lived through a male student onslaught, survived a scrape with the CCAP clergy, came through with minor scars and keeps her spirits undaunted'. This was a great honour to me because it showed me that I had big support from both men and women in this country. My suffering is not in vain. Secondly, the newspaper article came out a day before the new academic year started. Therefore, it gave me the courage to go to work with my head held high to meet the student and staff community of Chancellor. I felt as though the public declared me 'Not Guilty'. I was vindicated.

The Police – a Crime Worth Prosecuting

I was most disappointed with the role played by the Malawi Police. At the beginning, colleagues in my department and my husband reported the incident to the police. Indeed the night after the incident, the police patrolled regularly outside my house. After that we never heard from them again. There were rumours that a few students were called in for questioning in October 1995. Ten months later nothing has been done. No one has been persecuted despite the fact that the students involved are known to the college administration. This raises a lot of questions as to why nothing has been heard of. Was there a conspiracy?

A Case Worth Hiring a Lawyer

Due to the criminal nature of the case and also to defend my academic freedom, I was forced to hire a lawyer to represent me. I wanted to be represented by a female lawyer, but there was none readily available. They are either working for the government or are employed by private companies. However, the male lawyer that I hired started very well. He reminded the college administration that besides the damage caused on personal property, there was also physical as well as mental damage caused on my child, my mother and myself. He argued that:

> Our client and her colleagues, by presenting the paper after conducting a thorough research, merely exercised their freedom of expression academically, a thing that ought to be encouraged at a place of learning. The academic community should not run away from expressions of truth and the public ought to know what is actually happening in our institutions of higher learning.[24]

He reminded the College Administration that its role was to work hand in hand with the police in order to bring to book those who were involved in vandalism so that nothing of this sort should happen again in the University of Malawi. He also demanded that I be given another office. Since the College Administration was failing to come up with the culprits, he demanded that the College should bear the responsibility of everything which included compensating me for harassment, the irreparable physical and mental shock suffered by my family and for repairing of my car.

I felt that I was not ready to face a court case therefore my lawyer and I agreed that the settlement should be done out of court. The University agreed. However the University lawyer then left on leave of absence before the settlement was finalised. Therefore the University has put the case on hold until it employs another lawyer.

The initial reaction of the College was total disbelief that I hired a lawyer against the University. On the positive side, the College Administration allocated me another office.[25]

The Church and Fellowship Groups

The day that I returned from Mangochi I was visited by my church minister who offered his apology and explained to me what he observed and heard from the student demonstrators. He prayed with me. I took it as a sign of solidarity. It was then that I also learnt that I had missed my chance of being blessed to join the women's guild. I had attended all the women's guild classes for a year and sat the oral examinations in June 1995, which I passed with no difficulty. All the women's guild students were just waiting for the church minister to choose a day for dedication. When I left for the Mangochi conference I was not aware that the minister had chosen the same Sunday for dedication of new members. I therefore missed my chance. On the day that he came to see me I mentioned to him the possibility of choosing another date for me and two others who were also left out. I was told that everything would be conducted after he had returned from holiday in October.

When I went to see him in October, I was told that I had been put on hold because of the Chancellor College issue. I was only going to be dedicated after I was cleared by my employers. I asked him why he did not inform me of the church's decision and I wanted to know whether there was a committee that had been set up to conduct an investigation as to whether I was in the wrong or not. He said no to both issues. Seven months have passed since then and nothing has been communicated to me as to what the findings of the church were and whether I can be dedicated as a member of the women's guild or not. When I went to ask for a transfer letter, I was told that the minister had gone to his village on sick leave and that he had not communicated to anyone his decision that I was on hold or that anyone should investigate my case with my employers.

Contrary to the stand taken by my church minister, the new General Secretary of Blantyre Synod Church of Central Africa Presbyterian, the Rev Kansilanga visited me at home in February 1996 to inform me that I had his support in all that I was going through at work. Even though he did not find me at home, he left a message of encouragement to me as a member of Blantyre Synod CCAP. I appreciated that a lot.

My greatest spiritual support during the difficult period that I found myself in was at a charismatic fellowship in Chitawira, Blantyre known by the name of Holy Ghost Christian Fellowship. I shared with them my burden and they fought with me through earnest prayers. It was through this fellowship that I being admitted to mental hospital and experienced the love of Jesus Christ in a new way. I also experienced a Jesus Christ who solves people's problem in concrete terms.

Conclusion

Not a New Issue

My clash with the student body was not new. An earlier example was a one day seminar, organised by the Department of Theology and Religious Studies and the Department of Sociology held on 12 February 1994. This seminar was on Violence Against Women and it was attended by both female students and female members of the Zomba community. It was at this seminar that the Chancellor College female students complained about the kind of violence that they were experiencing on campus. A week after the conference, a mob of 50 male students came to my house to insult me for being one of the organisers of the conference. Since they came in the early evening, it was difficult for me to identify them. However, some people who managed to identify them and through the efforts of all academic staff, the culprits were brought to book. My college house became an easy target for the students because it happens to be the first one after the college campus.

Accountability
The Chancellor College administration took a negative attitude to my issue in 1995 because they were not accountable to anyone. Most of those who wrote to protest were foreigners within the country but no international body was involved. As a result, the University did not feel obliged to defend academic freedom. At a meeting with the Principal in November, he made it very clear that he had no apology to make because whatever he said was influenced by the mood of the occasion. The College Administrators did not consider to look at the recommendations that we had made which are of help to the running of the college and the lives of female students.

Positive Effects
The Chancellor College female students that I have been in contact with in the 1996 academic year have reported that there is a great improvement in the relationship between male and female students. The female students have been sensitised as to what are their rights on the issues of rape and sexual harassment. Most of the female students have learnt to be assertive without being aggressive. They have said with confidence that the college has now become a learning centre with friendly atmosphere for both male and female students.

As for me I was forced to apply for sabbatical leave so that I can sort myself out emotionally and psychologically. More especially I needed to give our son space to heal as he is still afraid of crowds of people and especially students. My application for sabbatical leave for one year was converted to leave of absence which can be extended up to four years. This was done by the University administrators. This is a welcome move as I did not qualify for either sabbatical leave or leave of absence. However, giving me an option to be away for a longer period raises questions as to whether the administration think my going away is better for them or not.

It has also become clear that the major problem with the dissemination of our research findings was the failure to differentiate between rape and sexual harassment. In the Principal's memo to the Vice Chancellor, and in the students' report, as well as the first article that appeared in the *Daily Times*, it was reported that 67 per cent of the students had been raped and suffered sexual harassment. This mistake was enough to raise an alarm to whoever heard or read about it. But when the correction was made, no apology was offered.

It should also be understood that this research was breaking new grounds. People used to talk about rape and sexual harassment in their homes behind closed doors. A topic which is a taboo was brought into the open through scientific research. Hence the violent reaction from the most learned society in the land. However, this reaction meant that the research findings were speedily disseminated. Many more people read the paper than would have been the case if there was no controversy. The continued debate in the newspapers on issues of rape and sexual harassment is a welcomed development because the Malawi nation is being continually made more conscious about gender issues.

Notes
1. Refer to paper P. 3
2. Report 'Students Demonstration' from Chairman, Students Union of Chancellor College to Principal.
3. No copy of the text read has become available since then.
4. This statement was to be released only after the students had finished their examinations, three weeks after the event.
5. Full copy of the text written on a note with the complement of the Principal dated July 31, 1995
6. See the Principal's memo entitled, 'Violent Demonstration by Students', dated August 3, 1995.
7. See my memo to the Principal of Chancellor College dated September 5.
8. See memo to the Principal dated July 20, 1995.
9. See Department of Theology and Religious Studies minute 11 dated August 1, 1996.
10. See the Vice Chancellor's letter to Mrs J.M. Walker dated July 24, 1995.
11. See minutes 92/95 of Minutes of the 122nd meeting of Senate Research and Publications Committee held at the University Office on Tuesday, September 17, 1995.
12. See prof J.R. Minnis' memo addressed to the Vice Chancellor dated July 20, 1995.
13. See the memo of the Head of Law Department to the Principal dated July 20, 1995.
14. See Dr Nyovani Madise's letter to Dr E. Fabiano dated September 20, 1995.
15. See a memo from Chairman, Students Union of Chancellor College, addressed to the Principal, Chancellor College dated July 20, 1995.
16. Chairman's report page 3.
17. Chairman's report page 6.
18. See *Daily Times* newspaper of Thursday, July 20 1996 page 1 article by Sitha Katumbi.
19. The second reporter from *Daily Times* was Ranken Nyekanyeka.
20. See the article by Justin Kalima which appeared in *The Nation* newspaper of September 6, 1996 entitled 'Women are Sexual Offenders'.
21. See the article by Janet Karim which appeared in *The Nation* newspaper of October 19, 1996 entitled 'Someone Found Women Guilty'.
22. Check for the Newspaper article.
23. This appeared on the front page of the *Saturday Nation* of December 30-July 5, 1996. The full story was carried on page 5 as a special profile. An outstanding comment of the feature was 'She rides tall among them all, yet so humble. She fights like an Amazon for women's rights. The battle is still on, but slowly, surely victory is hers' by Jika Nkolokosa.
24. See letter from Chizumila, Msiska and Co to the Principal of Chancellor College dated September 20, 1995.
25. See letter dated October 31, 1995 from the College Registrar to me. I never took up the office because the head of Curriculum Studies challenged the reallocation on the basis that the office in question belonged to her department and they already had a staff member who was using it.

4. Academic Freedom and the Gender Issue: a Report from Senegal

Penda Mbow

I will open my examination of the notion of academic freedom and the gender issue by relating a personal experience that illustrates the topic's relevance. On March 8, 1992, I was attacked by minor Muslim extremist factions for having aired my views at a conference on Women and AIDS organized by the SWAA. The case came to trial and made the headlines of every newspaper in Senegal. A fellow researcher from the department of Islamic studies at the IFAN (Negro-African studies research institute) at Cheikh Anta Diop University publicly castigated me during a talk held at the unfinished Mosque of Yoff, and the Imam of the university mosque also condemned me during one of his Friday sermons.

What had I said? I had merely attempted to establish the possible relationships between certain types of behaviour and the spread of the AIDS endemic, based on concrete examples. In the northern part of Senegal, it has been noted that returning emigrant workers who contracted HIV in foreign countries were quick to take new wives, and that they transmitted the virus to these new wives along with the other wives already waiting for them at home. After the men's death, the widows then marry their husbands' brothers and cousins. Although faithfulness in marriage can protect people from AIDS, in some cases the same cannot be said of polygamy.

I had also pointed out that the djawaz al muta'a, or temporary marriage, which resurfaced during the Iran-Iraq war, can also be a factor in the spread of AIDS due to its short-lived nature. My words were twisted by others, and the very same day (March 8) I received a letter containing death threats and was physically attacked by young Muslim extremists. I was insulted over the telephone, and was accused of having sold out to Freemasonry. Were it not for the intervention of El Hadj Abdoul Aziz Sy, the grand caliph of the Tidjanes, the incident would have been very serious indeed, for it divided Senegalese opinion.

I withdrew the charges, and the Imam of the university mosque apologized, saying he had been misled, while the grand caliph publicly condemned the fundamentalists' activism. However, my colleague from IFAN repeated his behaviour at a subsequent conference organized by the Association of Muslim Students of Senegal (more on this association later) on 'Contemporary challenges and Senegalese women' which took place on March 12, 1997. At this meeting, he said I was 'very brilliant but extremely dangerous since I had sold myself to the Americans'. I was one of the speakers at the conference, along with the Imam of the Unfinished Mosque and another social science researcher, who violently criticized the social sciences, saying, 'you cannot name a branch of social science whose conclusions are not disproved 50 years later. This type of science only exists in order to lead people astray...'. Once again, the university was the scene of obscurantism.

There is a reason why I am using this personal example: it strikes at the heart of the debate. In trying to understand what lay behind these actions, I realized that it can be dangerous to have a scientific approach to Muslim society, especially when you are a woman. All forms of knowledge in Senegal about Islam are the unique province of recognized families and preachers. Only a few women belonging to religious families are tolerated in this sphere. Sometimes certain of my students even openly rebel against my teaching, accusing me of misrepresenting historical facts. My studies, research and teaching centre mainly on the Middle Ages (the fifth to the sixteenth centuries AD). The early days of Islam, the formation of the first Muslim States, their evolution and the crusades constitute much of my main focus. Sometimes, my students have a hard time admitting facts, such as the human origins of the Shari'a or Muslim law. The early days of Islam were rich in interesting philosophical debates. For a young Senegalese whose only knowledge of Islam is dogmatic, the Mutazi'lites' debates over the creation or non-creation of the Koran are blasphemous, even more so if the classes are being taught by a member of the so-called weaker sex.

But historical reality is often different from basic beliefs, which have more to do with ideas, with one's conception of things. It often happens that historical facts disturb a certain intellectual comfort and prejudice. Furthermore, it must be admitted that it is not easy for a woman to make her way in certain branches of science. In order to reach a clearer understanding of this situation, I shall begin by analyzing the issue of gender in education, and women teachers in higher education through a look at the status of women in the University of Dakar and their role on campus, and a description of Senegalese women students at the dawn of the third millennium.

Gender and Education

My analysis of my personal experience ties in with an important debate raised by Nadia Ramsis Farah (1994) in her chapter in *Academic Freedom in Africa*. Civil society, overwhelmed as it is by the dominant religious discourse, has become sensitive to issues formulated in religious terms. While it is true that the conflicts between religious society and the public authorities are less intense in Senegal than in Egypt, we do encounter that form of opposition whereby fundamentalist groups use scriptures to undermine the legitimacy of the government and other rival social groups. Intellectual women are a favourite target, especially when their field of research is religious history.

Religious studies are a vital research area for women, since religion, which controls our collective psychology, lies at the heart of women's concerns. Relationships of dominance and submission and the unfair social division of labour should not be explained by biology, since they are the result of historical changes and cultural and linguistic constructs of which religious discourse is a part (Mbow: 1996).

Some struggles will never be won if the number of women in higher education is restricted. According to the National Ministry of Education, in 1995, 78 per cent of Senegalese women were illiterate. Like most uneducated women, they are victims of two-fold oppression: inequality in education and in work. This is why the education of girls is a fundamental feminist issue. Senegal seems to have caught on to this quite late, since it only became a high priority in this country fewer than two years ago.

Thus, we can observe with some bitterness that the democratic era is not necessarily favourable to women. For although in theory, women are not excluded from the public sphere nor confined to domesticity, democracy has not yet developed a system whereby this exclusion is eradicated, although it sets up the principle of equal rights. Feminism whose goal is to achieve sexual equality in practice, can only express itself through a collective, social and political movement.

In the context of structural adjustment, the economic dimension, which we will examine later in this chapter, dominates all other issues. It deeply affects not only the structures in place but also the men and women that operate them.

The issue of women's place in the democratic process in Africa centres fundamentally on the issue of education but also the development of the social sciences. The pertinence of the question posed by Mamadou Diouf indicates the complexity of the debate. He asked: Is not the whole problem surrounding this issue deep down the African intelligentsia's painful adjustment to the events of post-colonialism, the end of nationalistic messianism and the social, ideological, and, of course, economic deconstruction due to structural adjustment policies?

Even more than for their male colleagues, the issue at stake for women researchers is how to overcome the isolation that has always been the fate of teachers and researchers in Africa – social isolation in their relationships with society, and intellectual isolation. There is the problem of African women's integration in the modern world, which is really a matter of achieving the status of a subject (not an object), a real individual and a citizen, and wresting their economic, legal and symbolic autonomy away from their fathers and husbands (Duby and Perrot).

Democrats and laypersons should support intellectual women and work towards a policy that liberates women. Yet very few democrats or laypersons denounce the tendency towards totalitarianism or the different forms of morality that seek to hinder women's freedom of action and of thought.

Similarly, social science has a fundamental role to play in women's liberation. It should explain the nature and the sources of human behaviour through objective empirical observation and rigorous analysis that satisfies the curiosity of both researchers and the general public. Although social science is not monolithic, at least it presents a common front, since its various components are necessary to establish democratic, efficient, realistic and modern social order. When we truly understand what is at stake, the notion of academic freedom can be properly defined while taking into account the concerns and constraints affecting women in the university.

Women in Higher Education
In his introduction to *Academic Freedom in Africa* (Diouf and Mamdani, 1994: 1) entitled 'In search of academic freedom?', Mahmood Mamdani defines education as one of the main demands of the nationalist movement. The postcolonial state acceded to this demand, not only in response to enormous social pressure, but also because it recognized the difficulty of Africanizing the administration and the semi-public sector without a pool of qualified administrators.

The need to train women administrators became obvious very quickly, since colonization had only accentuated the marginalization of women. Colonial companies introduced cash farming and export farming. In its efforts to modernize rural Africa through rural development projects centred on developing new lands and new structures, the colonial administration brought its own role models to the traditional chiefs and farming became a man's job. Technical training to increase yield was offered only to the men, who were introduced into the monetary circuit by trading companies. Thus, men entered the modern world of progress while women remained in their traditional world.

Men were involved in cash crops and women in subsistence farming; this bipolarization accentuated the dichotomy in gender roles. Since women were not included in the circuits of modernization – education, training and credit – they came to be thought of as inferior (Heritier, 1984; Mbow, 1996). At the time of independence, most educated women had gone no further than their primary leaving certificate or secondary school entrance exam. Very few reached higher education: perhaps one or two in their first year of arts courses, one in fourth-year law. Women students rarely exceeded two per cent of the total. The presence of women researchers and teachers at universities came gradually and the percentage is still low.

The study of history is a fundamental field for female African academics. More than any other, it allows them to determine the depths of acculturation reached by African women. Indeed, only a historical and cultural perspective will enable us to define the evolution of gender relationships, since male domination can be historically dated in different societies and in the structures societies invent for themselves. Systems of civilization, means of economic and social development, and even the opposition between the rural and urban worlds must be taken into account.

The Situation at the University of Dakar

In a survey on women in higher education, and educational research, planning and management, the United Nations Educational, Scientific and Cultural Organization (UNESCO) came to some interesting conclusions. While the number of women pupils and students is considerable, and women are obtaining higher and higher level degrees, their numbers are still very low in areas where access usually depends on the possession of diplomas. It cannot be denied that women have achieved increased participation in cultural life through education, and that they have also achieved a certain prestige. But the education they receive does not repay them in gaining access to economic, social and political power. Thus we note that women's access to professions which confer recognized influence, especially when they are well paid, remains difficult. This is the case with most liberal professions.

However, even if the process is very slow, women have made undeniable progress in professional fields that were until recently reserved for men. In 1985, of 449 teachers at the University of Dakar, 11.1 per cent were female. In the highest rank, which includes full professors and assistant professors, only 7.3 per cent of a total of 192 were female. In the second highest rank, which includes lower-ranking assistant professors and teaching assistants, 14.0 per cent of the total staff of 257 were women.

The percentage of women instructors and/or researchers per field of study was as follows:

Overall:	11.1 per cent
Education:	15.9 per cent
Social Science:	10.7 per cent
Natural Science:	9.3 per cent
Medical Science:	11.6 per cent
Agriculture	–
Others	–

However, in 1995, according to Education Office statistics, the University of Dakar had 115 women teachers out of a total of 741, and 10 women researchers as compared to 36 men.

This survey also assessed criteria for hiring and promotion. It included a question on the reasons for choosing between various people for positions, including a) past experience, b) recognized skills, c) mobility, i.e. the ability to relocate for work, and d) gender.

The situation is more or less identical to that in Europe, since hiring is largely based on research, which is generally seen to be favourable to women; teaching is considered of low importance for hiring and advancement in universities, a fact considered unfavourable to women. It is thought that the mobility factor is either neutral or unfavourable to women.

Almost all the people surveyed considered research work to be the most important aspect for hiring and advancement. The practice of teaching is seen as either of equal or average importance. It is noted that there are too few women in higher education and that they lack mobility. We could add to those reasons the weight of tradition and family responsibilities.

As for their position in the hierarchy and type of posting, the analysis of the staff according to grade and sex indicates that in the highest positions in the administration, which are generally occupied by teacher-researchers, there are very few women. What few women there are are positioned at the lowest levels of the hierarchy. Certain measures are recommended in order to correct the inequalities between men and women in higher education, such as:

Improving women's access to higher education.

Improving training for women.

Offering women financial support to pursue higher education.

Improving information.

Increasing girls' presence in secondary schools.

Offering women job opportunities, especially early in their careers.

Improving family working conditions by developing services (for example, household helpers, babysitters).

Taking action in favour of equal pay (women pay more income tax than do men).

Offering job opportunities early in their career.

Offering incentive to take on responsibilities.

Improving equal opportunity on hiring and throughout their careers.

However, there is a huge difference between these declarations and the reality of our universities. Ayesha Imam and Amina Mama have written at great length on the limitation or enlargement of academic freedom in relation to the gender issue (Imam and Mama, 1995).

Freedom is always relative because it is a function of social relationships and of the political economy of the academic world and society in general. Within the university institution, most of those in charge either deny existent social divisions (religion, class and gender) or claim they are natural. In both cases they contribute to the perpetuation of inequalities. Housing and equipment are among the problems faced by female teachers, especially unmarried ones. Their male colleagues are loath to agree to any special treatment for women. When scholarships are offered, married women with children are obliged to pass up trips and special courses at the expense of their careers. Material constraints and their consequences are in evidence at the University of Dakar. Women have much more difficulty finding consultation work to make up for their lack of funds. They are often dependent on their husbands and their lack of autonomy makes them hard to distinguish from ordinary women.

The general social conditions directly affecting academic work are more severely felt by women academics. Given the gender-based division of labour that prevails in Africa, women are responsible for reproductive work and domestic work and its organization, to which we could add numerous social duties. Ayesha Imam and Amina Mama are quite right when they say that women's extra workload is often ignored in discussions on academic freedom and the social responsibilities of intellectuals.

Although universities are supposed to be institutes of teaching and research, they are almost all under-financed and only a tiny portion of their budgets is dedicated to research. Consequently, when governments give out research funds, they are most often intended for quantitative gathering of statistics for state institutions or for work oriented towards specific policies that accept government objectives and seek the means to achieve them, and not for empirical, innovative or theoretical research. Research on women's and gender issues very rarely receives even minimal financial support. It is almost nonexistent in Dakar.

Women's studies are completely ignored at the university, and very few women academics are willing to lend their expertise to gender issues. On this level, the social responsibility of women academics is a critical issue. Often, in their fear of being labelled feminists, they steer clear of the fundamental debates they ought to initiate in order to help their society move forward. Who will fight against polygamy with scientific arguments? Who will ask for a revision of family law? What is the role of women academics where sexual mutilation is concerned? Only Fatou Sow and Awa Thiam have addressed these issues. Who will confront the aspects of African cultures that have negative consequences on the status of women? The foundations of inequality, which are perpetuated by women in our societies due to their own ignorance and the general climate of obscurantism, really ought to be more closely studied. West African societies are faced with caste and slavery problems that increase the precariousness of women's positions and disperse their energies. Indeed, what is more important for a woman of servile origins, the fight for freedom from slavery or women's emancipation?

The tasks awaiting women academics are truly complex. Attacking the anaemic structures of African societies is a major challenge. As the former General Director of UNESCO stated in a plea for a new status for women, 'the fundamental obstacle to full equality of the sexes lies in tradition and mentalities. Cultural factors embedded in mental attitudes and traditional systems of ethics explain the behaviour of most men' (Mbow, 1980). It is especially important to reveal changes, making women's history relevant by showing that they have been active participants in history and not mere onlookers. (Duby and Perrot).

Senegalese women academics are truly behind the times. They have no women's journals or magazines, and certainly no seminars or updates on gender issues. It seems they do not clearly perceive the issues, which would explain why they dedicate very little time to feminist studies. Certain male researchers have managed to convince them that discussing women's concerns is secondary and will only further marginalize them, trap them in a ghetto. It is urgent that we change the social relationships in university institutes, research centres, research and publications as well as within civil society. This would demonstrate our commitment to linking the universities to other educational and civil institutions, as well as mass organizations (unions, women's movements and organizations, etc.). Even more importantly, it is vital to work in liaison with other progressive forces in society to integrate intellectual undertakings into the broadest social movements that defend the general interest and popular concerns.

Since the 1990s, the University of Dakar has been engaged in reform which has not made room for women's studies or women's publications. There is a continued absence of women in decision-making centres and unions. Thus far, union platforms have ignored women's specific demands. And the university's statutes, for instance, make no reference to maternity leave or widow's leave.

Union operating methods sometimes drive women away. The 1989 congress of the independent union of higher education (Syndicat Autonome de l'Enseignement Supérieur, or SAES) lasted an entire weekend and delegates were obliged to spend the night to elect new officers. The situation was very difficult for young women with children.

The reform process has also concentrated on decision-making within the university. But women in decision-making positions are still rare. Not a single faculty is directed by a woman, and only two faculty institutes have woman heads. However, women play their part when the university is in crisis. It should also be mentioned that, although such situations are rare, women teachers sometimes have difficulties with their male students. In 1995, a colleague at the Department of Modern Letters was obliged to call some of her students before the disciplinary council because they had pushed her around and assaulted her in the classroom. The lack of sufficient classrooms and chairs creates situations where tensions sometimes run high on campus. Misunderstandings can arise, and persist, between students who are increasingly impolite and women professors who were trained under different circumstances.

The same year, the case of another woman colleague at the Faculty of Legal Science, who was attacked by her students while pregnant, was held up by the rector of the University of Dakar as a justification for the presence of law enforcement officers on campus, a serious breach of the university franchise. This raises a serious dilemma for teachers: does their need for protection from their students contradict one of the basic demands of African universities: the respect of the university's franchise? African women academics are in sore need of mental and psychological strength to face the uncertainties relating to the future of African universities whose role and functions still need to be defined.

In the 1960s, universities were perceived as a place for training the manpower that would handle the development process. It was believed that the independent state should play a fundamental role in the management of the universities themselves. But all the reforms then were carried out concomitantly with the former colonial powers. Today the dominant partners are the World Bank and the International Monetary Fund. Structural adjustment policies have finally discredited our African universities. On the other side of things, women students have been even more severely affected by the reforms.

Women Students
Statistics
Between 1967-8 and 1990-1, the percentage of women students in higher education rose from 9.7 per cent (147 women compared to 1336 men) to 22.3 per cent (3630 women for 12,642 men).

The percentage of female students tends to be higher in certain faculties (arts, pharmacy, dental surgery, economy and legal science) whereas their numbers are fewer in medicine and in the scientific and technical institutes. Thus in 1983-4, the number of female students in the Faculty of Arts was 439 out of a total of 2072 students, or 21 per cent. Women were even more numerous in pharmacy, where they made up 52 per cent of the total of 341 students. On the other hand, of the 1609 students at the Faculty of Science, only eight per cent were women.

Constraining factors on female education can be explained by the deterioration of the educational system, but also by the sociocultural prejudices that minimize the importance of modern education for women. Given the economic difficulties experienced by most families, educational opportunities are offered to boys in priority, since they are considered future heads of families.

Early marriage and motherhood and the domestic chores little girls carry out in the home, especially in poor urban areas, are responsible for the high rates of attrition and failure among girls (Ministere de la Femme, 1993).

Impact of the Crisis

From 1960 to the present time, there has been a clear evolution in the number of girls entering university, but repeated crises and unemployment among holders of higher education diplomas have tended to discourage girls.

Since 1968, Dakar's university campus has undergone regular and cyclical crises. As in most other African countries, the campus has served as a permanent battleground for governments and students. Students have always confronted the authorities, usually over the autonomy of the university or important social concerns. Purely academic issues have been of little concern, except when demands were made for multiple examination sessions or reducing an excessive workload.

As might have been expected, devaluation reinforced inflationary tendencies brought on by the longstanding budget deficit. Every school year, students demand that their scholarships be indexed to inflation and that the number of students receiving assistance be increased.

The government views the increasing campus activism, occurring as it does in a context of inevitably stringent budgets, as a threat to law and order. Accordingly, it has responded to that threat by using the forces of law and order. The presence of law enforcement officers on campus and the inevitable confrontations with students led to an invalidated school year and the closure of the campus in 1988, following the political crisis engendered by the elections of February 1988. As I write, in March 1997, it seems the same scenario may repeat itself this year. Budgetary restrictions imposed by the World Bank and the elimination of the campus social programme for a huge majority of students, combined with transportation and housing problems, may well compromise the school year. New survival strategies need to be developed.

While the effects of the crisis are familiar to the population (and to women in particular) in the form of difficult living conditions, unemployment, the debt problem, rebellion against budgetary restrictions and rising prices, the cultural crisis is rarely central to people's concerns and reflections.

Yet, due to the economic crisis, families are becoming unstable or falling apart completely, social and moral references are becoming unsure, political ideologies are growing uncertain and modernity is being questioned.

The lack of economic and political perspectives has caused or deepened a crisis in values and cultural references. Fatalism, cultural nationalism, a return to the origins of African tradition and the emergence of religious fundamentalism (Muslim or Christian) are among the various responses that have been put forward so far. They help fill the void, reassure and guide the population in their quest for economic and social well-being and psychological and emotional balance. Unfortunately, they often threaten women's advances, accentuate their marginalization and weaken them emotionally and psychologically in order to better control them.

Because the oppression of women is integrated into both the economy and the culture, it appears as a coherent, natural situation beyond the control of men and women who can only submit to it.

In our societies, women and young people form the overwhelming majority of the population and they are also the most oppressed due to their status and social position. However, they are also the most dynamic members of the population and the most likely to seek out new solutions.

On the Dakar campus, ethnic nationalism is on the rise with the multiplication of identity-based associations based on ethnic origins, geographic origins and religious creed. However, the most serious aspect seems to be the rise of fundamentalism and its impact on female students. On March 8, 1997, women lay students organized a round table in a room in the Claudel building. This was met with indifference by most female students, and the room stayed half empty. On March 12, the Muslim students' association celebrated International Women's Day. This time, the room was full by 2.30pm. In separate areas, boys and veiled girls took their seats in a disciplined manner. These women receive guidance, but they are completely manipulated and visibly lacking in experience, their speech is biased. They barely raise their voices.

Their discourse is worrisome. The numbers of these women grow from year to year while the university authorities remain indifferent. Small scholarships and personal disappointments make them more vulnerable and are, to a certain extent, responsible for their choice. They find mutual assistance and solidarity in the association. The chador has become a familiar item on the Cheikh Anta Diop University campus in Dakar.

Relationships between male and female students are another highly interesting aspect of gender relations at the university. It has been noted that, in the classroom, female students are completely intimidated and rarely speak, even though they may obtain very satisfactory marks on their examinations. The presence of woman teachers may have a positive impact on these students. Female students are sometimes suspected of using their charms to get good grades from certain professors. Although there sometimes are personal relationships between teachers and students, in most cases, woman students earn their marks through hard work.

This problem touches on another form of slander that is spread against female students living in university residence: it is said they practice prostitution. A decade ago, a Muslim non-governmental institution, Jamra, raised this issue which has recurred ever since. In March 1997, female students once again went on strike when this issue of prostitution was raised in one of Dakar's daily newspapers, *le Matin*. Once again, they were charged by the law enforcement agencies for having demanded that visiting hours be extended past 10pm and that people stop accusing them of prostitution.

Special attention should be paid to women from other African countries who are alone and unsupported. They may go for months without receiving money, as well as being students from very poor backgrounds. For some girls, this may be an alternative answer to the economic crisis. However, one must not lose sight of the fact that denigration has always been used to contain feminism and hold back women's emancipation.

In conclusion, we can say that academic freedom should be a priority for woman academics due to their relatively fragile position in the institution. As it was defined in the Kampala Declaration, the struggle for intellectual freedom is an integral part of the struggle for human rights. One of the major challenges facing Africa's women intellectuals is the fulfillment of their social role, which depends on the recognition of their right to knowledge and science, and their ability to participate in all fields of research.

In order for society to recognize itself in women's research work and their approach to reality, the entire scientific community must operate a change in epistemology, and examine the obstacles encountered in order to take a different tack. Women intellectuals need to realize that only feminist thought can effectively contribute to a more equal reconstruction of gender relations. African societies are in dire need of a social movement to spur modernization, which is inevitable because Africa's salvation depends on it.

Furthermore, structural adjustment policies should spare universities because it is nearly impossible to do research without minimal facilities and better conditions. Destroying higher education means punishing future generations and making even a minimal level of development impossible.

Careful attention should be paid to the role of religion in social and political life, and teaching and research on religious topics.

Appendix

SUMMARY TABLE OF AFRICAN TEACHING AND RESEARCH PERSONNEL, December 1995

Institute → Rank ↓	Legal & Pol Science M	W	Economics & Management M	W	Medicine Pharmacy & IOS M	W	Science & Technology M	W	Arts & Social Science M	W	ESP Polytechnic M	W	ENS Teaching M	W	EBAD Library Science M	W	IFE French for foreigners M	W	CESTI Journalism M	W	IFAN African studies M	W	CLAD Applied ling. M	W	Micro-biology Lab M	W	TOTAL per Rank M	W
Prof. & Dir. de recherche	07	-	01	-	41	03	15	-	15	01	04	-	-	-	-	-	-	-	-	-	01	-	-	-	-	-	84	04
Maître de conf. & Charg de rech.	09	01	03	-	35	06	26	03	13	02	04	-	-	-	-	-	01	-	01	-	02	-	01	-	-	-	95	12
M.A. & M.A. de rech.	07	01	03	-	36	06	70	13	58	11	24	02	11	02	06	-	02	-	03	-	12	07	04	-	-	-	236	42
Maîtres d'encad.	-	-	-	-	-	-	-	-	-	-	-	-	04	01	01	-	-	-	-	-	-	-	-	-	-	-	05	01
Assistants & attachés	32	04	26	-	87	30	44	07	23	04	50	03	44	06	05	02	01	02	10	-	-	-	-	-	-	-	322	58
Assistants de recherche	-	-	-	-	-	-	-	-	-	-	-	-	-	-	-	-	-	-	-	-	12	01	-	-	-	01	12	02
Chercheurs (MEN)	-	-	-	-	-	-	-	-	-	-	-	-	-	-	-	-	-	-	-	-	-	-	04	-	-	-	04	-
Prof. Cert. & Ens. Tech.	-	-	-	-	-	-	-	-	-	-	02	02	05	02	-	-	-	-	-	-	-	-	-	-	-	-	07	04
PTA – Adj. d'Ens. & Adj. de rech.	-	-	-	-	-	-	-	-	-	-	08	01	-	-	-	-	02	-	-	-	-	01	-	-	-	-	10	02
Chefs de trav.	-	-	-	-	-	-	-	-	-	-	02	-	-	-	-	-	-	-	-	-	-	-	-	-	-	-	02	-
TOTAL/INSTITUTE	55	06	33	-	199	45	155	23	109	18	94	08	64	11	12	02	06	02	14	-	27	09	09	-	-	01	777	125

Total Teaching Staff = 741 Men and 115 Women   Total Researchers = 36 Men and 10 Women

Total Teaching Institutes = 213   Total Faculties = 643   Total Research Institutes = 46

Source: C.A. Diop University, Dakar Rectorate / Bureau of Human Resources

Notes
1. The organization is a West African Women's network for the prevention of AIDS. It was formerly led by Professor Awa Marie Coll Seck who currently works for UNAIDS, whose headquarters is in Geneva.
2. Temporary marriage, an old Muslim practice which had fallen into disuse, allows a man and woman who do not know each other, but would like to know each other in the Biblical sense, to do so without sinning through a legal simulacrum of marriage. They merely declare their intent in the presence of two adult Muslim witnesses. After consummation, the marriage is dissolved by another ceremony, which also requires just two witnesses. Cf. Zeghidour (1975).
3. The first man to criticize me on March 8, 1992 is well-known as a preacher in women's issues since he very often speaks at talks and conferences, especially during the month of Ramadan. He is also an appointed exegete of the State media.
4. The Institute of Odontology and Stomatology headed by Madame Ndioro Ndiaye and the Institute of Applied Foreign Languages headed by Madame Marième Sy.

References
Diouf, M., (1994) 'Liberté intellectuelle et démocratie : les intellectuels dans la transition démocratique', in Diouf, M., and Mamdani, M., (eds.), *Academic Freedom in Africa*, CODESRIA, Dakar.
Duby, G., and Perrot, M., *Histoire des Femmes, le XXes*, Plon, Paris
Farah, N. R., (1994), 'Civil society and freedom of research in Egypt' in Diouf, M., and Mamdani, M., (eds.), *Academic Freedom in Africa*, CODESRIA, Dakar, 1994.
Héritier, F., (1984), 'l'Africaine, Sexe et signe', *Cahier du GRTF* no. 29, 1984.
Imam, A.M. and Mama, A., (1994) 'Limitation ou élargissement de la liberté académique : La responsabilité des universitaires' in Diouf, M., and Mamdani, M., (eds.), op. cit. *Academic Freedom in Africa*, CODESRIA, Dakar.
Mama, A., (1996), 'Women's Studies and Studies of Women in Africa During the 1990s', CODESRIA Working Paper Series 5/96.
Mbow, A.M., (1980), Speech given at the conference of the United Nations Decade of Women. Copenhagen, July 1980.
Mbow, P., (1996a), 'Femmes, violence et religions', *Revue Démocraties Africaines*, April-May-June.
Mbow, P., (1996b), 'Violence et démocratie', AFARD seminar June 1996, UNIFEM.
Ministère de la femme, de l'enfant et de la famille, (1993), *Femmes sénégalaises à l'horizon 2015*, Dakar.
Zeghidour, S., (1975), 'Homme-Femme en Islam,' *Revue Notre Histoire* 75, February.

5. Social Dimensions of Intellectual and Academic Freedom in Egypt

Helmi Sharawy

Introduction

Intellectual and academic freedom in Egypt is related to its heritage of cultural and political development as well as the conflicts in this field. The permanent presence of 'history' in the cultural life in Egypt represents a problematic, the effect of which extends to the present as well as the future within the limits of the current social dynamics. Therefore, the issues discussed in this study are affected by the character of the trends for solving conflict in this field.

The reader may feel the weight of history more than he or she expects, while the aim of our endeavour is to address reality and the future. Within this framework, this chapter deals with a number of apparently diverse but integrated issues: a) The religious institution and its roots in the religious and political heritage, b) The great influence of the heritage in the economic, social and political systems of the state (the problem of political culture), c) The position of universities and the educational movement in the development of the modernization process (the question of freedom), and d) the position of women in religious secular thought and their exclusion from the participation process in the society. We might call this the 'structural violation' of women's role, which determines the gender issue (the societal and citizenship problem).

The social history of Egypt is not a simple history of conflict between tradition and modernity as in many Third World countries. Neither the cultural issue nor the intellectual crisis can be limited to their emancipation from a group of restrictions imposed by the social reality or by the contact with the 'other'.

Egyptian history is an articulated component that has its weight in many phenomena, including cultural and intellectual ones. So, intellectual aspirations – oriented towards the future – always radically contradict with dominant historical phenomena. Periods of building of a central state to face 'historical enemies' have reoccured frequently over thousands of years and were accompanied by attitudes of 'ideological and social mobilization' under the so-called 'collective' goal.

These periods formulated ceilings that seemed to be 'optional' for the intellectual and social movement. Since the Pharonic time, the strength of creed, with its limited space for freedom, has exercised power for prolonged periods. The church has also had its own intellectuals and the Islamic Sunni religious institutions have had a significant established hegemony throughout fifteen centuries, during which the role of the intellectuals (ulama), and many social groups and political institutions have been defined (social classes, woman, the limits of participation, etc.).

The state and religious institutions exchanged roles over these periods to define the fields and limits of freedoms as well as the nature of participation of the social groups, but always from a male viewpoint.

The case of Dr Nasr H. Abu Zeid, the university lecturer, accused of infidelity (Kufr) because of his research on 'the interpretation of *Koran* according to modern methods' (1993), is an example of the overlap of this 'heritage' in the structure of the political culture in Egypt and most Arab world countries and illustrates the extent to which this affects this issues of freedoms and scientific research. This case represents an introduction to a debate which still exercises great influence on the future although it may seem to be related to the past.

In brief, the case and its development were as follows:

Dr Abu Zeid submitted a number of studies for professional promotion. He discussed various topics, among them the re-interpretation of the *Koran* as a text of a human character, the embodiment of the human discourses on human-holy tradition of the Prophet Mohammed and how these holy discourses developed over many years into political and social discourses which sought to deepen the hegemony of the political systems and organizations. The discourse of the modern Islamic left wing itself is not free of this evasiveness and bias to the religious trend.

The strong right wing in the senate of Cairo University (the oldest Egyptian university) rejected the promotion of the lecturer, after a report written by influential Islamist professors accused the researcher of infidelity and Ridda (apostasy). No academic or administration authority interfered to stop this trend of linking scientific research to religion.

The case exploded outside the university, in a campaign in Cairo's biggest mosque and a number of Islamic newspapers (some of them owned by the government) called for the dismissal of the lecturer from his job and the prohibition of the circulation of his books. A group of Islamist lawyers then resorted to the court. Their case was dependent on the fact that the state constitution is Islam, and Sharia is the major source of legislation (article 2). It is noteworthy that the 'Hisba' principle gives the individual Muslim the right to act directly or through law, to apply the Shariat Allah (law of God). Three years later they succeeded in getting judgement from the Supreme Court of Cassation; which stated that the professor is a Murtad (apostate). Then the main demand, according to Sharia, became his separation from his wife, a 'Muslim' university professor, despite her declaration of her refusal of this interference in her private life. The Sheikh (Grand Imam) of Al-Azhar approved this judgement.

The case became an issue of public opinion and the government justified its silence by citing 'its respect for the law'. Its representatives declared that they are unable to stop a 'religious judgement' at a time when attacks by 'Islamist terrorists' were on the increase. This case has been followed by more than a hundred cases of apostasy in the courts of the Cairo and other governorates against many intellectuals, writers and film directors. The wave of attacks extend to those on the works and personality of Najeeb Mahfouz, the Nobel Prize holder and the pride of the 'state and its intellectuals'.

Finally, the state tried to interfere to stop this 'confusion' through the People's Assembly, (95 per cent of PMs belong to the ruling party), but the Assembly enacted a law to approve the 'Hisba' system which has been removed from Egyptian legislation since 1957 (Seif, 1996). The Assembly tried to balance this by limiting its use to the General Prosecutor, the government legal representative, not to individuals, 'when the state sees that this goes against the interests of the society'! The new legislation includes discontinuation of the current cases if they are not yet settled. Thus, Abu Zeid's case remained the only one as it was actually settled.

So what are the implications of this case to our issue?

The wish of the state for political stability was demonstrated by its acceptance of the hegemony of the religious culture (regarding Abu Zeid as an infidel), while confronting the Islamist movement (as a terrorist political force). It tolerated the social instability (charges with infidelity), while it controlled political instability. While the Islamist movement challenges the state with violence, the state itself resorts to religion instead of developing political culture or popular participation (the involvement of elements of civil society). What is the basis of this unstable triple relationship between the state (political), the society (religious) and the social interactions (civic)? Are we facing the typical characteristics of a historical religious society, or a secular state in crisis? What is the status of the movement of intellectual and academic freedom in this scene?

Taking the religious reference as the source of legitimacy, the state did little towards the development of the social institutions whether ideological (education), organizational (jurisdiction) or legislative (constitution), because it can control, from above, the social situation which is in deep crisis.

The state pretends – in a case such as Abu Zeid's – that it is unbiased, while it is actually relying on an arsenal of laws accumulated over two centuries. Moreover, it controls the production of these laws by the party whose regime has dominated between 1952 and 1996 in an atmosphere that it maintains it is pluralistic and secular, while it is in fact dominated by conservative forces.

The significance of the courts' endeavour to link apostasy to the change of the relationship between man and woman (separation of couples) is relevant to social norms, which are supported by the religious institution and the state, therefore it governs social and intellectual relations, rather than being subjected to the public movement of freedoms or social interactions.

The Religious Culture and Institutions

Following the religious purity period in the age of the Prophet Mohammed and the orthodox caliphs' era, along with the stability of Arab-Islamic state, the religious culture settled on the opinion that national unity in the 'Islam land' is represented by the Sultan – The Imam, 'God's shadow on earth', although holy *Koran* stated generally that 'the succession in the earth (Istikhlaph) is reserved to man'. This made the legislative power and even the source of political culture represented in the 'Caliph' Imam role, representative of the nation's unity at the same time. Thus, the 'Imamat' in itself became the source of legitimacy, and the Sharia became the 'central' instrument of the 'Imamat'. Since man is no more a partner to the 'Caliphate' or involved in legislation, the state-caliphate became the only power which could approve the dominant religious doctrine, establish the religious institutions and recruit jurists.

At some times, the religious texts, whether Islamic or Christian, have clearly downgraded woman's rights as a citizen, such as inheritance, testimony at courts and leadership position (Imamat) etc. But the historical realities of the Islamic society and state have made most of these rules changeable according to the 'religious' relations in the society and the social economic developments. Women have been respectfully treated in the traditions and practices of the prophet Mohammed. They have even been introduced as a principal source of religious knowledge (for example, Mohammed told Muslims to take half of their religious knowledge from his wife Aisha). In fact Aisha had been a prominent figure for the Umyad state and certain Sunni traditions have followed from her lead.

This view of the position of women has not moved from the level of estimation by the individual to the social level to match the progress made by the state system when it moved away from being an Arab Bedouin political and cultural society in the Arab Peninsula. Women's presence in politics and religion remained subjected to those individual estimations in governance (Shagarat al Dur) or sufism (Rabaa al Adaweya), while the socially dominant image was the woman of the royal palace (during the Umyad and Abassi state) or the Turkish harim (Ottoman state). This was all reflected in the modernization launched by M. Ali's reign which did not premise its programme on any social programme of citizenship that involved women. This is the same heritage which remains dominant among the socially conservative classes and which is currently used by the fundamentalist culture.

We will see later that political culture in the region depends on this mechanism to exclude some social strata, such as peasants and workers, from the political participation process because of the elitism of the religious legislative power which is based on cultural stratification of citizenship as well as social hierarchy.

However, the Arab-Islamic society in Egypt, North Africa and Mashriq covers various types of 'civil society' such as jurists, writers, soldiers, traders, artisans, Sufi sects and other religious denominations in large cities such as Cairo, Fas, Damascus and Baghdad (El Jabri, 1995). Nevertheless, the society was still viewed as a united Umma (Nation) and the 'Islam land' rather than a diversified society. Rebellion (Fitna) against the Sultan-Imam was regarded as a form of disbelief and apostasy. Even when there was competition for the position of Imam in different parts of the 'Islam land', the 'other' was considered disobedient and infidel. The role of the jurist apparatus was to exert every effort to assert obedience and to win the support of the forces of the society to the unity of Islam Nation behind an Imam. Any Muslim has no right to spend a single night without paying homage to an 'Imam'. Accordingly, Ibn Taimiya (the jurist of the current fundamentalist movements) declared in the 12th century that 60 years under an unjust governor (Imam) who realizes 'the nation's unity' are much better than a single night without an Imam. Fundamentalists in all ages have been preoccupied with the religious preconditions the governor must enjoy. In fact they were more preoccupied with the unity of the 'Islamic Umma' (nation) more than with the 'society'. Therefore, apostasy represents, in their perspective, a threat to the 'nation's unity' because it threatens the belief rather than influences the social or cultural interactions.

Hence the demand for the implementation of Sharia is related to the establishment of power (Caliphate), rather than a specific social, cultural and political system. Proving that a governor is not committed to Sharia is a proof of his illegitimacy. Therefore, Islamists fight violently under the slogan of the Islamic solution – Sharia, because the Imam of the Islamic Solution – the Caliph should come from among them and realize the unity of the nation and belief. Hence the literature of the alleged apostasy becomes a counter action (fitna) to the Imamat project and not just an intellectual work which it is worth engaging in dialogue. The current governments which claim that they draw their legitimacy from Sharia (e.g. Egypt, Morocco, Algeria, Sudan and the Gulf States) inevitably counter the fundamentalists with this concept even if the state's structure is of a secular character (e.g. Egypt).

Islamic history provides different forms of religious support institutions, such as Al-Azhar in Egypt, Al-Zeitouna in Tunisia, the religious sects in

Morocco and Sudan, and the Wihaby religious institution in the Gulf. A strong state may choose its custodians and supporting institutions from the modern and developed space, but a weak state may resort to bootlicking and dissembling of religious trends, to face the forces of instability, which have a religious nature, and to avoid dialogue with the social, economic and political demands of civil society.

In Egypt, Al-Azhar's position for over more than one thousand years was not the source of legislation, but it has always served as a symbol of Sharia on the side of the Sultan, whether he was a Shiite, in the Fatimist era, or a Sunni, since the twelfth century. Its jurists shared some of its protest actions with the movement to create a civil society, but it remained as the apparatus of power and a source of legitimacy against rebelling movements.

Al-Azhar's jurists and intellectuals had participated in the rebellion movements during the period when the state went into stagnation in the 18th century, but it succumbed to Mohamed Ali and his descendants' plan in the 19th and 20th century to build a modern state. It had accepted obediently a position as a subordinated apparatus within the state. Hence, since the national state has always preceded it in development, Al-Azhar's position did not strengthen except during the periods of deterioration of the state and its social role. When the achievements of the national state led to some structural advances in its feudal form in the 19th century, the religious reformist movement revived by Gamal Al-Afaghani, Mohamed Abdou and others (radical Azharist jurists at the beginning of this century), Al-Azhar did not cope with this development. It resisted the reformist movement and linked it to modernization and Westernized secularism. When, between the two world wars, the intellectual movement raised the project of modernizing Al-Azhar alongside the modernization of the education system by Taha Hussein, the Al-Azhar community resisted. They still accuse Taha Hussein of being infidel! When the National Nasirist state attempted to make some progressive changes in Al-Azhar and other religious institutions, it succeeded only in the cancellation of the Sharia Courts, while Al-Azhar resisted the structural change. The state did not want to challenge it further because of its generally moderate policy in both social and cultural fields. It was satisfied with the change from within Al-Azhar (introducing some modern sciences) instead of changing the entire institution.

During the last two centuries, Al-Azhar is no longer the grantor of legitimacy to the state, as it had been before, but at the same time it remained the voice of the religious legitimacy to which the state resorts at the times of its stagnation, or with which the arising political religious powers dialogue. The Muslim Brothers remained appreciative of the role of Al-Azhar since their inception in 1928, despite their dissatisfaction with its political silence; and the current political Islamist movements ignored what from their point of view they see as its 'negative role'.

The success of Al-Azhar in crippling the religious reformist movement made this more traditional and conservative and made the modern state's attitude to Al-Azhar appear very weak. This motivated the emergence of the political Islam trend represented in 1928 by the Muslim Brothers, and later by the period when President Sadat pulled Egypt out of the socialist block, aspiring to gain some religious support. The competition between the traditional religious movement and the fundamentalist political trend led to their competition in combating the modernization trends in the cultural movement and in universities. In 1924 the two wings of the religious institution dismissed one of the great liberal Islamic intellectuals, Sheikh Ali Abdel-Razzik, from the religious community and the Azhar jurists body, because of his criticism and denial of the Islamic Caliphate ideology. At about the same time, in 1925, they isolated Taha Hussein of Cairo University because of his Descartestic interpretation of the Koran and the Jahili (pre-Islam) Arabic poetry (Hussein, 1937). They even dismissed him from the university for a period. Now the religious institution – in both its political and cultural wings – is trying to get rid of Nasr Hamid Abu Zeid and complete its cultural hegemony by widening the campaign against dozens of his intellectual colleagues.

Because of the weakness of the state's cultural apparatus and its withdrawal from any transformational role in the society since the Sadat era, and in the absence of any joint project between it and the secular intellectuals (despite its commitment to some forms of secularism) it has favoured the traditional religion (Al-Azhar and its institutions and the similar elements in universities) in its relations with the political Islam fundamentalists and their Islamist solution. This is the context during which the case of Nasr Abu Zeid emerged. Despite the implicit condemnation by the political Islam of the conservative stance of Al-Azhar towards the politicization of Islam, the fundamentalists realize that, by combining broad cultural activity with direct violence, the relationship of Al-Azhar to the state can also benefit them in mobilizing the weapon of the law against the modernizing elements.

This is the essence of what has happened over the last two decades in a number of different cases. By withdrawing from its developmental role, the state started to behave falsely towards the acceptance of plurality, commitment to democracy and support of the 'state of institutions'. Since the Sadat era it maintains it has adopted the principles of supremacy of law and separation of powers, but the current arsenal of laws, the dominant party and the highly conservative religious institution emphasize that these slogans are false.

We can list a number of laws that allow Al-Azhar to act as a censorship institution towards the cultural and intellectual movement of the society, as it shares with the state its patriarchal role, particularly in the periods of its decay. The Egyptian constitution (article 137) states that Al-Azhar and its Sheikh who is appointed by the president are part and parcel of the executive power (El Burai, 1992). So, constitutionally he is a secular power, rather than a holy religious one, but his assignment for life and his presentation in a clerical form by the state gives him this 'papal' status. By understanding the strong relationship between Al-Azhar (the Research Assembly), the Ministry of Religious Endowments (in charge of mosques and the presentation of Friday sermons) and the fundamentalist intellectual characters (academics and other members of the Research Assembly and Friday sermon givers), we can see the influence of Al-Azhar on restricting freedoms. This influence becomes more apparent when we add the impact of more than 40,000 private mosques established by the Islamist groups, to a further 40,000 mosques which belong to the government, all of which assert the top-down religious hegemony against all forms of freedom (from the freedom of thought through to the position of women).

Cases such as that of Abu Zeid do not remain as a university or academic concern. The complete hegemony displayed against freedom of thought and academic freedom by the statements of the Sheikh of Al-Azhar (who actually approved the court decision against Abu Zeid), the announcements of the Al-Azhar Research Assembly or the Friday sermons in thousands of mosques become an issue of religious and public opinion. The Islamist groups are given strength in attacks against the civil society, let alone their violence against the state by this breadth of support. The groups actually apply the most violent forms of punishment, in the form of assassination, on intellectuals, such as in the case of Farag Fouda.

It is noticeable that the patriarchal atmosphere imposed by the Islamic religious institution has recently tempted the Christian clerical institution (both Orthodox and Evangelical) to similar practices. While the Orthodox (Coptic) church of Egypt used to be satisfied with its religious and social role as well as dealing with the problems of citizenship for the Egyptian Copts, it has been observed recently that it has anathematized and excluded some intellectuals from the church because of their writings. The cases of Dr Imad Nazeeh (Orthodox) author of a book on Renaissance and Dr Rafik Habib (Evangelical) who published a book, *The Psychology of Religiousness Practices among Copts*, are cases in point (Howedi, 1992).

It is clear that the religious and paternalistic institutions which restrict intellectual freedom in society, are not isolated from the hegemony of the state which is mobilized against the Islamic violence with several forms of violence of its own (intellectual violence practiced by the government institutions such as control and security apparatus, media and legislative institutions).

Political Culture Under State Capitalism and the Capitalist State

The sources of political culture in Egypt varied from one historical period to another according to the variation of modes and relations of production. But these different developments created some principles that greatly influenced the structure of the state's power, the content of legislation and their relationship with the popular classes and the dominant social formation. This is what Aziz Al-Azma refers to as the 'penetration of the civil society by the state' (Al-Azma, 1992). We will outline below the major aspects of the development of the modes and relations of production to define the nature of the currently dominant mode and to determine to what extent it allows social interactions that nurture freedoms.

A central state has been a characteristic of Egypt since the days of the Pharaohs. It corresponded with the character of the tributary and quasi-tributary social relationships in the Nile valley (the hydraulic state). Creed, the development of science and the materialistic civilization served in asserting the type of central state. Militarism also played a prominent role, whether through external expansion or defence of political regimes, in the building of the state and its hegemony, making concerns such as wealth, education and development belong to the central state. This constituted an early alienation of the social forces.

In the early Arab Islamic era, the state in Egypt had been integrated into the system of central Islamic Caliphate which was, in turn, a tributary one. The strategic location of Egypt facilitated long distance trade. Also, in the Islamic world Egypt's location, along with its long history in the production of culture and thought, made the Egyptian Sultanate one of the centres of the Islamic Caliphate.

These factors also made the state's religious institutions, such as Al-Azhar and the jurist schools, major sources of political and religious culture. Expansion and defence of the boundaries of the state are relevant in securing the long distance trade paths to the far East, Far Magareb and Africa. Despite the variation in the forms of what we might describe as a civil society (jurists, judges, Sufis, merchants, artisans, harafish (laymen) and even Mamluki soldiers) the centralization and the dichotomy between the creed and the nation, separated the state from the society – it even allowed the state to identify the margin and function of the civil society. Furthermore, it prevented any type of civic participation under the central state and creed. The Sharia issue was not raised. It was not associated with any revolution or rebellion throughout the long history of rebellions in the Arab-Islamic world. Intellectual and legislative jurisprudence (Ijtihad) remained within the frame of the moderate Sunni tradition (Wasateya) and the support of the central Caliphate. Since the Mohamed Ali era at the beginning of the 19th century, the modern national state inherited centralization, militarism, and external expansion. The state remained within the Caliphate and at the same time, attempted to compete with the Ottoman Caliphate with an independent regional Egyptian influence. Mohamed Ali emphasized, in the first stage of his reign, the state dominance over society and the tributary system that would channel the national wealth to the building of the new strong state. In fact he began this process under the escalation of international capitalism and its success in the integration of the Middle East in its market. The aspiration to build a modern state and to modernize the public life in the country, led Egypt to fall within the international market. But the state was not been fully subordinated to international capitalism, at least during Mohamed Ali's era. However, Mohamed Ali's descendants failed to keep this independence. They integrated Egypt, throughout the following hundred years into the colonialized international market, with all it social and cultural implications. This lasted until the 1952 revolution led by Nasir.

The modernization process, led by the state, resulted in its gradual penetration into the structure of the society for the first time. A certain degree of separation between belief, Sharia and legislation occurred here, although the religious institution remained active. The social formation of the agricultural bourgeoisie confronted the traditional religious education and the influence of Islamic clergy at Al-Azhar. This made modernization seem to be connected with Westernization and infidelity, particularly with the collapse of the Pan Islamic (the nation's unity). It is very important to bear in mind these elements when discussing fundamentalism, even on its current agenda.

Some intellectuals feel that the trend of the Ottoman Caliphate itself and the national state in Egypt or Tunisia, for example, to modernization did not create a large divergence between the centralization of belief, which suggested the presence of the religious nation, and the pragmatic secularization, which made it prone to development under independence. It had been destroyed mainly by the colonial dependency and hegemony. It is obvious that the colonial administration supported traditionalism rather than secularism, contrary to the received idea that colonialization had been accompanied by modernization or secularism (Al-Azma, 1992). This pragmatism could explain the relative advancement of the position of women in the modern 'Islamic societies'.

This statement, of course has its strength in the Egyptian reality, and its credibility almost until now if we replaced the colonial administration with the independent despotic state. On this basis of national Egyptian culture, Nasirism has furthered social transformation and determined the cultural process within the framework of a populist approach based on 'revolutionary legitimacy' and the personal charisma of the leader. Many intellectuals contributed to the formulation of this approach as can be found in the documents of 'revolution', which range from the *Philosophy of the Revolution* (1954), *the National Action Charter* (1962) to the *30 March Declaration* (1968). The revolution, said a significant segment of intellectuals, asserted 'the unity of the nation and society' (single party), that 'freedom is for people, no freedom for its enemies' and that the state 'leads the nationalist project' by deepening modernization in industry and bringing about large projects such as the High Dam, steel, chemicals and electricity industries, agrarian reform and the dissolution of feudalism and the nationalization of large politics. Through this national 'legitimacy', the July Revolution was to transcend its previous negative attitude against freedom and constitutionalism, shown in the 1954 crisis when the regime confronted the political parties, university intellectuals and the professional unions (more than one hundred university professors were dismissed). Thousands of communists and Muslim Brothers were arrested for periods ranging from five to ten years. When it came to the so-called social justice procedures, the state prohibited any free organization for intellectuals, workers, farmers or women, thereby asserting the concept of 'the just despotic', which had been used by some intellectuals at the onset of the revolution as an Islamic conception emphasized by some Islamic reform leaders at the beginning of this century. It was linked to the national state project in the second half of this century. Therefore, the Sadat coup did not experienced any direct opposition in the 1970s when he suggested democracy instead of 'social justice' procedures, following the open door policy and the deepening of dependence on the international capitalist market.

The Sadat regime and its inheritors announced 'law supremacy' and 'constitutional legitimacy' instead of the revolutionary legitimacy (Abu Zeid). It also announced multipartyism (1975-6) and allowed parties or large capitalist organizations to issue newspapers. At the same time, it kept major media corporations (Egyptian radio and television and five old large journalistic institutions) under its direct control. It also controlled the largest publishing house (the Public Book organization). At the same time, the regime revived the political role of Islam through the Muslim Brothers, who returned from the Gulf to nurture conservative religious trends in society. From the beginning, political Islam devoted its support to the new capitalists, according to Islamic principles on private ownership and the refusal of interference of state. This helped the Islamists to achieve in the 1970s, with the Sadat regime's support, what they had failed to achieve through the last 50 years. For a time Sadat went on with his policies moving from the strong position, since the October 1973 victory over the Israeli enemy granted the regime nationalistic legitimacy for some time. With this, the Egyptian militarism not only restored its social and political position, but also established its economic project. Hence, the regime realized its traditional balance between economy, militarism and politics under the protection of both the army and the Islamists - until Sadat was assassinated by Islamists from within the army!

Despite the instability this caused, some felt that there were some apparent features of capitalism present that would make Egypt regress to the national bourgeoisie project prevalent before 1952. They also felt the capitalist orientation would be associated with a parallel liberal orientation, according to traditional Western history.

But the capitalist project was an economic project only, aimed at eliminating the national state's dominance on the sources of accumulation. This is evidenced by the lack of the growth in the civil society as well as any features of political participation, while religious conservatism and the concentration of the Islamists on undermining the role of women in the society were growing, making use of the increase in unemployment under the new economic policies. This expressed itself in the limited space for liberalism since the 1970s. Despite the dominance of the ruling party and state bureaucracy in the government institutions, the success of the opposition parties in winning five per cent of the seats in Parliament in 1976 took the 'freedoms' issue into the national and legislative arena. The government's plan for privatization faced influential parliament campaigns, manifested in the 'Bread Revolution' of January 18-19 1977. This was a popular Intifada extended to more than ten large cities and would have toppled the Sadat regime and its new institutions, if it had had a properly organized leadership. Despite that, hundred of communists were accused of acting against the new liberalism. The coincidence of the bread and freedom crises signalled the end of the national state project and, even, the collapse of the move towards a new liberal capitalist orientation. This can be adduced from the following points:

First, Sadat went too far with his visit to Israel in 1977 and signing of the Camp David Accord with Israel and the USA, to find a single-handed solution for the Arab-Israeli conflict, without the Arab countries, the Arab League and also the African boycott of Israel. The solution appeared to contradict to the achievements of the 1973 war. It prevented the reaching of a fair comprehensive peace until the late 1990s, because of the superior position of Israel through different stages.

Second, the unsettled situation in the national and Arab arena led to the failure of Sadat in presenting himself, to Western investors and the USA, as a substitute for Israel at a time when the Arab oil capitals abstained from investment in Egypt.

Third, after the national development project was dissolved, the state turned into a tributary nation, dependent on revenue from the Suez Canal, tourism, the transfers of its expatriates in Arab countries and its own oil income. The total of these revenues ranged between 13 and 15 billion dollars each year since the 1980s. These revenues did not help to realize the dream of building a national capitalism. Because he had this income and also a great desire to attract Jewish and international capital to support him in Egypt, Sadat thought that this would be enough to substitute not only the Arabs but also the civil and political social forces. Therefore he restrained freedoms and abandoned his alliance with the Islamists to prevent the expansion of their power, the same as he did before with the Nasirists and the leftists. He started oppressing them and subjecting them to the new arsenal of laws at a time when they were settled and had developed a broad popular grassroots base, over a period of ten years, with the support of the state's own religious media. It was this clash that led to his own assassination in September 1981 after he detained many prominent figures from all political forces and arrested 1500 people.

Fourth, the limited openness at the beginning of Mubarak's reign, after the assassination of Sadat, gave an impression that the new presidential institution had learned Sadat's lesson and would link the economic open-door policy with true liberalism.

This gained Mubarak some sympathy among the different 'secular' forces from both the right and the left. However Islamists decided not to give up their gains, especially since the Irani wave was rising after the success of the Islamic revolution in Iran. This had been very helpful for the radical political Islamic movement. The influence of supporters of the tributary mode of production (the new compradors) and the nature of the new class (the rural bourgeoisie, real-estate brokers, ex-soldiers and bureaucrats who had left the public sector) pushed the new presidential institution to complete the suppressive procedures and legislation started by Sadat. The new actions included a new emergency law and an arsenal of legislation against various freedoms, the role of universities in public life and even some of the gains attained by women in family law. (Sadat had presented his wife as a 'liberator of women', as the Shah of Iran had done before him.) Therefore the false change in the political culture which Sadat heralded after Nasir completely collapsed, while the open-door policies (Infitah) proceeded to an acceptance of privatization and structural adjustment programmes that denied the social role of the state. This policy affected not only economic or social life of the nation, but also the space for freedom and popular participation. We will outline some of these aspects in the following section.

The Legislative Violence of the State and the Building of the Privatisation State

The legislation that has been enacted during the last two decades in Egypt is not only related to the restricting of traditional civil and political freedoms, but also to the reorganization of the state to further its new phase of hegemony. It is also related to the control of the relationship with the different social and political forces in an explicit contradiction to the margin of freedom that might be expected under the new capitalist phase. This has established a base for the 'violence of the state' which, along with the increasing poverty, necessarily led to the escalation of counter-violence in poor and marginalized areas (both rural and urban), as we will see later. This violence was led by the fundamentalists who, unlike all other groups, enjoyed some degree of freedom which enabled them to build their popular support under the Sadat regime. The intention of the regime to control the sociopolitical situation and face counter-violence led it to extend its procedures to unusual gaps in its pretended liberalism, such as the strictness towards the small political parties and even the prevention of the moderate Muslim Brotherhood from forming a official party, the regime's hegemony on the university, and absence of seriousness in addressing the laws on family and women. It also had contradictory policies promoting 'traditional religious feeling' and combating of fundamentalist extremism at the same time. This legislative state violence led some intellectuals and academics to accuse the regime of practising violence and thus take the responsibility for the counter violence. The legislative violence of the state moved gradually into police violence which lost it the sympathy of both civil society and the intellectual community, despite the condemnation of the terrorist violence of the fundamentalist groups. Here we will briefly outline some aspects of the legislative violence practiced by the state.

When Sadat started manoeuvring in the margin of the liberal agenda to build a political movement to get rid of the influence of Nasirism and communism, he announced this policy as if it was a political act rather than the reorganization of the state and society to ensure the regime maintained the upper hand and was consistent with the traditional heritage of political culture in Egypt. In 1974, after the October war, he announced his recognition of three forums inside the Socialist Union (a single party) right, left, and middle. He considered his official organization as the middle forum. One year later Sadat recognized these forums as political parties. In 1977 he issued the act of political parties' organization (no.40), making it possible to establish other parties - according to the regulations applied by the Political Parties' Committee, formed by the regime! The committee comprised the president of the Council of State (Shura) and three ministers and jurists. Article 45 stated the consistency of the party's programme with Sharia, the principles of the July 1952 revolution and the May 1971 revolution amongst other matters. The regime had the right to dissolve the party, confiscate its journal, hold back any of its decisions and prevent individuals from joining it (political isolation law). It also prohibited the formation of parties on either a religious basis (to ban Muslim Brothers) and a class basis (mainly to ban the communists).

Many other important laws belonging to the 'totalitarian power' structure, such as the 'Interior Front Protection and Social Peace law' (no.23/1977) and the 'Law for Protection of Values Against Disgrace' (no.95/1980) which were known as the 'laws of protecting national unity aiming at jeopardizing the regime's opposites', were issued at the time (Khalil, 1993).

This arsenal of laws has been complemented by the Emergency Law issued after the assassination of Sadat (October 1981) to face any protest against the regime by the security forces. The 'Law for Combating Terrorism' has been declared as an alternative for to this in 1994, as has the 'Law of the Formation of Exceptional and Military Courts and Supreme State Security Courts'.

To legitimize its hegemony and empower its instruments of ideology, the regime moved away from totalitarianism and the militarization of power. It did this in a number of ways.

First, the religious institution's influence in intellectual freedom issues was expanded. The pragmatic secularism of the Nasirist state prevalent in the 1960s had limited the influence of the religious institution. This encouraged the Orthodox Church to take on a similar role, although this is restricted by laws dated back to 1856 which control its expansion and activities.

Second, it took steps to control the media. Egypt has one of the most influential media systems in the third world. The media were nationalized in 1961. and large state monopoly institutions were established including the major five journalistic outlets, radio and television and cinema. Although there had been attempts to liberalize the economy since the 1970s, it had not included the media institutions.

Third, it restricted the organizations of civil society. The state's aspiration to control the accumulation process lay behind the preoccupation with 'mobilizing the nation's capacity' in the Mohammed Ali and the 'popular mobilization' in the Nassirist phase, under the slogan of 'the state of workers, farmers and national capitalism'. Single party rule served to create the philosophy for the state's hegemony on farmers, students and workers' unions, as well as crippling the development of any women's organization. This was followed in the 1970s and 1980s by a number of laws, aimed at controlling groups in civil society.

University and Scientific Research
The concept of the university is deep rooted in Arab culture, especially in Egypt, and goes back to before modern times. Al-Azhar was known in Cairo as one of the oldest universities in the world since the Fatimist era, in the 11th century. For hundreds of years, religious science students (males only) studied different jurisprudence disciplines, taught by the Sheikhs of Al-Azhar. Cairo also had Dar Al-Hikma (knowledge houses) as a university for Sunni and Shiite jurisprudence, and four famous schools of jurisprudence.

The situation deteriorated from the 13th to the 18th century and the Arab Renaissance came to a close. During this period, the 'Sheikhs' of jurisprudence schools were nominated by Mamaleek rulers, to whom the Arab culture was foreign. The intellectual religious institution became one of the state's tools for coercion, not just an ideological organization, due to its newly developed apologist function. The door was closed by formal pronouncements to prevent many jurists forming independent opinions (Ijtihad). Shiite schools, as well as other jurisprudence schools, were prohibited by one ruler or another. The schools that had previously brought religious debate into the public arena, influencing the formation of social consciousness, were regarded as a source of 'sectarian trouble' (fitna) among the people. Particularly in the Ottoman reign, due to the development of the 'Touranist' militarism, the establishment of schools and technical institutes had not been neglected. But this in itself played a retarding role for five centuries when the traditional heritage remained conservative and not a force for enlightenment. Any move towards modernization became a technical rather than cultural or enlightenment endeavour. The ruling regimes kept the support of the traditional religion, while 'importing' modern education for technical development, building of 'the state' and the support of external expansion. Within this frame no room for free thought was reserved, and development of the situation of women or a distinctive role of the university community, except under resistance and with wide social interactions, was not allowed. This was what happened, to a degree or another, for 150 years.

Mohammed Ali, for example, sent Rifaa Raf'i al Tahtawy, the prominent 19th century Egyptian intellectual, to be educated as a religious intellectual. But after his return he adopted modern thought and new different modes of civilization that actually motivated enlightenment although 'he did not wish its evils to happen' (Emara, 1973). He asserted the difference between the Egyptian and the European realities. He translated about 2000 European texts in physical science and technology and established the languages school and technical institutes. But all this remained imprisoned within the frame of technology. They had nothing to do with culture, philosophy or social sciences. He warned, in his writings, against intellectual extremism and the development of women's situation in a way that does not fit his call for a modern civilization. The efforts of Rifaa Al-Tahtawy were followed by those of Ali Mubarak in the late 19th century to further the education of the poor to provide government with officials and turn poor women into bourgeoisie, while still rejecting modern education. Egypt's integration into the international capitalist market in the late 19th century and the emergence of a modern role for the local bourgeoisie in the early to mid-20th century, laid the foundations for a different type of modernization, accompanied by resisting colonialism while conserving the traditional position. This, in turn, led to the continued separation between modern education institutions and those of traditional (Azharist) education.

Cairo University was established in 1908 as a modern non-governmental university, then it became the Royal Fu'ad University in 1924. In the 1950s and 1960s the number of universities in the country was increased from four universities, reaching a total of 14 by the end of the 20th century, with about half a million students enrolled. The universities were associated with modernizing liberalism during the first half of this century. Campuses witnessed in-depth intellectual debates on the Koran, the Caliphate and the situation of Al-Azhar itself (for example, the Taha Hussein and Ali Abdel Raziq cases). However the Nasirist national state limited the role of the university to the nurturing of the 'modernization revolution through technical sciences'. In 1954, the regime also rejected the universities' liberal role in a crucial battle between the Revolution's government and political forces that were influential in the university.

Technical aspects of education have always been given a higher priority. Hence the legal education role (producing legal jurists and advocates) was reduced since the 1950s and the role of engineers (with the building of the High Dam), doctors (with the initiation of a clinical unit in each village) and technical institutes (with the establishment of a thousand factories) were increased during the 1960s.

Military technical colleges were established within the frame of the increasingly growing army. Scientific research academies dealing with physical sciences (needed for the construction of atomic reactors in the 1960s) were also established. However, despite these other changes, Al-Azhar remained the power centre for traditional religious education although there were attempts to develop it by introducing some modern sciences and 'secular' university faculties like medicine and engineering. Culture was not divided between the religious and the secular in the modernization era, because so-called secular education, based on technology and pragmatism, does not establish by itself secularism. Just because there has been a high percentage of women at universities since the 1960s it does not follow that the position of women in terms of political or civil freedoms has made progress. The faculties of medicine and engineering sciences, which in the 1950s and 1960s were centres of Marxist thought, became dominated by Islamists in the 1970s and remain so now due to the absence of the enlightening role of the university.

Despite this, the regime's need for a cadre that believed in the July Revolution's objectives against reactionary and colonial forces, left a limited margin for the Youth Organization members, most of whom were university students, to embrace the national liberation movement. This made the youth movement exert pressures on Nasir for freedom and democracy to the extent of organizing prohibited demonstrations and building alliances with workers after the 1967 setback and till his death in 1970, then later against Sadat in 1972-3. In this atmosphere Sadatism saw that its superficial adoption of some liberal procedures must not include liberalization of the universities. The government even supported the Islamist students' organizations bid to crush the Nasirist and leftist student movement. This artificial Islamic movement formed the base for a populist Islamic movement immediately afterwards, in the late 1970s.

In this framework, laws and procedures restricting freedoms at universities and scientific research centres were enacted, among them law no. 40/1972 concerning university organization which restricted all forms of free action and collective expression and law no. 809/1975, including the bylaw concerning the organization of students' unions, which prohibited their political activity and politicization. This was complemented by decree no. 1088/1987, issued by the Minister of Education. This group of laws prohibited any union organization at the university as well as peaceful strikes or mobilization, demonstrations, organization of any associations, publication or distribution of newsletters, etc. As for professors, the regulations included cancellation of deans' elections, the subordination of the Higher Council of Universities under the supervision of the Minister of Education and control of the procedures of the promotion committees, in addition to prohibiting the formation of professors' unions, thereby limiting their activities to university clubs.

Despite this, Islamists enjoyed great freedom inside and outside the university campuses. This atmosphere motivated some professors to support anti-progressive thought campaigns.

There is also a problem that bureaucratic procedures against freedom of thought in universities are encouraged in Egypt. This is because universities are no longer a place of scientific research but limited to the educational process. Professors are asked to produce an 'educational product' known as the 'university text book', very different from 'university reference', the same as the difference between education and research.

It is a bureaucratic hierarchical structure that governed by the bureaucratic hierarchy rather than by creativity. Outside the traditional university frame there are the Scientific Research Academy, the National Centre for Social Research, Research Academy, the National Centre for Social Research, and Economic Planning Institute, as well as important research centres at institutions like Al-Ahram newspaper and non-governmental centres set up in the privatization process. A university professor has to conduct and publish his intellectual product outside the university. If he conducted it at the university, it would be an intellectual shock for the traditions of educational writing. The conservation of traditions, the national heritage and stability of society has been used as an argument to justify the prohibition of intellectual work. This explains why liberty is extensive outside the university but conventionalism inside it. The traditional frame of the university prevents free thought as well as women's position in it, the same condition as in the traditional society.

Although the university was the basis for the entry of women into public life, especially in the cultural field, it is no longer the path that public figures follow to enter social life.

The Women's Movement and Intellectual Freedom

The women's issue in Egypt is linked to the modernization problem in a number of ways. Women have significant presence in social, cultural and economic activities, and in the modernization process and its institutions. But these two aspects do not lead to a process of radical political change or cultural transformation. Therefore, religious fundamentalists relate them to a single external factor – Westernization. This gives the gender issue its real societal dimension, rather than becoming a mere feminist question (El Zayat, 1996). In many ways, the obstacles for the progress of woman are the same as for men's progress. This is related to problems of social transformation, how to place the modernization process in its right position, and how to confront the central tenet of fundamentalism, i.e., the linking of religion to state.

By international comparison, Egypt is not backward in the fields of modern education, labour regulations, political participation forums, laws on equality between sexes and intellectual freedom in general, in all of which progressive steps have been taken for at least two centuries. This is evident in the statistics for men and women in labour, general and higher education, and presence in public positions and political bodies. Nevertheless we have seen above, how the modern state has limited education to its technological aspects, political form to the limits of 'the just despotic' and the dominant political party, and forced culture to serve the state's hegemony.

This gave the elements of civil society the power to resist the expected forms of intellectual freedom produced by the materialistic and social progress. During many periods of time this, in turn, resulted the civil society and state uniting on the basis of religious traditions to maintain stability and defend male traditions. The outcome was a weak situation of both men and woman in political and social participation, and the isolation of both from decision making on the major issues, whether national or social. This reinforced the idea a number of prominent women and men in Egypt still have – that the social problem is still the major question in political and cultural life, contrary to several other Arab or African societies. Of course this does not exclude some bright moments during which women realized the specificity of their cause and led political and social changes.

A review of some modern historical developments reveals these actions which are asserted by any sound dialectic perspective.

The modern state started introducing women into the modern labour force in the 1820s by employing them in textile factories, when the state had a pressing need for this industry as its military forces developed. Despite this, Mohammed Ali himself denied women the right to education when the Education Bureau (Majlis Diwan al Madaris) led by Tahtawy approved this right. At the same time he gave his own daughters education, despite the opposition of the religious community to such a step. The situation remained the same until the 1870s until Tahtawy published his book *The Sincere Guide for Girls and Boys* (al Murshid al Amin lil Banat wal Banin) in 1872, which was followed by the establishment of the first school for girls in 1873. The Coptic Church and some foreign bodies in Egypt had also assumed undertaken earlier activities in this field.

The beginning of the 20th century witnessed an obvious rise in the position of women. This was achieved by the cooperation of men and women, some Turkish and foreign aid, the work of some liberal religious leaders such as Sheikh Jamal Eldin Al-Afghani and Sheikh Mohammed Abdou, and the trend amongst the political and cultural elite towards the establishment of the National University in 1908. The book *Woman Emancipation* by the enlightened intellectual Qasim Amin was published and was supported by some religious men in the face of an attack by the religious institution. This attack led to girls being prevented from enrolling in the universities, except as associates, until the 1919 farmers bourgeois revolution. This was immediately followed by the establishment of the first higher level school for girls in 1920. The first batch of girls – 17 students – were officially enrolled in the university in 1929 despite large social protest.

Social and political action against British colonialism and its policies led to the extensive participation of woman in the 1919 revolution. The bourgeois women stood beside men in political and social issues. They not only refused, for the first time, the hijab (veil) but also some leaders like Huda Sharawy, Siza Nabrawy and Shareefa Riad challenged the conservative popular leadership of Saad Zaghloul by setting up the Central Committee of Wafd Ladies and the Saadist Committee for Women in 1920. This was followed in 1923 by the establishment of the Egyptian Women's Union which supported some demands for women's rights and equal opportunities in voting and prohibition of polygamy (Moawad, 1995). It is worth noting that these years cover the same period from 1920 to 1925 when the Egyptian Workers Confederation and the Egyptian Communist Party were established, in the face of severe opposition from the state as well as the bourgeoisie society.

Progressive developments occurred in the period between the two world wars, with the entry of women into the regular labour force, particularly as women labourers were just as oppressed as men. This was caused by the retreat of the local bourgeoisie in the face of foreign investment. However, the same period witnessed the activities of women in political and cultural fields where many university graduates emerged into public life, such as Malak Hefni Nasif, Nabaweya Musa and Ma'y Ziyada. Others worked within the new political parties. This activity included school activities, publication of journals, and the establishment of both the Party of Egyptian Women in 1945 led by Fatima Ni'ma Rashid, with a programme of social and political demands and the Ittihad Bint Al-Nil (Union of Nile Women) in 1949, led by Dorrya Shafik. Meanwhile in 1946, girls led the student movement which allied with the workers movement when Latifa El-Zayat, beside Fatima Zaki, as a representative of the communist movement, was elected as secretary of the National Committee for Students and Workers which organized the largest demonstrations against the British after Second World War. The universities reflected the movements in society up to the emergence of the Nasirist national state project in 1952, with the women's movement being an echo of the social situation and the free intellectual movement brought about by national developments.

During the 1950s and 1960s, the development of many sectors of society including women was connected with the other major changes that took place during this period. The national state ruled with a tight grip. Its concepts of modernization was limited to industrialization, development through technical education, maximization of the service role of the state, and putting culture to the service of 'revolution's' mass communication system. In this secular pragmatic framework women's education and the application of equal opportunities in employment and education emerged. By the early 1960s, 5.9 per cent of women were participating in the formal labour force, compared with 30.9 per cent of men. This development was also expressed in the new Egyptian constitution in 1956 which stated the right of women to vote and to be elected. The first woman to be elected to the legislative council was in 1957.

Between 1967 and 1976, several circumstances contributed to placing the male-female relationship in a relatively new framework. At the beginning of this period the Nasirist regime mobilized more than one million men to confront the Israeli aggression. Since then, women have occupied different professional positions, despite their increasing duty towards their families. This gave women a sense of a new social status, and this was represented in their eminent participation in the cultural and informational fields under famous leftist leaders. During this period, the student movement pushed many young women to the front, during its opposition to Sadat in the early 1970s. The decision of Sadat to 'grant' political plurality and the liberalization of public life offered women the opportunity to continue participation. Emigration of men to Arab countries, during the oil boom after 1973 similar to their previous mobilization in the army, also helped to activate the social and political role of women.

As a result, many prominent women emerged: for example, in the press,

Amina Shafiq, in literature, Nawal Elsaadawy, and as university professors, Shahinda Maqlad and Fareeda El-Naqqash. In the face of these radical figures, the wife of the president (Jihan al Sadat) attempted to mobilize the bourgeois wing of the women's movement either by winning their support for government policy or by confining them to a social services role, leaving no room for the two parts to establish an independent women's union. The government also refused to amend the law of association for non-governmental organizations (32/1964) that strongly prohibits intellectual, religious or political activities. Because of the politically escalating Islamist movement against Sadat, his wife then paid more attention to the mobilization of women's efforts. Accordingly, law No. 44/1979 (personal conditions law) was enacted, which gave some additional rights to women in their family life. This was objected to strongly by the religious institutions until it was finally cancelled by Mubarak (law 100/1985) (Arab Woman Movement, 1995) to please traditional religious trends and the political Islamist trend at the same time.

There is no doubt that social interactions and political and economic developments in Egypt through two centuries have largely improved the status of women in social, economic and cultural life, compared with many Third World countries. But the different forms of restrictions on the women's movement, or what might be called genderization – the societal relationships between men and women – do not fit with these materialistic gains. Some recent facts will help in looking at this lopsided relationship (Kazim, 1995; Halloda, 1995; Kamel, 1995; Rushti, 1995).

In university life, females represent 40 per cent of university students (1992 statistics) who total more than half a million in 13 universities. The percentage of women teaching staff is 24 per cent of a total 18,451 university staff. Women even make up 30 per cent of the staff at the universities of Cairo, Ain Shams and Alexandria.

In scientific research, there are 37,400 researchers in the scientific community, of whom 10,000 are women ranging from the social sciences with 27.3 per cent women to the physical and technological sciences with 30 per cent. This is due to the increasing number of women with PhDs (4900 from 16,100) and with masters degrees (3800 from 12,500) in scientific research. Women also occupy 2037 professorship positions at universities representing 25.3 per cent of the total professors and 2184 of associate professors, 30.5 per cent of the total number.

This high percentage of women is also observed in the field of general education. Women in this sector make up 487,000 from a total of 1.2 million personnel. The percentage of women occupying technical posts at Radio and Television Union is 40 per cent, and in the governmental and national press, the figure is 25 per cent.

The presence of women also extends to jobs in the public sector, where there are 1.1 million women from among 3.7 million employees – but only 13 per cent of leading jobs are occupied by women. This leads us to the increasingly wide gap between the position of women in different fields of work and their absence from the senior positions due to traditions and some official laws which restrict their promotion to these positions in the judiciary, military and at universities. Here the pressures of the traditional and religious pressure groups are clear.

The 1956 and 1972 constitutions do not deny women equality in rights and duties (article 194). By contrast, they give women several guarantees of protection and welfare. But the unified employment laws and the laws for nomination instead of election for senior positions now limit the promotion of women to the positions of deans of faculties at universities, chief editors in the press and the executive committee of the General Federation of Workers, where the first women to join arrived in 1996.

From 1979, 30 seats for women in Parliament were granted by Sadat. But this law was cancelled in 1992 thanks to a number of different pressure groups. There were only three women, two of whom were nominated and not elected, in the last parliament which included 450 members.

With women absent in such numbers from senior scientific and political positions despite their actual scientific and social advancement, the bureaucratic as well as the traditional religious leadership justifies the dangers of giving women such rights with their fear of the fanatic fundamentalism. In this context, the wife of the President continues her traditional role in carrying out some enlightened and cultural activities, and her appearance is required at international conferences on women issues. She often sponsors national conferences on women's issues (for example, the 'Reading for All Festival' and periodic national women's conferences between 1994 and 1996).

In opposition to these few liberal manifestations, however, government newspapers participate in some campaigns led by fundamentalists, including those for the 'return of women to the house' and 'protection of the family'. The weakness of the family unit is blamed by them for the phenomenon of street children. This attitude conceals the relationship of this situation to the increasing unemployment and suffering of the whole population caused by the effects of structural adjustment which lead to increasing of numbers of women in low-paid jobs and in the informal sector, and the increase of illiteracy among women to 60 per cent in urban areas and 70 per cent in rural ones. This socioeconomic situation cripples women's participation in political life or in the leadership of the NGOs which cater for women's affairs. Bureaucracy interferes with and restricts the activity of active women's groups and societies such as the Arab Women Solidarity Society, led by the eminent writer Nawal al

Saadawy, the New Woman group and the Progressive Women's Union.

Governmental organizations were very keen to mobilize support for their side and created a semi-governmental umbrella for women's societies to control the voice of women in the 1994 ICPD in Cairo and in the 1995 Beijing Conference.

If the 1960s witnessed active political and social participation under the dominant party during the Nasirist national state being impeded, this was, at least, connected to the development and modernization plans that pushed forward the social and economic situation of women. The plans even gave practical preparation for women to lead their own progressive movement at the first opportunity when plurality came about. Claims for emancipating legislation or an improvement in the political and social role of women in Egypt seem fragile in the atmosphere of accelerating economic oppression caused by the SAPs and an overwhelming escalation of the role of the traditional religious institution. Improvements in social welfare or women's political participation will not be realized without seeking comprehensive solutions for the entire crisis. They will never escape the daily violence led by fundamentalists in their propaganda for the hijab (veil) and for women to stay at home and satisfy themselves with the cottage economy (family production) and the informal sector. Women were also likely to be concealed from the social presence in rural areas and poor districts in towns.

Constraints on Intellectual Freedom for Women
A number of studies have outlined the factors that impeded the development of women's social and cultural status or the promotion of their role in academic and intellectual life in the same proportion as their contribution to the labour force or to the social formation of the middle class. Women have not been of great interest to the projects of the modern national state.

As well as the historical factors we have already listed, there are other contemporary considerations with which they interact to constrain women from advancement, even in the academic arena. These include:

First, the weight of the cultural male history, or what Bourdier called the 'habitus'. It extends male dominance of academic space since the old days (over jurisdiction, Koran interpretation etc.) to possess modern university space. One researcher stated that a significant proportion of female academics take for granted this dominance which constrains their professional status and academic freedom (Tabour, 1992).

Second, some women may have liberated themselves from this heritage, but not because the indigenous culture has developed, but because of their identification with the Western culture. This has led to their alienation and to attempts by the conservative environment to attack their intellectual activities and professional progress.

Third, because of women's social environment, their status in the household, the professional labour force does not allow them to make distinctive academic achievements in a way that would empower them to exert pressure for their freedom in this field. One researcher observed that the scientific contribution of women in university is estimated to be 50 per cent of the contribution of men.

Fourth, the media influenced the image and social status of women during the infitah period by encouraging the image of a householder and guardian of children, the nature of her consumption and the sources of her importance to society (sex and fitness). This means that society does not expect any contribution from women in the intellectual or academic life (Abu El Naga, 1997).

Fifth, the dominance of the 'gulf oil culture', backed by the Islamic Wihabi fundamental trends that have prevailed in Saudi Arabia and the Gulf region and serve to promote the above mentioned image.

Sixth, the absence of a strong women's social movement that support progressive intellectual contributions by women or stimulate such contributions. The associations' law in Egypt does not allow enough freedom for NGOs in general in addition to the fact that, since 1964, it has not admitted the right of women to organize associations. There are no women's unions in Egypt except within the limited activities of the political parties.

This situation has led to the exposure of prominent women intellectuals to severe attacks when they dared to publish or adopt radical ideas or social stances in favour of women or even tried to organize women associations (for example, the case of the Arab Women Solidarity Association, led by N Al Saadawy).

References

Abu El Naga, Sherine (1997), 'The Cultural Constrains for the Egyptian Woman Progress', in The New Woman (ed), *The Woman, The Law and Development*, Centre for the New Woman Studies.

Abu Zeid, N. Hamid, (1990), *The Concept of the Text (Mafhoum El Nass)*, Dar Sinai Cairo.

Abu Zeid, N. Hamid, (1992), *The Religious Discourse, (Al Khitab Addini)*, Dar Sinai, Cairo.

Abu Zeid, Ola, 'The Legal and Political Frame of Pluralism 1976-92' in El Sayed, M. K. (ed), *Political Pluralism in Egypt*, Arab Research Centre, Madbouli (in collaboration with CODESRIA).

Al Azma, A., 1992, *Secularism from Different Views*, Centre for Arab Unity Studies, Beirut.

Arab Woman Movement, (1995), 'The New Woman, Egypt Case Study', in Conference on Egyptian Woman and the 21st Century Challenges, Final Report, Cairo

Chill, A., (1993), *The Legal Constraints for Civil and Political Rights in Egypt*, EOHR, Cairo.

El Burai, N., (1992), 'The Religious Institution Control on Publication Liberty', in EOHR, *The Freedom of Thought and Belief*, Cairo.

El Jabri, A., (1995), *The Intellectuals in Arab Civilization*, Centre for Arab Unity, Beirut.

El Zayat, L., (1996), 'My Life', in: El Bahrawi, S., (ed), *Literature and Nation*, Dar Nur and Arab Research Centre, Cairo.

Emara, M., (1973), *The Complete Works of Rifaa R. El Tahtawi*, Arab Institution for Publishing, Beirut.

Halloda, M., (1995), 'The Egyptian Woman in Educational Process', in Conference on Egyptian Woman and the 21st Century Challenges, Final Report, Cairo.

Howedi, Fahmi, (1992),The Religious Institution Control on Publication, in EOHR, *The Freedom of Thought and Belief*, Cairo.

Hussain, Taha, (1937), *The Future of Culture in Egypt*, Cairo.

Kamel, M., (1995), 'The Egyptian Woman Participation in Academic Research', in Conference on Egyptian Woman and the 21st Century Challenges, Final Report, Cairo.

Kazim, H., (1995), Egyptian Women in Higher Posts, in Conference on Egyptian Woman and the 21st Century Challenges, Final Report, Cairo.

Moawad, N., (1994), 'Egyptian Women in Political Life', in Conference on Egyptian Woman and the 21st Century Challenges, Final Report, Cairo.

Rushti, J., (1995), 'Egyptian Woman Participation in Mass Media', in Conference on Egyptian Woman and the 21st Century Challenges, Final Report, Cairo.

Seif, A., (1996), 'Hisab', In between the Civil and Religious State, paper prepared for Centre for Legal Aid, Cairo.

Tabour, E., (1992), 'The Knowledge and Power, in The Arab Society', *The Arab Academicians and Power*, Centre for Arab Unity Studies, Beirut.

Taiymiya I., *The Religious Politics*, Al Siyasa, Al Shariya.

6. The Challenges of Scientific Research in Mauritania

Mohamadou Abdoul

Introduction

The profound and generalised crisis affecting the continent is perhaps the major challenge with which African intellectuals are confronted. They are involved, both as researchers and as citizens, in their work of satisfying the objectives of the nation through critical observation of society in its evolution, its changes and deviations. Explanation of the causes, manifestations and. consequences of this crisis may result in the outline of a solution, if taken into account by decision-makers. However, research itself has not been spared by this crisis, which has deeply affected the structures which underpin it: the university, research institutes and centres. These places, designed for reflection and the production of knowledge, have recently been the object of growing attention precisely because of the numerous problems existing within them.[1]

If we were to tackle the issue of higher education in its entirety, we would certainly be led into a lengthy enumeration of the countless causes of the crisis which affects it. That would make a relatively exhaustive and, no doubt, instructive inventory of the problems encountered by the university and even of difficulties affecting the education system as a whole. But this approach, though enlightening, will not be used here for at least three reasons. First, there is a full description of the crisis in Mauritania. Second, such an approach might swamp our problem with general considerations on education. Finally, and this is very significant, it presents the issue away from its context.

There is, therefore, a need to adopt a dynamic and interactive approach to underline the mutual influences shared between researchers in social sciences, the society and the state. This tripartite approach makes it possible to carry out the analysis from the perspective of issues of intellectual space, social responsibility and academic freedom[2]. Consequently, their relations with socioeconomic, political and cultural realities constitute the framework of this chapter. Research, the conditions in which it is undertaken and its problems will form the guiding theme of the analysis. It is, in our view, one of the most important links between the 'intellectual community', the state and the society. Through thought, reflection and research intellectuals produce knowledge and devise judgements relative both to their society as well as to the political system that governs them. We will, therefore, look at several measures, which vary from the abolition of slavery (1981), democratisation (1992), national land reform

(1983), the Economic and Financial Recovery Plan (1985-8) and the Consolidation and Relaunching Plan (1989-91), to name only a few. These measures, we believe, have caused more problems than they solve.

The University of Nouakchott [3] was established in 1981, but it obviously could not discharge with success the objectives for which it was created. When established it had two faculties: Law and Economics, and Arts and the Humanities. Later, in 1995, the Faculty of Science and Technology was set up[4]. The institution was given the mission of 'contributing to scientific research, promoting and developing Arab and African cultural values in collaboration with others'. The content and meaning of the expression 'Arab and African cultural values' could be discussed at length. In Mauritania, such a formulation is deliberately ambiguous and imprecise.

The legislation and statutes above do not, at any point, make any provisions guaranteeing academic freedom. This is not unexpected in view of the nature of the political regime controlled by the military since the coup d'etat of 10 July 1978. Even though important measures were initiated by the Military Committee for National Salvation (CMSN), the body which forms the government, the establishment of the university was not the result of a desire to set up a space for intellectual freedom. Conversely, it was more of a response to find a place for baccalaureate holders who had become too many to be sent to universities abroad. This explains the precipitate nature and lack of preparation and unpreparedness that characterized the establishment of this 'nursery for adults', as some have ironically named it. Moreover, the university carries with it a 'congenital defect' related to this state of affairs (Ould Tolba, 1993 : 32). Other explanations have a different analysis. They attribute the university crisis to the increasing number of students. In 1989-90, the number of students pursuing higher education totalled 7800. In 1992-3, it increased to 10,500[5]. It is our view that this increase aggravates the crisis confronting the university because it results from the inadequacy between demand and supply in terms of education. Because of the enormous economic difficulties and the crisis in the education system, the establishment of this university defies every logic. One is even tempted to wonder whether, beyond the need to find a solution for new baccalaureate holders, it was not instituted also for reasons of national pride. The profound changes that took place in the education system illustrate well enough the results of the strict application of a policy whose motives are other than the search for efficiency, performance in the acquisition of knowledge and the training of administrators.

Trends of Mauritanian Education Policy

The reforms of education in 1966, 1967, 1973 and 1978 were successive stages of a progressive arabisation of the education system and consolidation of the preponderance of the Arab language (Gueye: 1992; Ba : 1993; Taine-Cheikh: 1994; Sounkalo: 1995). The linguistic reform of 1980 established two branches of Arabic and French education, during a transition period which is still ongoing. The creation of the Institute of National Languages (ILN) at the end of 1979 for the promotion of Black-African languages did not alter, in any significant way, this arabisation, whose ideological and political substructure are evident. It is misleading to say that there is equality between the systems since two parallel education branches have now developed and one (Arabic) has an advantage over the other (French). Each of the two communities – Moor and Black-African – identifies with one of them[6]. Therefore, it is wishful thinking to set up a school as a 'crucible of the nation' and a place in which all the social components of the country blend into one another. Consequently, we can observe that 'the decade of the 1980s – in the course of which the consequences of Arabisation in education and its career prospects appear – witnessed the intensification of national minority dissatisfaction.' (Taine-Cheikh, 1994: 62). From the perspective of the process of nation-building, the issue is central, the political challenge enormous and its sensitivity extreme.

The gap between the two groups of student populations corresponding to the two different socio-cultural groups of the country continues to grow (Amel, 1994: 4). The obstacle to comprehensive integration of these groups is that students have the option of which language to be taught in at every level of the education system, from the first to the third cycle. The example of the Arts and Humanities Faculty is edifying. In the 1993-4 academic year, 'the Black-Mauritanians represented less than 5 per cent of the total students pursuing the 'Arabic' option (corresponding to less than 10 per cent of the total number of Black-Mauritanians in the Arts and Humanities Faculty.' (Amel, 1994 : 4). This trend is going to intensify to the point of raising concern among many Mauritanians preoccupied with territorial unity, national cohesion and social justice. In the minds of most Black-Mauritanians, this results from a deliberate choice to marginalize them in the management of the affairs of the state.

It is not surprising that here, as in many other areas, people have strong convictions that are as varied as they are passionate. For some, such convictions boil down to their condemnation of others. Others attempt to explain the correctness of their option. It is almost impossible to achieve any change in the situation, given the stance of one of the major opposition parties, the Union of Democratic Forces (UDF). This stated, in a paper on general policy: 'the Mauritanian school should be adapted to our socio-economic environment and to our preoccupations in terms of development. It should aim at the future by strengthening scientific, technical and professional education. In this regard, there is need to adapt and develop our university system with a view to promoting 'fundamental and applied research.' This challenge is difficult to confront because neither the public authorities, nor the university administration and, to a lesser degree the students, intellectuals and university scholars do not seem to count it among their priorities, at least for the moment. The university is not ready to fulfil its real mission and to play its role in national construction, if it has any at all beside the production of knowledge.

Researchers and Social Science Research

Like other African countries, research in Mauritania is burdened with a heavy colonial heritage. Anthropological studies of colonial Mauritania has provided us with the image of a country associated with the desert, a nomadic lifestyle, camels, 'blue men', 'veiled men' or 'sons of clouds and freedom'. This exotic vision leaves tourists – including intellectual tourists – dreaming. Because there is this already-assembled framework, the 'whole Mauritanian cultural heritage' is in fact often limited to the heritage of just one of the country's social components (the Arab component). The other components are kept secret or treated as 'minorities', if they are mentioned at all. It is as if those minorities don't have a cultural heritage as well'. The political analysis of the minority components is focused on tribes, their organisations, tribulations and turbulences. They are generally described in very degrading terms[8].

Reports by colonial administrators described the 'political and administrative situation' in Mauritania using the term 'the Moor tribe' for the black population of the south. These administrative documents are the primary source of Mauritania's colonial history still used by researchers who, very often, repeat the classifications and methods of presentation in their writings.

This 'tradition' is revealed in the way in which political, cultural and socioeconomic issues are still approached in post-independent Mauritania. Most cases still draw comparisons and parallels between white and black. The underlying reason, whether it is acknowledged or not, is to use this method either justify or invalidate the viewpoint of another. Objectivity is difficult to establish. Marchesin (1994: 111) gives a very edifying example of this situation : 'let's examine two Master's theses in history defended, a few years ago in Nouakchott and relative to the period we have just discussed (1946-1956), the first by a Moor student and the second by a Black African student . While the theme is strictly the same and concern the general evolution of the country, we discover two different analyses, one focused on the Moor community, the other on the Black African organisations even in the bibliography which, for the former contains no Black African, while the latter mentions no Moor!'[9]. This could be considered as an extreme example. Maybe it is. Whatever the case, this passage clearly describes the state of mind and the intellectual atmosphere prevailing within the Mauritanian 'intellectual community' in 1986. With a few limited exceptions, such as groups known as 'parlour circles' or 'Nouakchott groupings', there were practically no intellectual exchanges between the communities. Besides, these circles were more interested in political activism than in the critical and objective analysis of their economic, social and political environment. The small amount of intellectual space that could have existed was transformed into a political arena.

However, since 1991, with the advent of press freedom, many newspapers have been launched, thus providing the Mauritanian intelligentsia with possibilities to express themselves outside the confines of parlour debates. Promoters of these newspapers have often facilitated intellectual exchanges and their development by creating 'Debate' and 'Essays' columns and other free supplements [10]. In these columns, researchers, intellectuals and academics give free expression to their ideas, reflections and points of view. However, the support of the press, while still important, is not enough to provide the support for results of extensive research and providing space for in-depth reflection.

One of the university's most important functions is to provide a space for research. This dimension, even though fundamental, has serious limits in Mauritania. Despite a budget that could be regarded as relatively substantial (360 million ouguiya in 1994), an insignificant part is set aside for documentation, publications and intellectual and cultural manifestations – 93 per cent of this budget is absorbed by the payment of salaries and fellowships. The remaining seven per cent is even more inconsequential when we consider that it also covers equipment and the purchase of consumable material (Amel, 1994: 4).

Consequently, apart from a few very episodic publications, most of the research work constitutes theses written for degrees. Unfortunately, these generally have very serious gaps, for which the students alone cannot be held responsible. In an article entitled 'How deplorable these theses are... But whose fault is it?' a head of department, who wanted to stay anonymous to avoid loosing his colleagues' support, wrote that these works were 'incredibly mediocre' in both form and substance (*Espaces Calame*, 1994: 4). The supervision of students who are just taking their first steps into the field of research was severely criticized. This mediocrity is primarily the responsibility of the thesis director, the guide, the 'initiator' of the research.

Various different factors – education policy, 'bad governance', the incitements offered by international financial institutions with their ill-timed conditionalities and their devastating social consequences – have all contributed to the crisis faced by African universities in general, and that of Mauritania in particular. These should, however, not be used as a pretext to absolve other causes. The international financial institutions, for example, have deliberately imposed drastic restrictions on university expenditure, on decision-makers. This dealt, and continues to deal, a heavy blow on intellectual reflection and production. Those inside the institution responsible for running it are also to a large extent responsible for the crisis[11], even though such responsibilities are very often concealed. Some lecturers – quite a substantial number it seems – direct 10 or even 15 masters and doctorate students per academic year. A thesis directed and validated by the jury is equivalent to 20 hours overtime. Because the obsession with making money takes pre-eminence over research, the existence and quality of research is thus compromised (*Espaces Calame*, 1994: 4). Some lecturers also teach for an excessive number of hours each week, well above the norms set for adequate preparation and the relatively correct transmission of knowledge. Some also teach in private schools, while others work occasionally as consultants.

Many hours of work can also be justified by publishing research. Five issues of the Annals of the Faculty of Arts and the Humanities were published between 1989 and 1996. This publication aims to develop serious scientific research at the university. The articles it publishes are supposed to set out the conclusions of research work on Mauritania and its 'cultural values' and at the same time attempt 'to contribute in remedying certain deficiencies affecting other areas of knowledge.'[12]

The Faculty of Arts and the Humanities wants to use these Annals to circulate material and consolidate the objective spirit in which articles are published, to popularize and develop diverse methodologies, and to provide a forum for the exchange of scientific knowledge, methods and experience, both within the university, and between the University of Nouakchott and other institutions. Even though there is a degree of uncertainty about its publication, the will to make it appear exists.

France has given financial help to establish two study and research laboratories. These should improve the situation for researchers in history, and for training trainers, as well as providing data-processing and reproduction equipment for geographers.

The Mauritanian Institute for Scientific Research (IMRS), was founded in December 1994, and has succeeded in some of its work, despite encountering numerous difficulties. It has three sections: Arab manuscripts; sociology, oral tradition and linguistics; and historical studies. In 1993, the fourth issue of this institute's review (Al Wasit) had been prepared but could not be printed because of lack of funds. The Mauritanian Oral Tradition and Written Tradition (TOTEM) project, launched in collaboration with the French Co-operation, provided the second tranche of funding which unfortunately will soon disappear just like the first[13].

Because there are now more Mauritanian graduates, there has been an observable increase in the number of publications by Mauritanian researchers. However, most of these publications, appear outside the country in foreign reviews, particularly French[14].

Research in Mauritania is impaired mostly by the limited circulation and the very little interest shown by both the State and the public.

Universities and the State

The diverse relations between social science researchers and the objects of their research are extremely complex, partly because of the situation described by Boubacar Ly (1989: 4):

> *The social sciences exist in Africa in a context which - while being in its various aspects, the object of their attention and, to some extent, transformed by them - has an influence over it. The social context indeed has repercussions on their conditions of existence and on those in which their activities are carried out. It is the diverse aspects of the social as a whole which are involved in the determination of the social sciences. These aspects are social, political, institutional, administrative, economic, financial and even cultural.*

This quotation perfectly summarizes the complexity of the issue and also raises problems of what position the country's intellectuals should take. What attitude should intellectuals, researchers and academics have in relation to the state? What gives them the right to pose as pioneers of national construction - for this is a function they claim quite often? Whatever their differences of opinion and their contentions, they carry forward the ideal for a modern and democratic society[15].

At the time of the Aleg Congress in May 1958, the opportunity to reflect on the form and nature of the Mauritanian state was wasted by the emerging intelligentsia. At that point, the intellectuals – called the elite at that time – could have made their contributions to the new independent country, but there was also the need to unite all its social components. Moktar Ould Daddah stated a year before the Aleg Congress: 'We are a Nation coming into existence. Together, let us construct the Mauritanian Nation.' They should have worked harder to build sentiment and conscience in the community. Yet 'the intellectuals had the means to participate in the democratic life based on legal and economic competence and on the understanding of statements made. The latter requires the ability to handle words and concepts' (Schnappen, 1994: 149). Under the one-party state, however, no political, socioeconomic, cultural and intellectual activities existed outside party officials, nor could these activities stretch beyond the course determined by its organs. Intellectual freedom has always been muzzled by slogans such as 'respect for the party line and for the major options and orientations of the State'. Fortunately, the democratisation which occurred at the beginning of the 1990s, has begun to erase the persecution mania that frequently inhibits university lecturers[16].

It is these people who may, consciously or unconsciously, upset the system.

They may try to expose the political and social contradictions and practices which go against the general interest, pointing an accusing finger to the state and to some sectors of society. This can lead to trouble, which can be quite serious when the information provided is considered as 'subversive', undermining state security, social stability and cohesion'. Furthermore, social science researchers are very often influenced, in their research and publications, by 'the sensitiveness of the authorities whose despotic inclination makes it difficult for them to encourage anything that is not in line with propaganda, and the strengthening of a line of action already determined at the highest level (Ould Cheikh 1994:8).

Because they are endowed with the 'power of knowledge', academics are respected, feared, wooed and closely watched in the positions they defend publicly as well as in what they produce. It is for this reason that, even in their discussions with journalists, they often prefer to remain anonymous. This occurred, for example, when a professor and a researcher made a recent study tour to Saint-Cyr Coëtquidan School in Mauritania on behalf of a French newspaper[17]. In the report, some statements and explanations are attributed by expressions such as 'a sociologist indicated' or 'this same sociologist explains', or 'a professor at the university explained'. The practice of hiding behind anonymity or other disguising subtleties is very common in Mauritania. However, thanks to democratisation, more people are willing to declare their identities. Now they can openly offer their services and expertise to the different state structures (Diallo, 1996: 7).

The government has enormous resources to influence both the decision-making process and the way in which decisions are applied. These resources can be legal, but they may also involve pressure, threats, censorship and other obstructions of intellectual freedom[18]. This was demonstrated by the seizure of the second issue of Al Wasit, the Mauritanian Institute of Scientific Research (IMRS) review and the censorship of an article in its third issue. In fact, the power granted to the Ministry of National Education by statutory acts is too great. The university resources emanate from state subsidies, donations, and various receipts, and the funds can be authorised, approved, suspended and nullified (clause 5 of decree no. 81-231, 20 October 19XX relating to the organisation and operation of the University of Nouakchott). The design and organisation of courses and exams as well as the disciplinary administration of faculties and institutions of the University of Nouakchott are determined by the Minister responsible for higher education (clause 1 of decree 95-047 of 2 November 1995).

It is obvious that the issue of the autonomy of decision-making is higher up the agenda than ever. Notwithstanding democratisation and decentralisation, the university has still not been provided with the means required to obtain greater autonomy. The following question should then be asked: what are lecturers doing to obtain university autonomy and freedom to lecture and conduct research? The union of university lecturers leads a vegetable-like existence. At no level of the institution does one witness a debate on intellectual and/or academic freedom, whose promotion and/or protection are mentioned only in very rare statements. Does that mean that this union is satisfied with decree no. 86-212/PG of 25 December 1987 relating to the status of higher education personnel? Does the Commission on Higher Education function normally? What actions and measures were taken when a French professor at the department of philosophy was presumably dismissed arbitrarily? (*Al Bayane* no. 65 of 10-16 March 1993, p.11). Does the recruitment policy meet the needs of the University. The answer to the last question since 'the integration of new recruits in the professorial corps creates real obstacles'. (Ould Ahmed Izid Bih, 1995: 12). There are an excessive number of applications for jobs. The dates for meetings of the candidate evaluation and selection committees are fixed only with the good will of the authorities. One may wonder whether the authorities' attitude constitutes a barrier against new recruitment inside the university[19]. More generally, what is type of relations exist between the university and society as a whole? How do the authorities react in relation to the predominant mental attitude?

Universities and Society

Mauritania is a multi-ethnic and biracial society, but it is also hierarchical and unequal – only 37 per cent of adults were literate in 1995. Given this, it is difficult to expect social science researchers to be assisted and encouraged in their research work. Ould Cheikh (1994: 8) says: 'it [social science research] is rather meant to disturb, its vocation is essentially critical, and it puts its fingers on things that the society does not generally want to have unveiled and expose publicly – political ideologies, social taboos, madness, genealogy'. Because of the tribal and/or ethnic context, the population can be extremely sensitive and easily roused when some unpleasant realities are exposed. For example, in 1993, a number of aggressive attacks were made on Khadijetou Mint El Hacen, Professor of History, following a critical comment she had made on a rhyming account of the history of Trarza, by a 19th century scholar. Her aggressors accused her of adverse comments on some tribes mentioned in the chronicle. A petition was opened to support her and condemn the reprehensible attacks on her. Called a petition in favour of the freedom of research it was signed by 214 university lecturers, researchers, teachers of all levels of the education system, librarians, journalists, lawyers, economists, doctors, administrators, engineers, businessmen, various officials and members of human rights organisations). The petition's introductory passage stated:

Such actions, apart from the prejudice they have inflicted on a researcher, constitute an unacceptable obstruction of the freedom of expression and research. They furthermore contribute in reviving archaic, illusory and dangerous tribal solidarity to the detriment of the national conscience... They [the signatories of the petition] draw the public authorities' attention to the fact that freedom of thought cannot exist if, in its exercise, it is not protected against interference, whatever its origin. They emphasised that if third parties feel wronged by revelations contained in a publication, they have various means provided by the law (the right to reply, taking the matter to court) to assert their claims and obtain, if necessary, the reparation of the prejudice suffered. They, consequently, appeal to all freedom lovers to condemn the pressures, threats and aggressions used by all forms of obscurantism to block researchers' activities (Al Bayane, no. 75 May 19-25, 1993, p.11).

This reaction and the denunciation of violations of freedom of research are encouraging to researchers. Researchers are now beginning to be conscious of the need to have a community of their own, defending their rights and working instruments as well as their means of existence.

However, incidents such as the plundering of the offices and equipment of an independent newspaper by a group of people to cleanse an 'insult' to their clan is not likely to encourage researchers despite all the support and sympathy they may have been offered (*Le Calame* no. 60, November 14, 1994). Some clan members who hold political positions felt 'insulted' by the newspaper. This is especially so when in such cases, the victims themselves, the journalists, were then sentenced by the courts.

It is difficult for objective research to develop in Mauritania. Self-censorship is also very common. Furthermore, in many cases, 'those who still show an interest in research [are], most of the time, trapped in semi-traditional issues [and are] suspected of being biased.' This further hinders the formation of an intellectual community concerned and jealous of its freedom and autonomy of thought and reflection. One might comment that the university simply reflects society and its lethargy.

In Mauritania, the social demand for intellectual work, other than the exegesis of religious texts and Arab poems, is very insignificant[20]. Marchesin (1992: 14) describes it thus: 'besides the fact that the research profession is neither valorising nor valorised, the concern to pursue an interesting personal career requires the researcher to be neutral not only in relation to the authorities but to all other persons, no matter how weak, who are criticised in their works. In a society in which people know each other, reputation is a fundamental value'. In Mauritania, the tribal issue dominates all other relationships. Going beyond this framework in the name of scientific objectivity is considered as treason. Lecturers and researchers leave the university for other sectors and posts not only earn more. It means they can avoid losing the respect of the tribe, the ethnic group or even of some very influential personalities. In this unfavourable environment, it is no wonder that intellectuals are generally regarded as people detached from reality and living on books and newspapers. They are described as 'great theoreticians', 'good orators' or 'dreamers'.

Conclusion

We have looked at the role and place in society of the university institution and research institutes, as well as their material, financial, infrastructural and human problems,and their relations with the state. Intellectuals in general and academics in particular are primarily concerned in reflecting on the future of the society to which they belong and in which they may pride themselves that they are the cream of 'the elite'. Academics are faced with the challenge of forming an independent intellectual community, a 'middle class', counterbalancing the political elite, and to some extent, the business elite (traders, entrepreneurs, financiers, etc.) and even the traditional authorities. This challenge involves coming together in a plural intellectual community within which frank and healthy debates will be organised. It should identify with the values of freedom, tolerance, objectivity, the respect of differences and of the diversity of opinions. It is urgent for Mauritanian intellectuals, whatever their theoretical orientations may be, to concentrate on their existence as a community. They are bound to construct 'a professional memory' and to coin a collective conscience. It is only by so doing that they will survive.

Taken from sub-regional seminar on 'Academic Freedom in Africa' (Ouagadougou, August 1996) in CODESRIA Bulletin *no. 4, Dakar, Senegal, p. 4-5.*

Notes

1   The creation in 1994, by CODESRIA, of a programme on Academic Freedom is a fundamental contribution to this impetus. In addition to numerous publications including *Academic Freedom in Africa* (1994), under the direction of Mamadou Diouf and Mahmood Mamdani, and *The State of Intellectual Freedom in Africa* (1995), CODESRIA has already organised with other partners, two national conferences in 1996 in Ivory Coast and in Egypt on 'academic and intellectual freedom', and 'the social responsibility and autonomy of institutions of higher learning', respectively. In 1996 with other partners, a sub-regional seminar was organised in Ouagadougou on the theme 'Academic Freedom in Africa'. The whole process has been launched since April 1990 during the Dar-es-Salam meeting on academic and university freedom, followed in March 1992 by that of Ouagadougou and in November of the same year by the Kampala meeting.

2   In this text, we adopt the definition of intellectual freedom given by Ardiouma and Philippe (1996 : 4) in terms of 'a group of advantages instituted into laws granted to the academic community of a society, with a view to allowing it an intellectual productivity of quality aimed at contributing in easing the ills and improving the quality of life of the society as a whole : freedom to think, to conduct research with adequate means and to publish its results, freedom of opinion in the exercise of their functions, freedom of association, of the press etc..'

3   This text does not aim to deal with these theoretical and epistemological aspects. Its main object is to underline certain aspects related to research, intellectual production and academic freedom in order to arouse a wide debate within the Mauritanian 'intellectual community' as well as within the African intelligentsia on these aspects and those more generally related to human rights in this country. It is to be noted that writings on intellectual production in Mauritania exist even though they are rare. One can quote the interesting but unfortunately short-lived contribution of Mahmoudy Ould Mohamedou entitled 'The Moor Renaissance' in *Le Calame*, no 94 from July 25-30,1995, p13

4   For more details on the establishment of the university institution of Mauritania cf. General Order no. 81-208 of September 16, 1981 relative to the creation of the University of Nouakchott, in the *Official Gazette of the Islamic Republic of Mauritania*, no. 552-553, of Wednesday October 28 1981, p.450; Decree no. 81-208 bis of September 28 1981 establishing the Faculty of Law and Economics, and decree no. 81-209 bis of September 18 1981 establishing the Faculty of Arts and the Humanities in the *Official Gazette of the Islamic Republic of Mauritania* no. 576-577, of Wednesday October 27 1982. The Faculty of Science and Technology was created by decree no. 95-046 of November 2, 1995, in the *Official Gazette of the Islamic Republic of Mauritania*, no. 866 of November 15 1995, p. 544.

5. See *La Calame* no. 67 of 4-10 January 1995, p. 12 - article entitled 'University 2000 in Mauritania' which gives a report of a conference organised in Paris on December 23 1994 by the Executive Committee of the Union of Mauritanian students in France. The theme of the Conference was 'Franco-Mauritanian Co-operation : higher education sector' and was animated by J Y Hoisnard, Agrégé in Arts and head of the Higher Education and Research Office at the French Ministry of Co-operation.

6. The duality of the education system makes the definition of the term intellectual even more ambiguous. Depending on whether one sees it from the viewpoint of Arab cultural orientation or of that of a western type State, federating all the cultural identities in a single Mauritanian nation, the meaning of intellectual is different, at least in the past and present situations in Mauritania. Their judgements are indeed different and very often opposed. For detailed developments on the situation, all things considered, of the

separation between these two judgements, cf. Abdallah Laroui (1978), *The Crisis of Arab Intellectuals, Traditionalism or Historicism?* Paris, Franáois Maspero, 221 p.

7. It is regrettable that the cultural policy of the post-colonial period and all the national research projects are in keeping with this logic of marginalising the so-called minority cultures.

8. Since independence, little has been done to 'rectify' this biased approach of colonial history and anthropology. 'Forgetting' to introduce other social groups that are an integral part of the country is still common practice. Thus, the Chinguitti Colloquium of October 13-19 1995 organised by the International Centre for Saharan and Sahelian Research whose proceedings are published in *La Nouvelle Revue Anthropologique* of the International Anthropolgy Institute shows no trace of Black-Mauritanians, either in the topics discussed or among the participants to this colloquium. The topics were: a) Identification, protection and cultural valorisation of cave art stations (prehistoric and historic), archaeological sites and ancient cities in danger in presaharan and Saharan Morocco , the Malian Sahara, the Canary Islands, Mauritania and Niger; b) Research and protection, restoration, classification and examination of ancient manuscripts of the Sahara and the Sahel; c) The social and human environment: cultural anthropology and sociological problems referring to the survival and preservation of the cultural identity of inhabitants of urban and rural zones of archaeological and historical sites in danger; d) Government projects, international co-operation interventions as well as programmes realised or being realised in geo-historical cities.

9. Cf. Mohamed Ould El Hassan, (1983-4) '*Aperçu de l'histoire politique de la Mauritanie, 1944-1961*, Ecole Normale Supérieure, Nouakchott, and BA Ciré Ismaïla (1985-6) *L'Evolution Politique de la Mauritanie, 1946-1960*, Faculty of Arts and the Humanities, Nouakchott.

10. *Espaces Calame*, a monthly paper, is the free supplement of the twice-weekly newspaper *Le Calame*. In each of its issues, it chooses an important current affairs topic. Its 4th issue of April 1994 deals with the University of Nouakchott. In it one finds 'the misery of research' p.8, discussions with Abdel Wedoud Ould Cheikh, Doctor in Sociology, former director of the Mauritanian Institute of Scientific Research (IMRS) which he headed from 1987 to 1989. *Espaces Calame* and the 'Essays' column of the twice-weekly *Le Calame*, open to intellectuals for in-depth analysis, to some extent, compensate for the rarity of university publications on crucial issues that concern Mauritania.

11. On working conditions at the university, see the 'students' list of grievances' in *l'Etudiant*, free general information paper for students, trial issue April-May 1996, pp. 14-16; and on lecturers' responsibility, see 'The students speak' in *Espaces Calame* (1994 : 6) in which the university, faculties and lecturers are generally criticised.

12. See the presentation of the second issue of Annals of the Arts and Humanities faculty, 1990, p.5

13. This important project has made it possible for a professor of the Arts and Humanities Faculty to publish a book in Arabic entitled: *Fiqh, Société et Pouvoir en Mauritanie*. In it, the author explains the relations between the tribal organisation and the State by presenting the viewpoint of theologians of yesterday and today.

14. In this regard, refer to issues dealing with Mauritania in which Mauritanian researchers have participated in collaboration with specialists on African issues. They are: *Revue du Monde Musulman et de la Méditerranée* no 54 entitled 'Mauritanie between Arabness and Africanity', Paris 1989; *Diagonales*, no. 26 in its Special Feature entitled Special Mauritania, relative to education in general and its problems, pp. 19-40 Paris, Hachette/Edicef, April 1993; *African Politics* no. 55 entitled 'Mauritania a democratic turn?', Paris Karthala, October 1994; *Notre Librairie*, Review of books: Africa, the

Caribbean, the Indian Ocean, *Mauritanian Literature*, no. 120-121, Jan. - March 1995; *La Nouvelle Revue Anthropologique* of the International Anthropological Institute, *Proceedings of the Chinguitti Colloquium*, July 1995, 305 p. We also observe that Mauritanian researchers have begun publishing books. For example: Oumar Moussa B, (1993) *Noirs et Beydanes mauritaniens, l'École, creuset de la nation?* Paris, l'Harmattan, 167p.; Mohamed-Mahmoud Ould Mouhamedou (1995) *Societal transition democracy in Mauritania*, Dar-el-Ameen, Cairo, and to be published by the same author, *Economic stagnation and political transformation: The primacy of politics in Mauritania*.

15. We refer here, like we have done all through the text, to intellectuals who have chosen the western way of thinking and behaviour and who openly or implicitly advocate that Mauritanians prefer to remain abroad at the end of their university training. In addition to the unfavourable research climate, the possibilities of finding a post at the university or research institutes are almost non-existent. Thus, an intellectual Diaspora has started to spread in the United States, Europe as well as in other African countries.

16. University lecturers of all fields.

17. Ils notats: 'wars and temptations on all borders'.

18. Voluntary departures and forced exiles abroad of eminent Mauritanain researchers and intellectuals resulting from all sorts of harassment and diverse persecutions are very common. Among them are the historian Ibrahima Abou Sall; sociologist Saïdou Kane; jurist Gourmo Lo; film producer Med Hondo; sociologist Boubacar Ba; researcher Moussa Oumar Ba etc. Still today, an increasing number of Mauritanians prefer to stay abroad after their university training. In addition to the unfavourable research climate, the possibilities of finding a post at the university or research institutes are almost non-existent. Thus, an intellectual Diaspora has started to spread in the United States, Europe as well as in other African countries.

19. In its Tuesday November 28, 1995 issue, *Le Calame* no 113 noted the existence of unemployed doctors. These are organised and have decided to draw attention to their situation. Applicants to these teaching posts held a General Assembly and requested to meet the Minister of National Education. Those of them who are on contract have also addressed a letter to the pResident of the Republic explaining the difficult conditions they have been working in since their return about four years ago. By the same token, they underscored the existence of budgetary posts that have not been used by the university administration. They observed that the Faculties have already expressed their respective needs and several heads of department have stressed the need for the urgent satisfaction of their requests.

20. According to the definition given by the *Social Science Lexicon*, Dalloz, Paris, 1981, p.99, the social demand is an 'imprecise expression indicating the need for all social practices to fit into a general social system.'

References

Assié-Lumumba, l'Enseignement supérieur en Afrique fracophone : *Évaluation des universités classiques et, des alternatives pour le développement*, The World Bank, technical note no. 5, human resources division,Washington D.C.

Ba Oumar Moussa (1993), *Noirs et Beydanes mauritaniens, l'école, creuset de la nation?*, L'Harmattan, Paris.

Cabal, Alphonso Borrero (1995), *L'université aujourd'hui*, CRDI/UNESCO, Paris.

Diallo, Alpha Cheybani (1996) 'Université, Société, Pouvoirs publics et développement' in *L'Eveil-Hebdo*, no. 228 du lundi 25 novembre 1996, p.7.

Diouf, M., and Mamdani, M., (1994) *Academic Freedom in Africa*, CODESRIA, Dakar.

Espaces Calame, (1994) Free Supplement, Monthly, No. 4, April 1994, 16p.

Imam, A M. and Mama, A., (1994), Limitation ou Èlargissement de la liberté académique : la responsabilité des universitaires, in Diouf and Mamdani, op. cit., pp. 82-123.

La Nouvelle Revue Anthropologique, Proceedings of the Sedjenoume colloquium, (1996), 'Séminaire sous-régional sur Les libertés académiques en Afrique (Ouagadogou, from 19 - 21 August 1996), in *CODESRIA Bulletin*, no. 4, Dakar.

La Nouvelle Revue Anthropologique, Proceedings of the Chinguitti Colloquium, (July 1996); 6th Euro-African colloquium of the International Centre for Saharan and Sahelian Research, Institut International d'Anthropologie, Paris, Octobre 1995.

Le Calame, no. 48, 4 to 10 July 1994.

L'Etudiant, General information paper for students, trial issue, April-May 1996, 17p.

Guèye, Bakary, (1992), 'L'Arabisation en question', *Al Bayane*, no. 3, 1-7 July 1992,

Laroui, Abdallah, (1978), *La crise des intellectuels arabes, Traditionalismme ou historicisme?*, François Maspero, Paris.

Lexique des sciences sociales, (1981), Dalloz, Paris.

Ly, Boubacar, (1989), *Problèmes épistémologiques et méthodologiques des sciences sociales en Afrique*, CODESRIA, Dakar.

Marchesin, Philippe, (1992), *Tribus, ethnies et pouvoir en Mauritanie*, Karthala, Paris.

Office National de la Statistique, (1995), *La Mauritanie en chiffres*, édition 1995, Noukchott, Imprimerie Atlas

Ould Ahmed Izid Bih, Isselkou, (1995), 'Enseignement supérieur: l'urgente réforme' in *Le Calame*, no. 66 24 décembre - 3 janvier 1995.

Ould Cheikh, Abdel Wedoud, (1995), 'La Mauritanie: un pays qui descend? In *Notre Librairie, Revue du Livre, Afrique Caraïbes, Océan Indien, Littérature Mauritanienne*, no. 120-121.

Ould Cheikh, Abdel Wedoud, (1994), 'Misère de la recherche' interview in *Espaces Calame* no. 4, April 1994.

Ould Kharchi, Ahmed, (1994), 'L'université en projet(s)', *Espaces Calame*, Monthly Supplement - no. 4.

Ould Mouhamédou, Mahmoudy, (1995), 'La renaissace maure' in *Le Calame*, no. 94, 25-30 July 1995.

Ould Tolba, Yehdih, (1993), 'Quel avenir pour l'université?', *Diagonales*, no. 26, EDICEF, Paris.

Pons, Roger, (1994), L'éducation en Afrique de l'Ouest: Situation, enjeux et perspectives, Etude des perspectives à long terme en Afrique de l'Ouest, Document de travail no.7, OCDE/OECD, CILSS, BAD/ADB.

Schnapper, Dominique, (1994), *La communauté des citoyens, sur l'idée moderne de la nation*, Fayard, Paris

Sounkalo, Jiddou, (1995), 'La situation linguistique en Mauritanie, langues et politique des langues en Mauritanie', *Notre Librairie, Revue du Livre, Afrique Caraïbes, Océan Indien, Litttérature Mauritanienne*, no. 120-121.

Taine-Cheikh, Catherine, (1994), 'Les langues comme enjeu identitaire', *Politique Africaine*, no. 55, Paris Karthala, pp.57-65.

UNDP, (1995), *Economica: Rapport mondial sur le développement humain,*, Paris, July.

UNESCO, (1995), Rapport mondial sur le développement humain, 1996, PNUD, Rapport mondial sur l'éducation.

UNESCO (1995), Female participation in education in sub-saharan Africa, Statistical Profiles prepared by Division of Statistics, Paris, in co-operation with African Academy of Sciences, Nairobi, Kenya.

Union des Forces Démocratiques, (1991), Déclaration de politique générale, 1er octobre 1991, Nouakchott.

Appendix: An effort should be made in connection with the under-representation of women and the gender issue

Issues relative to gender are not completely taken care of in Mauritania. They, however, deserve particular attention because their impact on the future of the country is crucial. According to the 1988 census, women constituted 50.48 per cent of the population and projections for 1994 estimated them to be 50.33 per cent. In both cases, the number of women was largely higher than that of men. Still, according to these projections, the classification, according to sex, of the population old enough to go to university was thus presented:

Age	Men	Women
20-24	93618	94991
25-29	74926	85658
30-34	65878	77145

Source: *Mauritania in Figures*, National Statistics Office, 1995 edition, p.11

In 1990, the university had 6000 students, 5200 of whom were men and 800 women. In 1993-94, the student population of the Faculty of Arts and Humanities classified according to sex was as follows: 85 per cent were boys and 15 per cent girls. The issue of women's representation within the university institution as well as in all other institutions is an aspect that deserves to be given particular attention. Moreover, on the basis of revelations of female students who have been victims of male segregation and provocation: Fatiha, a female student from Tunisia states that 'the head of the university library counter often repeats to them that women have no right to speak, and that male guarantee is always required for them to lend their books out to female students.' The latter declare that their professors 'sexually harass them continuously'; they qualify their professors as obsessed, as blackmailers! A male student even advised the 'girls of the university to sue their professors for sexual harassment' (*Espaces Calame*, 1994 : 6).

Sources: World Bank (1995), World Bank report on human development; UNDP (1995) *Economica*, July 1995, Paris. *Espaces Calame*, Free Supplement, monthly paper no. 4, April 1994. Pons, op. cit., p 11.

7. Academic Freedom and Female Academics in Nigeria

Olutoyin Mejiuni Fashina

Introduction

Although academics in Nigeria are concerned about academic freedom, in practical terms, the debates, discussions, policies and attitudes that can ensure academic freedom for all academics are generally gender blind (not gender conscious) and are at times discriminatory.

Male and female academics in Nigeria are both well aware, at least at the cognitive level, of the existence of international and regional human rights instruments which guarantee certain rights for all human beings regardless of race, class, sex etc. Relevant examples of such instruments are given below.

The United Nations Universal Declaration of Human Rights, in particular Articles 1, 2, 16 (1), 19, and 25 (2), sees everybody as having been born free and equal in dignity and rights; sees all as entitled to all rights set forth in the Declaration irrespective of race, colour, sex etc., proclaims the right to freedom of opinion and expression which include freedom to hold opinions without interference and to seek, receive and impart information and ideas through any media and regardless of frontiers and proclaims that motherhood and childhood are entitled to special care.

The UN's Convention on the Elimination of all Forms of Discrimination Against Women, amongst others, recognizes the need for states to take special measures to correct the view that women are less important or of less value than men and to abolish all existing laws, customs and regulations that discriminate against women.

Also, Articles 6, 21 and 25 of the Kampala Declaration requires academics to 'approach and resolve differences in the spirit of equality, non-discrimination and democracy' and 'encourage and contribute to affirmative actions to redress historical and contemporary inequalities based on gender, nationality, or any other social disadvantage' and states that:

Every African intellectual has the right to pursue intellectual activity, including teaching, research and dissemination of research results, without let or hindrance subject only to universally recognized principles of scientific inquiry and ethical and professional standards.

Should Female Academics Think About Academic Freedom?
Attempts will be made to answer this question by focusing on three issues – female academics and the subject of research and work in the university, motherhood and female academics, and unjust laws and female academics. The question is pertinent because contrary to Articles 6, 21 and 25 of the Kampala Declaration, the UN's Convention on the Elimination of all Forms of Discrimination Against Women and the UDHR, some male members of the academic community act in an oppressive manner towards their colleagues of the opposite sex and those issues that concern them.

Female Academics and Intellectual Work in Universities
For an examination of this issue, the following example should prove useful. Until recently, there was a Women's Studies Programme based in the Department of Sociology and Anthropology of this author's university. Members of the group organized monthly seminars and published some of the papers in book form. Thus, they contributed to debate about gender, equality and issues that concern women. In order to extend the range of issues to be covered by the existing programme, encourage participation by academic members of the university community in different areas of studies and ensure that the programme had an impact on both the university community and the wider community, a proposal was put forward for the expansion of the Women's Studies Programme into an academic unit.

The papers proposing the unit had to, as is the case with such papers, pass through the necessary committees in the university. Many of the women who had an interest in the centre had anticipated the reactions of their male colleagues, so they mobilized other women to the board and committee meetings, prepared all their arguments as if they were going to 'war'. The proposal was said to have met with stiff resistance from male counterparts. It was said that when the male colleagues failed to convince everyone that the centre was not necessary, they resorted to very snide remarks about equality, feminism and the usefulness of the centre.

Now that the Centre for Gender and Social Policy Studies has been established, it is finding its feet. It has organized workshops, it organizes a monthly seminar, and it is trying to organize gender sensitization programmes for governmental and non-governmental organizations and training programmes for women in different settings. Plans are afoot for coordinated research on women's issues. On the way to attending the workshops and seminars organized by the Centre, women have heard male colleagues refer to the workshops and seminars as 'a women's nonsense going on up there'. It should be said that there are some male colleagues on the coordinating committee of the Centre and they are active participants in its activities. It appears that the most important reason why some men believe that the Centre should not be taken seriously is that it concerns itself mostly with issues concerning women.

For many of our male colleagues, there is no reason why issues that are important to women should be taken so seriously as to be a subject of study for a researcher or a unit within the university system. However, when such male colleagues are asked whether women are needed and issues of concern to them are important, their answer is almost always in the affirmative: for procreation, keeping the family and general social order.

Another example of the nature of discrimination against female academics who take an interest in what affects people of their own sex will suffice. A female lecturer in the Department of Economics of the author's university had been promoted to a senior lecturership based on the research she had carried out mainly on women's issues. At the end of the promotion exercise, a 'concerned' male colleague had pulled her aside and advised her now to work hard at 'more serious issues and forget about all those things about women', for her subsequent promotions. This 'concerned' colleague's attitude differs considerably from that of another male colleague, who has worked with her on the analyses of some of her research data. It was said that this other male colleague expressed surprise at the seriousness with which she undertook the work, with regard to conceptualization, choice of variables, paradigms, methodology etc. He was quite enthusiastic and helpful with the analysis.

So, even though the first colleague, the 'concerned' one, had access to research works that had been done by his colleague on women, he still thought issues that concern women were not just serious enough. Whereas, the second colleague, unaware that issues of concern to women could be researched into seriously, was pleasantly surprised at the data before him, and was quite helpful thereafter.

The implication of this is that some of our male colleagues can be convinced by good, fruitful and seriously researched work in areas other than surgery, space technology, philosophy, or child and adolescent psychology can be carried on in a university. For others, no matter the amount of evidence, once your research work is about issues of importance to the psychology, economic and general well-being of women it is not serious research! Unfortunately, some of those who hold this last view want to be taken seriously when they talk about academic freedom.

When this writer raised the question of how issues of concern to women are treated by male colleagues with a colleague, he voiced the opinion that the real reason some people become engaged in research on women is because they think that they can make money from governmental, inter-governmental and non-governmental agencies for this work. I responded to that by pointing out that the university has a Centre for Industrial Development, just as it has an

Institute for Ecology. Also many of our male counterparts and a few female colleagues are involved in researches and writings about human rights and democracy. The question I ask is: have the people involved in issues such as these had the same level of snide remarks directed at their efforts by their colleagues as women who have tried to focus on women's issues? The answer is, no. A handful of men have accused some of the people in all the areas mentioned above of being involved for the financial benefits that their efforts bring. Many, they have conceded, are serious researchers, doing serious work. However, this kind of concession is not given to many of the people who have focused on women's issues, even though there is evidence to show that serious, good and fruitful research is going on in this area in our universities.

It appears that the reason our male counterparts still think research on women's issues is not serious enough research is that they object both to being confronted with their oppressive discriminatory conduct toward women and to discussion about the rights of women as a distinct group in society. In this regard, Fatou Sow (1994), observed that in some circles, alluding to women's oppression, the impoverishment of the African masses and the feminization of poverty, the impact of structural adjustment policies on the most under-privileged categories of the population, especially women and the youth, has become a trivial matter.

For our male counterparts who have to be confronted with their oppressive or discriminatory conduct towards women, it appears they recognize that women have certain rights as human beings, but having denied them such rights for so long, they find it difficult to admit to their own wrongdoing.

The second category, that is, colleagues who object to talk about the rights of women as a distinct group in society, are unable to understand why women should think they need rights that are distinct from what their husbands, partners, fathers or brothers wish to give to them. They think women belong to the private and not the public sphere of life. To them, issues of importance to women belong also to the private realm, and so should not be brought into public debates and institutions. Only when such debates 'promote family values' or are about procreation, do they become acceptable in the public realm.

Such men seem to think that if some women are 'allowed' careers 'in public life' they should be happy with their positions and not make noises about discrimination, oppression, their rights, and then even ask for more than they have presently.

Gender sensitization and similar programmes are needed to educate even those who are involved in the business of knowledge production and dissemination, despite the level of consciousness about academic freedom in Nigerian universities.

Motherhood and Female Academics

Another area that deserves attention is the issue of motherhood and the female academic. In 1992, the agreement between the Federal Government of Nigeria and the academic staff of Nigerian universities marked out distinctly, the conditions of service of academic staff. Provision was made for 12 weeks maternity leave for women in the following statements:

it was agreed that each female academic staff irrespective of marital status shall be entitled to twelve(12) weeks of maternity leave with full pay.

However, despite this provision, women who applied for maternity leave after the agreement was made were told to take maternity leave in lieu of annual leave.

In 1995, in readiness for the review of the agreement which was supposed to have taken place that year, the author's branch of the academic staff union called a meeting to discuss the review. When the issue of maternity leave in lieu of an annual leave was raised as part of what the union's negotiating team should look at, it was greeted with laughter. It is important to say that 90 per cent of members who were present at that meeting were men. The chairman of the branch promised to collate the women's point of view along with other suggestions for review. For the woman who raised the issue of maternity leave and this author this was a serious matter. We have since wondered why this should attract so much laughter from colleagues, many of whom are also husbands of female academics and women in other spheres of life. People may ask: where is your sense of humour? My response to this is: what is the joke about? Is the case that when matters concerning combining procreation with work are raised in public, why is that a joke?

The issue of maternity leave negates my earlier assertion that public discussions about matters of procreation (as an issue that concerns women) should be acceptable to men.

Unjust Law and Female Academics

For many female academics in Nigeria, the taxation laws which apply to universities are grossly discriminatory. Whereas a married man is given a wife and children allowance, a married woman is not, even though she and her spouse may both work for the same institution, and sometimes, even have the same job descriptions. Many women contribute as much as their husbands, and in some cases, more than their husbands, to the finances of the family. Even in these cases, husbands are given an allowance for a spouse and children and wives are not.

The tax laws were made when it was assumed that men were still the sole breadwinners in the family. The reality is different today, and this should be reflected in the laws. This problem does not apply to universities alone. Notwithstanding this, it is important that academics, in pursuit of non-discrimination as set out in the Kampala Declaration, should be at the forefront of those calling for the review of this law.

Conclusion

The intellectual work that goes on in the universities and reactions (often negative) of a certain section (male academics) to such work should be a cause for concern for people who are concerned with academic freedom in Nigerian universities. For many female academics who have taken an interest in matters of concern to their own sex, the important questions are: Are their teaching and research activities consonant with universally recognized principles of scientific inquiry and ethical/professional standards? Is the reaction by men to their academic work non-discriminatory, but critical as expected in an academic environment? Or is their reaction a product of long held biases and prejudices that have always checked fruitful debates on women, and on the social, psychological, economic and political relations between men and women?

Being able to have a baby and taking good care of it is, for many women, as important as having a fulfilling career with adequate rest. Maternity leave should allow a working woman time to prepare for the arrival of her baby, and at least a few weeks to take care of the newborn baby and herself, before she goes back to work. If female academics of childbearing age are told to take their maternity leave in lieu of annual leave, then this uses up the time which any working person needs for rest. Are female academics being subtly told to make a choice, give up having children, or give up their jobs? As for the reaction of male academics to the issue of maternity leave, the question for them is: is maternity leave really a trivial matter for people in an academic environment?

Finally, for academics who are serious about the rights of citizens and academic freedom, the taxation laws in Nigeria should attract their condemnation, and its review should attract the attention of all.

References
CODESRIA, (1993), 'The Kampala Declaration', *CODESRIA Bulletin*, no.3
Federal Government of Nigeria and Academic Staff of Nigerian Universities, (1992), Agreement of 1992.
Jobson, M., and Menell, K., (1995), 'The Convention and the Elimination of All Forms of Discrimination Against Women' in *Women's Rights in South Africa*, HSRC Publishers, Pretoria.
McQuoid-Mason, D., O'Brien, E.L., and Greene, E., (1993), 'Universal Declaration of Human Rights' in *Human Rights for All – Education Towards a Rights Culture*, Juta and Co, South Africa.
Sow, F., (1994), 'The Role of Gender Analysis in the Future of Social Sciences in Africa', *CODESRIA Bulletin*, no.2.

8. Academic Freedom and the Position of Women in Cameroon

Norbert N. Ouendji

Universities in Turmoil

The year 1996 was one of the most tumultuous years in the history of Cameroon's universities. Once again the winds of protest shook the campuses. The crisis began towards the end of April 1996 at Yaoundé I University, in the nation's political capital, before spreading to Douala University, in the economic capital, on May 23. The outbreaks and the generally inflammatory situation were a decisive answer to the huge and pernicious fraud operation perpetrated by university authorities with no concern for regulations. Penalized and frustrated, the students, who were increasingly exposed to poverty due to the suppression of scholarships and other university allowances, asked only for a return to reason.

Racketeering in Academia

University administrators seeking to line their pockets had been charging students numerous extra fees. Among them were: 5000 FCFA for early enrollment, 25 FCFA to use washrooms (poorly kept or non-existent), 100 FCFA per day to use classrooms for study, and 100 FCFA per day to use the library, on top of annual library card fees of 200 FCFA. They were also charged 1000 FCFA for each report card, 4900 FCFA for a yearly X-ray which was never performed, 3500 to 7000 FCFA per student for access to tutorials and labs, and 25,000 FCFA in tuition for the 'summer term' which used to be called the 'makeup term'. All these fees were in addition to the tuition fee of 50,000 FCFA, which was actually the only payment allowed under presidential decree no. 93/033 of January 19, 1993, which set the university tuition fee for students of Cameroonian nationality. Article 4 of this decree states quite clearly that the payment of 50,000 FCFA in tuition fees gives students the right to enrolment in classes, participation in sports and cultural activities, coverage by student insurance, access to the library, tutorials and labs, special training sessions and examinations.

In their determination to fight to improve their situation, and since talks had fallen through on a campus where the number of gendarmes was increasing at an alarming rate, students struck back. For instance, a wooden building at the science faculty in Yaoundé I University was burned to the ground on May 1 1996. The crisis grew severe, as total paralysis set in. Law and order forces were marshalled in Douala. Finally, the government realised the seriousness of the situation and recommended that the academic authorities stop all extortionary practices directed at students. Professor Obounou Akong, rector of Yaoundé I University, was even relieved of his duties by the head of state, probably due to his poor handling of the two-month protest movement. Obounou Akong was also behind the invention of tuition fees for the 'summer term', while he was rector at Yaoundé I University. He was replaced by Jean Messi, known as a specialist in repressive methods.

Arrests, Explosions and Revenge

The students say that one-third of their demands were met, at least for the 1995-96 school year. However, the negative consequences of their revolt received considerably greater attention. On June 12, 1996, the Minister of Higher Education, Peter Agbor Tabi, decided to expel most of the student representatives of Cameroon's universities. They included Christophe Ebanga Onguene, Patrice Kennedy Ikoe Natao, Alexandre Lebeau Mbaye, Patrick Asanga Nde, Rita Mbone and Valentin Azi. They were accused of 'attempted murder, death threats, assault and battery, disruption of the operations of Yaoundé I University'. They could hardly believe it. According to them, they were singled out because they were chosen by their fellow students on May 8, 1996 to represent them in negotiations with the government. Some of them were captured by vigilantes – a group of civilians armed with machetes, knives, screwdrivers, clubs and firearms – associated with the university administration. They were taken from their university residences between June 9-26, 1996, usually around 5am, and in most cases their doors were broken down. 'After being severely brutalized, we were taken to the police station and held for 50 days during which were subjected to unprecedented torture', they stated in their petition. 'We were called to court more than once under various charges with no grounds, such as inciting revolt, vandalism and forming an illegal association. Furthermore, our identity papers were confiscated by the police', they added. They were taken to court for the last time on September 4, 1996. Against all expectations, they have not been called up since, despite repeated requests. The case seems to have been closed, although they say they are determined to seek legal reprisal.

It should be noted that several other students suspected of participating in or supporting the May-June 1996 strike for the improvement of campus living and working conditions were also arrested and held in various police stations and torture halls in Yaoundé. Others were transferred from Yaoundé to the central prison in Kondengui on June 21 1996, after eight days at the central police legion and the central police station in Yaoundé. The officers in charge of the investigation had charged them with voluntary arson and the attempted murder of Ernest Menyomo, a teacher at the philosophy department at Yaoundé I University. He had been attacked by students for teaching classes while an order for a 'dead campus' (complete suspension of all teaching) was in effect. The Yaoundé county court, which tried them on a flagrante delicto basis, acquitted them on August 2 1996. However, it should be emphasized that only five of the seven students charged were present in court. The other two, Henri Anabi and Titus Ambe Tamgu, had been remitted to their families for medical care because they were in a coma due to the physical mistreatment they had received. The five students present in court were Jonas Diokdi Kotva, Maurice Tabot, Blaise Ova Pho Tashe, Roger Demghuo Tamno and Hippolyte Nkounga Kamdje.

According to René Tagne, one of the defence's lawyers, the prosecution flouted procedure in the case. He severely criticized the fact that his clients were arrested by vigilantes, and not by members of the Criminal Investigation Department which had legal jurisdiction. Furthermore, he said the youths were unjustly detained. 'It is strange that the prosecutor placed these young citizens under a committal order without witnesses', he reported to *Le Messager*, a bi-weekly independent newspaper. In addition, during the hearing on 19 July 1996, Menyomo himself, who had already been paid damages by the university, declared he was unable to identify his attackers.

Several young people were targeted arbitrarily at Douala University. The worst incident occurred in July 1996, when the rector, Ngando Mpondo, expelled seven students from second term examinations following a disciplinary committee meeting. Despite the fact that it is standard procedure, none of them were called to appear before the committee. They included Gnyasse Tonleu, Enone Eboht, Jean-Paul Kaga, Kaptche Tagne, Martin Pengou, Etienne Ndé Nseke and Guy Constant Njikam, from the Faculty of Science.

Support From All Quarters

Practically all opposition leaders and certain human rights associations demonstrated their support and encouragement for the oppressed students. They also called for the government to cease its barbarous practices, as did the national labour union of higher education teachers (SYNES). In a communiqué following the incident, the organization, which is feared by the government, called for 'teachers to refrain from all actions or behaviours liable to adversely affect the students' demands'.

Cameroonian students in exile also decided to make themselves heard. In a declaration dated June 28, 1996, the 'Parliament in Exile', more precisely the Niamey (Niger)-based branch of the National Committee of Cameroonian Students (forced to flee in 1990-1), wrote:

Dear brothers and sisters, all this persecution should not discourage you but encourage you to keep on fighting decisively and intrepidly until the final victory. For, every time an oppressed people shows its courage and its temerity, it wins out over even the fiercest dictatorships.

They also passed on encouraging messages from fellow student movements such as the Niger Union of Scholars, the Mali Pupils' and Students' Association (AEEM), the General Students' Union of Burkina (UGEB), the National Pupils' and Students' Union of Benin (UNSEB), the Students' and Schools' Federation of Côte d'Ivoire (FESCI) and the Union of Guinean Students. In an interview granted to the independent weekly newspaper, Challenge Nouveau, in October 1996, Corentin Talla, a member of the 'Parliament in Exile' living in Jacksonville, USA., who was one of the founding members of the 'Conscience du Cameroun' (September 1996) also expressed his support.

Furthermore, several months after the universities were rocked by upheavals, the students continued to suffer from gratuitous reprisals. For example, on the morning of Sunday October 27 1996, four students (Roger Alexis Wamba, Blaise Ngoune, Jules Armand Mbe, Edouard Tonang) were arrested on campus by order of Jean Messi, rector of Yaoundé I University. The SYNES, which strongly denounced this action, said that Messi had demanded they be held indefinitely because of what he claimed were acts of subversion and destruction committed on campus. 'They received degrading, inhuman and unacceptable treatment' at police headquarters, said Jongwanë Dipoko, President of SYNES.

Reliable sources said the real reason for the students' misfortune was that they had tried to organize what they called the Cameroon National Students' Movement (MNEC) in compliance with the law of December 1990 on freedom of association. On May 29 1996, the founding members of MNEC submitted an application to Mfoundi (Yaoundé) prefecture. Since two months' silence from the prefect legally signifies acceptance and the right to constitute a legal entity, they began their activities after the expiry of the waiting period. The university authorities, pretending to be unaware of the law, deemed this 'subversive'. The students were arrested on October 27 1996 and, apart from Edouard Tonang, who was freed after a week due to the intervention of influential parents, they were not released until mid-November, and only came before the Yaoundé county court on 27 December. They were accused of 'disrupting the university, inciting revolt, and breach of the peace'.

Later, on January 6 1997, the Prime Minister's General Secretary, Louis-Marie Abogo Nkono, told the MNEC that he took note of the movement's existence in conformity with the laws of the republic. He added that he would forward their file to the Vice Prime Minister in charge of Territorial Administration for his expertise. According to SYNES, the whole affair is a fiasco.

Jongwanë Dipoko, the union president, stated that these delaying tactics were merely an attempt to intimidate and silence the students who were only defending their legitimate rights.

It should also be noted that in 1993 Dipoko was suspended from Yaoundé I University for two years due to his union activities. This was despite the ILO's repeated warnings to the government of Cameroon. He has been re-established in his position, but continues to face frustration. Upon his return at the end of 1996, he found that the office he had occupied for over 15 years had been broken into and his belongings destroyed or thrown out. He claims it was under the instructions of the dean of the Faculty of Science, Amougou Akoa. Instruments and research findings from his years of studies and professional activity in France and the USA were lost, along with a personal computer and a large collection of books. In order to seek reparation for the material and personal loss inflicted on him, Jongwanë Dipoko laid charges against the dean. The outcome of the trial was not known at the time this chapter was written.

Ethnic Demands in the Academic Community

The academic community also faced a series of purely ethnic demands in 1996. When the situation grew tense at Yaoundé I University in early May, English-speaking students from the Northwest and the Southwest, and Bamiléké students from the West (who, like certain leaders from the same linguistic or ethnic groups were viewed as 'opponents of the Biya regime'), were told to 'go to school where they came from'. This hardly made sense since the victims came from a variety of backgrounds. However, tracts were distributed targeting these 'foreigners'. The authors were suspected of being Béti (the same ethnic group as the President). The authors said they did not want trouble on a university campus located in their 'village' and told the 'foreigners' to do whatever they wanted in the universities in their home areas, such as Buéa (anglophone, in the Southwest) and Dshang (Bamiléké, in the West). Contact between the groups became difficult and the climate was tense.

The 'English' and the Bamiléké faced considerable risk, especially since the university authorities were known to be behind the ethnic manipulation. There was even a rumour (denied by the administration) that members of the 'subversive race' would no longer be easily admitted to Yaoundé I University. There would be a quota to 'punish' them. A survey by Karl Obeng revealed that: 'Over 500 young secondary school graduates were refused admission to various faculties of Yaoundé I University directed by Jean Messi. Barring a very few exceptions, those who were not accepted came from the North, the West, the Northwest, etc. With the reigning atmosphere of tribalism, the incident quickly mushroomed into full-blown persecution of 'foreigners' at Ngoa Ekelle.'

Ethnic demands began to become frequent in Cameroon immediately after the President passed Law 96/06 of January 18 1996, which amended the constitution of June 2 1972. Contrary to the wishes of the people, the preamble to this basic law states that, 'the government ensures the protection of minorities and preserves the rights of its native populations in compliance with the law'. The President, aided by the National Assembly, thereby 'officialized' and 'constitutionalized' tribalism, and sowed the seeds of discord and internal conflicts.

In the political sphere, between February and March 1996, Sawa people demonstrated at Douala, where even traditional chiefs and high-placed politicians called for the departure of the area's (duly elected) Bamiléké mayors and their replacement by 'natives'. Their frustration stemmed from the fact that, at the time, only one out of five opposition mayors was of Duala origin. Now, there are two out of five.

In a memo to President Paul Biya, which was published by the newspapers in July 1996, Bamiléké students (one of 236 ethnic groups in Cameroon) reported what they called: 'the discrimination faced by students and teachers from the Western province' (see annex at the end of this chapter).

Given the rate at which events are taking place in Cameroon, it is generally believed there is a serious risk of the situation developing into another Rwanda. The public is demanding at least minimal security precautions. According to GERDDES (Study and Research Group for Democracy and Economic and Social Development), one of the forms these precautions should take is to modify the constitution, 'following discussions and negotiations which have the value of a social contract instituted as a fundamental law, a supreme, inviolable standard'. Thus, says GERDDES, such terms as 'foreigners' and 'natives', which institutionalize discrimination and foment civil war, should be eliminated. Tribalism should be expressly forbidden. In short, 'tribalism must be deconstitutionalized'. The same goes for the term 'protection of minorities', since the 'notion belongs to the same tribalistic semantics'. Unfortunately, the government in Yaoundé does not appear to be ready to implement that solution.

Women's Access to Education: The Problem of Discrimination
Women's problems are increasingly at the centre of debate in Cameroon. Their low level of representation at all levels of public life is constantly taken up as a reason to form associations and non-government organizations. Seminars and conferences abound, supported by the Ministry of Social Affairs and the Status of Women, which has been led by Aôssatou Yaou since its inception. The same conclusion is often reached: we need to fight for a law on quota systems to promote women in Cameroon. 'One thing is certain: quotas help overcome

prejudice and free creative energy', Aôssatou Yaou (1996) has pointed out. She has further asked the 'government to take the necessary corrective measures', while exhorting 'women to take charge of their own destiny'.

It should be noted, however, that these demands are heard mostly in the political sphere. For example, on the eve of the municipal elections of January 1996, the Women's Organization of the RDPC (OFRDPC) demanded (unfortunately without success) that the lists include 30 per cent women members of the party in power. In addition, the Federation of Cameroonian Women's Associations (FAFCAM), frustrated by the low level of women's representation in the government despite the changes in cabinet on September 19 1996, met on September 26 and 27 in Yaoundé to take stock of the situation one year after the United Nations international conference on the status of women in Beijing. They suggested that from then on, 40 per cent of government positions should be held by women. It should be noted that there are currently only two women in the Cameroonian government. And one of them, Isabelle Tokpanou, holds a position some would describe as a political appointment: she is Assistant Secretary of State for National Education. Generally, education appointments are notorious for discrimination.

It is as if it were a crime to be a woman in Cameroon, and the punishment were to be rejected out of hand, kept away from where the real decisions are made, and confined to the social sector. 'This is a source of problems. And it makes it painful to be a woman in Cameroon. Especially when you know that in countries like Burkina Faso where women are less educated, and where the Muslim religion is reputedly strict and conservative, there are more woman ministers with a great variety of portfolios: Economics and Finance, Commerce, etc.', journalist Marie Claire Nnana (1996) has said.

'The former Resident Representative of the World Bank in Cameroon, Joseph Ingram, who used to cite the example of Burkina Faso, noted the exceptional situation of the Cameroon, which has the highest percentage of educated women but keeps them out of public office', Nnana continued. The phallocratic nature of most countries in black Africa is being called into question, and regrets have been expressed that Cameroon, a country which has ratified the United Nations Convention on Discrimination Against Women, has only fulfilled its commitment in principle by rewriting its basic laws, and has so far failed to live up to this in practice not in practice.

Marie Louise Eteki Otabela, a defender of women's rights and leader of the Committee of Alternative Forces (CFA), a political party created on March 3 1997, believes that a huge risk is being run, especially in a country like Cameroon, where 51 per cent of the population is female. 'For centuries, the exclusion of women from the political sphere has deprived communities of half of their creative potential', she stated in an interview with the independent bi-weekly newspaper, *Le Messager*, on 10 March 1997.

The Situation in the Education Sector

The preamble to Cameroon's constitution stresses the fact that the state guarantees the right to education to all its citizens of both sexes. Furthermore, Law 63/13 of June 1963 grants equal access to institutions of technical education to all Cameroonians regardless of sex, race, or religion. A ministry circular of June 11, 1981 further reinforces these provisions, since it particularly encourages girls' orientation towards the industrial sector and boys' orientation towards so-called 'feminine' occupations. There is also Circular No. 10/A/MINEDUC/ESG/SAP of January 1980, which provides for the readmission of students suspended due to pregnancy. Despite these, however, there is still a flagrant discrepancy between the numbers of males and females in the nation's schools.

Several reports available from the National Ministry of Education indicate that at all levels, boys have greater access to education than girls. Although between 1976 and 1987 there was, 'a general rise in girls' level of education in primary school, the general level of female literacy and education is still too low', notes Ester Libam, a member of the Cameroonian Association of Woman Lawyers (ACAFEJ). The results of the latest census (1987) confirm this. They show that over 55 per cent of women aged 15 or more can neither read nor write, as opposed to 34 per cent of men in the same age range. Furthermore, over 58 per cent of women are uneducated, as opposed to fewer than 39 per cent of men. The same source also showed that the number of women in pursuit of knowledge decreases at each successive level of education, so that only 0.5 per cent of all women reach the level of higher education (as compared to 2 per cent of men). The difference is supposed to be due to the rate of attrition to which girls fall victim towards the end of the second academic cycle.

However, the enrolment rate for both sexes increased up until 1990, before declining slightly in 1991. The boys' enrolment rate fell from 75.6 per cent in 1987 to 71.6 per cent in 1991, while over the same period, that of the so-called 'weaker sex' dropped from 70.5 per cent to 60.4 per cent. We have been unable to obtain more recent statistics. But on the whole, it has been noted that women in general are still facing a serious problem. The 1986-7 and 1990-1 school year statistics of Cameroon's scientific and technical institutes are relatively clear in this respect (see annexed table).

Overall, one is given the impression by official figures that girls show little interest in scientific or technical studies. For example, in 1991, Ministry of Higher Education figures showed that only 139 women earned undergraduate degrees in science, as compared to 632 men. At the Masters (or equivalent) level, there were only ten women as opposed to 93 men. Of the ten students enrolled in the vocational training certificate program at the SIANTOU Institute of Yaoundé, there was not a single girl. Out of 15 students in electronics, there were two women and 13 men. This situation arises from several factors. One cause is that, 'in times of economic recession, parents prefer to pay for boys' education. The UNICEF-sponsored Girls' Education project was created in this context, according to the National Preparatory Committee for the World Conference on Women in Beijing, in 1995. The Committee also stated, 'Although education policy is egalitarian, there is still discrimination due to social perceptions of the role of women. This explains the high rate of attrition among girls due to early marriage or pregnancy'. Dr. Pauline Fotso, a teacher at Yaoundé I University, also cites early domestic responsibilities, the lack of female role models in science and technology, economic and financial difficulties, and laziness and lack of self-confidence.

There is no lack of examples to illustrate this last point. An example contributed by former Minister of Health Delphine Tsanga is quite revealing:

Once, I had ten scholarships for the Soviet Union, and I knew a girl who had just completed her secondary studies in science. I called her and offered her one of the scholarships, since I thought she would make a good textiles engineer. She asked me for some time to think about it and, a little later, she came to see me and told me she couldn't see herself as an engineer. I was very disappointed, since I felt like I had failed. I never forgot the incident.

It should be noted that Delphine Tsanga, who holds a State Diploma in Nursing (Toulouse, 1959) is one of the few intellectual women who have taken risks of late. Before resigning from the ruling RDPC party to join the National Union for Democracy and Progress (UNDP) of former Prime Minister Bouba Maôgari Bello in February 1997, she wrote an open letter to the head of state, Paul Biya. In it, she reproached him with having spoken disrespectfully and disparagingly of his political opponents and of the Cameroonian people in general during the second regular conference of the RDPC on December 17 1996. She was categorical on that account, saying, 'No, Mr. President, you no longer seem to be a statesman and a head of state'. The incident ended there, since on February 10 1997, Paul Biya made his traditional address to the nation's young people on the occasion of the 31st national youth celebration. During the seven-minute speech, he announced the creation of a special assistance fund for girls in science. Male students called it a 'discriminatory measure' against them. Women, on the other hand, saw the decision as an attempt to make things right, although public opinion did attach some political significance to it, coming as it did on the eve of important legislative elections (Cameroon had both legislative and presidential elections scheduled in 1997). According to Isabelle Tokpanou, Assistant Secretary of State for Education and president of the Association of Woman Scientists of Cameroon (FESCI-

CA), created in 1990, the gesture is intended to 'help young women play a real role in our future. Above and beyond feminist demands, the President is providing the means for equality between men and women. President Biya has struck a blow at a fundamental problem, a problem of social equilibrium. This is the beginning of a solution to the problem of fair distribution of responsibilities in our society,' said Tokpanou, who, it should be noted, is a member of the RDPC. No figure was set for the fund. Furthermore, the practical procedures for granting and managing the money have not been specified. Whatever the outcome of this 'gift from the President', the fact remains that the problems facing students in general and woman students in particular are heartrending and merit a more general solution.

Universities as 'Sex Supermarkets'

Cameroonian universities are no longer the temples of knowledge that were once the pride of the nation. Instead, they have become cemeteries where the government buries our nation's youth. The infrastructure is unfit; the teachers, sunken into apathy, have lost all social and economic status since they are humiliated in various ways and work under unbearable conditions; scholarships were abolished in 1992, and there are practically no social services on campus. In short, according to university professor, well-known literary critic and writer Ambroise Kom, the reforms initiated in 1993 have done nothing to change what in 1992 the national union of higher education teachers (SYNES) referred to as 'the university's downward slide'. The situation is so serious that, 'since 1991, diplomas from Yaoundé University are picked up like goods at a jumble sale, with teaching and examinations taking place in a chaos that hardly bears describing'. Things have only worsened since the introduction of the credit system, according to which students must pass each credit course in order to pass on to the next year of studies or obtain their diploma. The harsh realities of the hastily imposed system have put everyone in an uncomfortable position. And, since no one wants to take several makeup terms in order to earn a credit (which is often the case), cheating is on the rise. During examinations, supervisors often catch students with notes, which are called 'edges' in Cameroonian student slang.

It has been noticed, however, that young women suffer the most. Corroborating witnesses have reported that girls are even searched 'inside'. On the slightest suspicion, their private parts are 'inspected' by unscrupulous teachers who take advantage of the situation to blackmail them. At Yaoundé II University, in Soa, a town located 10 km outside the capital city of Yaoundé, it is said that: 'The victims are often forced to pay with their bodies in order to avoid penalties'. In some cases, it is purely a matter of personal revenge. Our investigations have led us to conclude that there are teachers who use their supervisory position as a way of 'handling' certain girls who previously spurned their advances. It has been reported similarly that certain teachers give marks based on sex rather than on merit. They believe their status as teachers grants them certain prerogatives, especially what the students call 'the droit de seigneur'. 'I know of cases where girls have taken longer to complete their studies because they refused the advances of certain professors', said a woman student at the grande école for teachers' training in Yaoundé, who asked to remain anonymous, for obvious reasons. However, she added that the professors are not the only instigators of sexual harassment, since, 'There are also some students who are really hung up and who count on sex to get good marks. These girls visit the professors and do everything in their power to convince them'. In a recent issue of the magazine of the *Club de Recherche et d'Action Culturelle*, a survey carried out in high schools and colleges revealed the actual strategies implemented; the same strategies are used in higher education. Apparently, the girls, 'do not hesitate to use their smile, their walk and their body language as serious arguments and factors to seduce and persuade their 'teacher/partners' to give them good grades'. The common term is STGs, or 'sexually transmitted grades'.

'As members of a generation that has been thrown to the wolves, these girls who rely on their sexuality have nothing left to lose', says Djuidjeu, a sociologist who teaches at Yaoundé I and is president of 'Promo-femme', a women's non-governmental organization. She further states that in certain fields, such as literature in particular, and in the 'grandes écoles' such as the Ecole Supérieure des Sciences et Techniques de l'Information et de la Communication (Superior Institute of Information and Communication Science and Technology) and the Ecole Normale Supérieure (teacher training), etc., the percentage of female students is growing and in some cases rivals the percentage of men. It could therefore be said that in these cases, men suffer 'sexual discrimination'. The richest students use their money to solve their problems, paying for credits. According to Djuidjeu, 'the impoverishment of the teachers has spurred the process of buying credits'. On the university campus of Yaoundé I, the price of a credit ranges from 10,000 to 20,000 FCFA, according to the subject. And women teachers are no exception, especially those who were trained under the racketeering system and received their diploma in the 'university market' before they were hired to teach.

This exacerbated academic terrorism is certainly what inspired the internationally renowned journalist and editor of the *Le Messager*, Pius N. Njawe, to describe the university as: 'a centre for debauchery of all kinds, a pleasure den, a shopping centre where sex and money can open or close any door, even those leading to the most prestigious diplomas'. In such an atmosphere, female students are freed from their scruples. However, even if they manage, by fair means or foul, to fill up the classrooms and receive their diplomas, it should be noted that the quality of their training rarely gives them access to stable employment. Furthermore, their qualifications are often regarded with suspicion. The end result is that Cameroonian universities mostly produce students who have to scrape by as best they can, and who, after several years of hardship end up returning to the neighbourhoods, streets or markets where they join those who, unable to afford higher education, left school early to work at menial jobs.

Everywhere in Cameroon, there are girls (and even boys) who hold a post-secondary degree but work in cheap eateries or bars, corner stores, telephone centres, hairdresser's salons, used-clothing stores, etc. In Yaoundé, in the student neighbourhoods surrounding the campus, there are a great many small businesses of this type. Here, survival is all that counts. Prostitution is the mainstay of some girls who sell their charms to get by. With the demise of scholarships and the economic crisis that has struck many families, a lot of female students resort to this nasty business to pay their way. A survey carried out by the independent weekly, *Generation* revealed that some girls can earn between 3000 and 5000 FCFA per night and that most of them believe that this will help them move on to 'real life', which, for most of them, means marriage. 'As you go through Bonamoussadi, (a student neighbourhood), you realize the extent of the sex market in Yaoundé. Here, girls of all ages, from all walks of life, intellectuals and illiterates, shamelessly sell their bodies to the first stranger who comes along', concluded the newspaper. Often, their career comes to a sorry end, with an unwanted pregnancy and a future baby whose father is in most cases unknown. On many campuses, young girls can be seen hanging about with swollen bellies or rocking their infants in their tiny rooms, looking miserable.

Conclusion

In conclusion, we can say that it is difficult to support the theory of academic discrimination or exclusion of the so-called weaker sex. There are no written restrictions, particularly where access to knowledge is concerned. Certain imbalances in the numbers of students can be explained by factors associated with the social role of women. However, most research indicates that the situation is changing for the better, although the gender gap in scientific fields remains a problem. 'Prostitution' in higher education seems to have contributed greatly to this situation. Some teachers have made the 'droit de seigneur' a condition for success. A number of girls use this to their advantage. Furthermore, some of them even make the first moves. Obviously, this casts doubts on their qualifications. During an official ceremony at Yaoundé I University in February 1997, the rector, Jean Messi, warned against these scandalous practices.

It should further be noted that academic discrimination is much more visible where appointments to administrative positions are concerned. For instance, of the six rectors in Cameroon's universities, only one is a woman (Dorothy Djeuma, of the English University of Buea, in the Southwest). There is also a woman Secretary General at Yaoundé II, Nicole Claire Ndoko. At the Siantou Institute in Yaoundé, only one of 15 department heads is a woman.

Furthermore, although Elomo Ntonga's appointment as head of the Institut des Relations Internationales du Cameroun (Cameroonian Institute of International Relations, or IRIC) was not unanimous, it must be said that she is one of the few woman fellows in Cameroon's universities currently at the head of a 'grande école'. There are many more examples of women's 'marginalization'. Obviously, some complain. Everyone recognizes, however, that while one may cite the lack of political will on the part of the country's leaders and the subjective attitudes of some, the fact remains that the percentage of women qualified for appointment to these positions is low.

Female Students, Protest and Repression

Universities in Cameroon, and especially in Yaoundé, are veritable hotbeds of protest and tension. Fabien Boulaga has described them as a 'powder keg' following the unfortunate events of May 6, 1992 on the Ngoa Ekelle campus. This particularly explosive day followed a period in which students had been demonstrating for better studying conditions. Tensions rose daily as the authorities refused talks. Security forces were let loose and fired into the crowds. That reaction, frequently sanctioned by Agbor Tabi, then the Chancellor of the Univeristy and now the Minister of Higher Education, continues to this day, resulting in dozens of victims each time.

Among them have been some well-known women activists, such as Ange Guiadem Tekam, whose story rocked public opinion. On May 5, 1992, this third-year economics student was arrested, illegally confined and led naked through the campus by police and members of the university administration's private militia, while she was menstruating. The incident occurred as she left a meeting with her fellow members of the National Committee of Cameroonian Students, otherwise known as the 'Parliament'. This was the third attack on Guiadem, president of the Club d'Accueil et d'Information (Welcome and Information Club) and head of the Voix de l'Etudiant (Student Voice) newspaper which had been suspended on 9 March 1992 by chancellor Tabi. She points out the seriousness of the treatment she was subjected to in an open letter to the chancellor of Yaoundé I University. But for the grace of God, I would no longer be here today because the obvious intent was to get rid of me', she wrote, adding that her attackers were armed with knives and pistols. She also said, 'if after such a heinous act, the chancellor does not know how to react [after the

1993 reforms, the term 'chancellor' was removed from the academic vocabulary and replaced by 'rector'], then he ought to leave his office vacant [since his presence has] prevented well-meaning people from taking action'.

It cannot be denied that in a system as repressive as that of Cameroon's universities, Guiadem was very daring. The chancellor whose resignation she called for was subsequently promoted to the position of rector and later became Minister of Higher Education. Thus, academic freedom continued to be flouted under Peter Agbor Tabi, so much so that a group of students, including Guiadem, went into voluntary exile in 1993.

Others, such as Fadimatou Nene, underwent a similar fate shortly after the death of student Djeugoue Kamga Collins, who was burned in his dormitory room on the night of April 26-27, 1993. Sixty-seven per cent of his body was covered with second degree burns. 'Two days later, without any investigation, the 'Parliament' was dissolved, and its leaders expelled from all Cameroonian universities and hunted down like animals', she explained. 'In such a dangerous context, exile was the best strategy we could choose to continue working for ourselves, for our country and for Africa', she continued. Nene initially settled in Ouagadougou, Burkina Faso, before being deported on September 11 1993 with some of her fellow students under suspicious circumstances. 'Today, thanks to help from sympathetic human rights organizations, most of those who were deported have been granted refugee status and enrolled in West African Universities, although not all of them receive financial assistance from the HCR'. Nene currently resides in Côte d'Ivoire, where she continues to fight for students' rights. At one point, her relationship with the authorities became strained. And on May 11, 1994, political police arrested the young woman nicknamed 'Winni Mandela' for her dedication to the cause, along with Oumar Mariko, a former student leader in Mali at the time of Moussa Traoré. The arrests took place during a demonstration by Ivoirian students in the streets of Abidjan. Nene got off with a warning, but Oumar was deported from Côte d'Ivoire. This unfortunate episode was reported in the Cameroonian media.

In many cases, female students have suffered along with their male colleagues. No one has forgotten the expulsion of Sidoline Lydie Malla and two other founding members of the Legal and Political Science Faculty Student Association (ASFSP), from Yaoundé II University in 1995. The then rector Dr Dominique Obounou was angry with them for having sent a memorandum to Prime Minister Achidi Achu on April 24 1995 (he was dismissed on September 19, 1996). In the memo, they described the difficult working conditions the students were subjected to and denounced the racketeering system whereby students could buy grades from teachers. A warrant was put out on all those who had signed the document. The warrant on Sidoline Malla (No.

150/OSP/CSP/ZA), made out on August 26 1995 by the District 2 police commissioner in Yaoundé, stated that she was wanted for 'activism on the university campus and seeking to provoke a strike'.

Overall, it can be said that no student activities or movements are limited to
men alone. On campus, both sexes often experience the same joys and the
same sorrows.

Women and Literary Production
Intelligence Has No Gender
'There are still people who have never heard of me even though I've been
publishing approximately two books per year since 1977, and they are all
available in the bookshops. I find that somewhat shocking'. This comment by
Werewere Liking, author of many works in a variety of genres including short
stories, plays, novels, literary criticism, raises the general problem of the marginalization of women writers. What Liking, who also works in the movies, in
painting and in music, expresses most of all is the domination of the literary
scene by male writers, who also attract more attention. For example, in 1969,
when Thérèse Kuoh-Moukoury published the first women's novel, *Rencontres
essentielles* (*Essential Encounters*) (Paris, Edgar), she did not make as much
of an impression as the likes of Mongo Beti, René Philombe and Francis
Bebey who were already famous.

'Today, with hindsight, we can say that the most immediate cause of the situation was the sociopolitical context of the day, coupled with our newly-
acquired political independence. Cameroonians were busy with nationalism
and 'nation building' and put women's issues on the sidelines', explains literary critic Joseph Ndinda. This position is understandable when you realize
that things have begun to change, especially since women writers, particularly
in the 1980s, have begun to go beyond feminism and explore other themes.
Thus, in recent years, there has been a sort of rehabilitation of women's literature. For instance, 'Women's Literature' classes have been taught at Yaoundé I
University since 1993, for students in arts and social science, especially in the
African literature department.

However, it should be noted that women's literary production is very limited. Since its creation in 1963, CLE Editions in Yaoundé has only published a
dozen works by women as compared to around a hundred by men (see table
no. 1). Furthermore, very few women authors write more than one book. What
is the explanation for this striking imbalance, since in Cameroon, as elsewhere, creative or literary activities are unrestricted? Are 'gender' or sexual
discrimination issues relevant to this area? Or do women lack inspiration?
Charly Gabriel Mbock, a Cameroonian writer and researcher, believes that an
examination of this subject should take into account the context and the imme-

diate working environment. 'The literary production of Cameroonian women suffers from certain sociocultural burdens that prevent women from enjoying the climate of creative liberty they need to be productive and devote themselves to their art,' he says. 'Because of this, when a woman, after a great many efforts, has been able to produce one or two works, her sociocultural burdens very often strangle her creativity despite her inspiration', he adds, clearly referring to women's social role. Odile Biyidi adds that, 'in every civilization, we have been assigned domestic and servile work, while noble work and access to power have been reserved for men'. She goes on to say that, 'this eternal division of labour bars women from access to culture, education and creativity'. Although women have the same capabilities as men, they are tied down to household responsibilities, which limit their field of action.

Evelyne Mpoudi Ngolle, author of *Sous la Cendre le feu* (*Fire Under the Ashes*) (L'Harmattan, 1990) points out that men can work in their offices until late at night, and go in to work on weekends, whereas this is difficult, if not impossible, for a woman who has children and a home to care for. Mpoudi Ngolle, who is head of Elig Essono High School in Yaoundé, also stresses that literary activity depends on one's level of education. And since, 'due to certain prejudices, women have less access to education than men', one can hardly expect miracles. In conclusion, she says that she does 'not support militant feminism', but rather 'action-oriented feminism'. By this she means that rather than defending broad principles on discrimination and making endless complaints about the male sex, she encourages women to try harder if they are really determined to be productive. 'When I am at work, I forget I am a woman. No excuses should be made for people because of their sex', she adds.

Using this type of approach, it becomes clear that intelligence has no gender, and literature even less. Everything seems to depend on the individual, although women are trapped by nature in an uncomfortable position, which is unfavourable to their self-actualization. Charly Gabriel Mbock has also pointed out that Werewere Liking and Calixthe Beyala, who live respectively in Côte d'Ivoire and in France, increased their production enormously as soon as they, 'freed themselves from certain domestic duties in order to devote themselves to their art', away from their native land. Beyala's case is particularly noteworthy.

She has been able to publish eight books in ten years. It is generally recognized that she made an impressive start, particularly with the 1987 publication of *Burned by the Sun*, (STOCK). Joseph Ndinda says, 'the novel was well received by both the public and the critics', although, 'paradoxically, certain Cameroonian critics considered it both agitating and provocative'. Despite this, according to Ndinda, *Tu t'appeleras Tanga* (*And you shall be called Tanga*), published a year later, in 1988, firmly established the Cameroonian novelist's talent. However, unlike Werewere Liking, whose work is both abundant and (of late) political, Beyala has earned an image as a woman caught up in an extensive and demeaning business of plagiarism. Certain passages from *La Vie devant soi* (*The Life Before Us*, Mercure de France, 1975) by Romain Gary and Howard Buten's *When I was five, I killed myself* (published by Seuil) were found in *Le petit Prince de Belleville* (*The Little Prince of Belleville*), which she published in 1992 with Albin Michel. Her silence when she was found guilty of 'partial pirating' by a Paris court on May 7 1996, was interpreted as an admission of guilt.

Beyala has also been accused of plagiarizing Paule Constant (*White Spirit, Folio*, 1992) and Alice Walker (*The Color Purple*) in *Assëze l'Africaine (J'ai lu)*, (1996). There was another incident last year, with *Les Honneurs Perdus* (*Lost Honours*, Albin Michel, 1996), which bore similarities to *La Route de la faim* (*The Road of Hunger*), by Ben Okri (Julliard, 1994). Pierre Assouline, editorial writer at the celebrated French literary magazine *Lire* stressed that Beyala had been 'caught in the act of literary kleptomania' and hammered home the idea that the Académie Française awarded her their 'Grand Prix du Roman' in October 1996 at 'their own risk and peril'. Despite the embarrassing controversy, it should be noted that Beyala was the first Cameroonian and African woman to be so honoured.

The case is still talked about, despite the denial or explanation given by the author in January 1997. 'I must say I have no idea what people mean by plagiary, since up until now I didn't know that a single sentence, or maybe (to use my African sense of exaggeration) ten or twenty, constituted the essence of a whole book', she wrote. 'All I ask [Assouline] is to kindly forgive me for not agreeing with his definition of plagiary. I appeal to his great generosity, so that he may forgive me once again for being nothing but an African woman, ignorant of so many aspects of the Parisian literary scene, and for being a Negress who has not stayed in her place', she continued. In certain circles in Cameroon, this 'explanation' was seen as mere whining. In the opinion of Charly Gabriel Mbock, she would have been better off remaining silent, since, 'it is better to keep a dignified silence than to try to manipulate obvious facts'. 'I say it's a shame, because, having had the opportunity to publish a few works of fiction myself, I believe one has a duty to be very, very careful', he added.

The famous Cameroonian writer Mongo Beti wholeheartedly approves of that approach. In addition, he believes he can explain these practices he describes as 'deviant'. According to him, writers who make that sort of mistake are, 'overambitious and seek success at any price, at the price of plagiary, for instance. In our opinion, that is not a good thing'. In fact, Beti goes even further, saying that plagiarism occurs because the authors are, 'given poor advice by their French publishers who, instead of encouraging them to work to improve their style, express themselves better and learn to write, tell them, 'we absolutely must win such and such an award this year'.

What is obvious is that this literary intrigue has tarnished the credibility of African artists in general and Cameroonians in particular. At any rate, the 'Beyala case' does nothing for the image of literature, particularly so-called 'women's' literature. However, the determination of certain women to set themselves apart and earn respect through the original and revolutionary quality of their works should be recognized. Their refusal to limit themselves to subjects related to the status of their own sex also speaks for the change in mentalities in a context in which men had long been the only ones who dared venture onto the slippery slope of politics. Marie Louise Eteki Otabela's *Misère et grandeur de la démocratie au Cameroun* (*The Misery and Splendour of Democracy in Cameroon*, L'Harmattan, 1987) is clearly such a book (see the excerpt from her interview with *Le Messager* in January 1994 below). It is also clear that aside from problems of publication and distribution faced by all writers, women are not subjected to gender discrimination that would explain their low level of productivity. It is unanimously agreed that the problem is linked to their social status. 'Women spend a great deal of time caring for others. Their occupations leave them little time in which to write', notes Aline Koala, Director of Publications and Literary Promotion in Burkina Faso. Women need to achieve a certain level of tranquility in order to reach their full intellectual potential. As Freddy Ngandu, of Editions CLE (publishers) in Yaoundé points out, 'writing requires a certain state of mind, a psychological predisposition, inner peace and a serene soul'.

Notes

1. Karl Obeng, 'Université de Yaoundé I: Jean Messi ferme les portes aux 'allogënes'' in Le Messager, No. 563, 25 November 1996.
2. Annals of the conference-debate on 'La démocratie l'épreuve du tribalisme', Yaoundé Hilton Hotel, 11-12 April 1996, GERDDES-Cameroon/Fondation Friedrich Ebert, Editions Terroirs.
3. Interview in the government daily newspaper, *Cameroon Tribune*, No. 6245, December 10, 1996.
4. Cf. *Cameroon Tribune*, No. 6245, December 10, 1996.
5. Cf. *Justice and Solidarite*, the trimestrial journal of the Cameroonian Association of Woman Lawyers (ACAFEJ), No. 1, April 1996.
6. Cf. the National Report on the Evaluation of the Implementation of the Nairobi Prospective Action Strategies and the Abuja Declaration on Participatory Development, April 1994.
7. Dr. Pauline Fotso, 'Etudes scientifiques et Techniques dans la dynamique du développement: cas de la jeune fille Camerounaise'; a contribution to Femmes Scientifiques du Cameroun (FESCICA), States General of Education, Yaoundé, 22-27 May 1995.
8. Interview with *Justice et Solidarite*, the trimestrial journal of the Cameroonian Association of Woman Lawyers (ACAFEJ), No. 1, April 1996.
9. Cf. the bi-weekly newspaper, *L'Expression*, No. 84, January 21, 1997.
10. Interview with the weekly newspaper, *L'Action*, a publication of the RDPC party committee (No. 66, February 21, 1997).
11. Ambroise Kom, Education et Démocratie en Afrique: le temps des illusions, L'Harmattan, *Etudes Africaines*, pp. 131-132.
12. *Le CRAC de l'Education et de la Culture*, No. 22, February-March 1997, p. 16.
13. Interview with the author.
14. Cf. *Le Messager* (Independent bi-weekly newspaper), No. 584, February 13, 1997.
15. Augustine Makon, 'UN SEXE MARKET au Cúur du 'Quartier Latin, in *Generation*, September 1996.
16. Guiadem, open letter to the Chancellor of Yaoundé University, published in *Le Messager*, July 17, 1992.
17. See note above.
18. Nene Fadimatou, in an interview with the weekly newspaper, *Challenge Nouveau*, August 21, 1996.
19. See note above.
20. Idem.
21. *Le Messager*, October 27, 1994.
22. *Notre librairie*, No. 79.
23. *Notre librairie*, No. 118.
24. From an interview with the author.
25. Odile Biyidi is the wife of Mongo Beti. Among other activities, she has been co-publisher and editor of the journal, *Peuples Noirs, Peuples Africains* (1978-1990). Her comments are taken from an interview with the author.
26. From an interview with the author.
27. *Notre Librairie*, No. 118.
28. *Lire*, February 1997.
29. *Le Figaro*, January 25-26, 1997.
30. See note above.
31. From an interview with the author.

32. From an interview with the author.
33. Interview published in *AMINA* women's magazine, November 1996.
34. From an interview with the author.

References

Obeng, Karl (1996) 'Université de Yaoundé I : Jean Messi ferme les portes aux 'allogënes'', *Le Messager*, No. 563, 25 November 1996.

Annals of the conference-debate on 'La démocratie, l'épreuve du tribalisme', Yaoundé Hilton Hotel, 11-12 April 1996, GERDDES-Cameroon/Fondation Friedrich Ebert, Editions Terroirs, 141 pages.

Interview in the government daily newspaper, *Cameroon Tribune*, No. 6245, December 10, 1996.

Nnana Cf. *Cameroon Tribune*, No. 6245, December 10, 1996.

Appendix 1: Marie-Louise Eteki: A Woman with a Cause

On 17 January 1994, Marie-Louise Eteki granted an interview to the Cameroonian newspaper, *Le Messager*, in which she spoke of her literary activities and her political misadventures.

Le Messager: You published a book entitled *The Misery and Splendor of Democracy* in Cameroon. Can you give us a synopsis of this work which made quite a few waves at the time of its publication?

Marie Louise Eteki: The book was published in December 1987, by Harmattan in Paris; that was after Ahidjo's departure and there was considerable debate on opening up to democracy. I found that the subject was often approached superficially: you may remember, the debate was often nothing more than quarrels about the New Men, etc.

My point of view, which is still unchanged, was that people should not forget that Cameroonians have been fighting for democracy for a long time – since the 1940s in fact. I think the issue should be treated more seriously. If we look at the history of African nations, I think Cameroon has always shown a certain grandeur in its quest for democracy. It was also important to realize who had problems with the issue of democracy, because to think all Cameroonians suddenly became democratic would be to lay oneself open to serious problems. And, finally, at the time I wanted to point out the limitations of the way we were opening up to democracy to the participants involved (especially women, intellectuals, and our foreign 'friends'). At the time, people used to ask me, 'Why does a book on democracy start with a chapter on women?'. For me, it was a sort of symbolism, and also a way of showing my colours: I am a woman writer and it was important to let my readers know what my perspective was. I am always on women's side.

LM: Do you think your book helped spark the new awareness that could be seen in Cameroonians in 1990?

MLE: Well let's say I'm still trying to set the record straight because people tell me the democratic process started with events in Eastern Europe, and that the democratic movement in Africa came from the East. Even here in Cameroon, President Biya's followers think he brought democracy to the country. I am always reminding people that in Africa, and in Cameroon, there are two traditional forces. As in all communities, there are people who have privileges and fight to defend them. And then there are those who feel that the way things are organized does meet their expectations, and so they fight to change the system.

I don't really know how much impact my book had on events, but I can at least say that it helped change the language of the debate, by bringing certain concepts into use such as the rule of law and now everyone uses the expression 'a pluralistic Cameroon' The term 'totalitarian' is now commonly used to describe the authorities in African countries. Only our Western 'friends' and their followers still talk about 'authoritarianism' as if they were referring to a handful of barbarian chiefs, and not a carefully thought out system which has been set in place and maintained and whose consequences we are now beginning to see.

LM: At the time you conceived your book and actually wrote and published it, all around you people were publishing *Paul Biya's Social Concept, Democratic Intent*, etc., in an environment where hagiography was prized above realism. Speaking as an intellectual woman, how did that make you feel?

MLE: I think that is a matter of personal commitment. Ever since I was old enough to think for myself, I have been fighting against everything I disagree with in our society.

When there was a new president in Cameroon, I went to see Mongo Beti in Paris with a draft of a fictionalized account of Ahidjo's departure. He asked the same question. He was very surprised that a Cameroonian woman like myself wanted to meet him. He asked me, 'How did a Cameroonian woman, married and living in Cameroon, manage to write a document like this?'.

Actually, it is a matter of commitment, but also of family tradition. It also helped that I went to university in France at a time when the African student union movement was still very dynamic. There were files on practically all of us and when we came back [to Cameroon] we were subjected to a lot of harassment. I had no choice but to react to the way the political authorities hijacked the debate. And I found it strange that they talked about opening up to democracy while the whole repressive system remained unchanged. Jean Marc Ela helped me a lot because he took the responsibility of sending my manuscript to Paris. At the time, I had also sent my manuscript to Henry Bandolo who was part of the political movement in favour of democratization. He sent it to the Ministry of Territorial Administration, who read it and sent him a note saying it couldn't be published because it dealt too harshly with France. When my father died in Brazzaville on 18 December 1984, he had the manuscript in his case because we had discussed it just the week before and he had tried to convince me to tone it down a little.

When the book was published, I was not personally harassed. Certain people took the risk of writing articles in the Cameroon Tribune, giving interviews on the radio and news flashes on television; they also published articles in other magazines. I received a wonderful letter from a woman in Douala.

The attacks, one could almost say the annihilation, were much subtler.

Appendix 2: Letter from Bamiléké Students to Paul Biya

To His Excellency,
The President of the Republic of Cameroon,
We Bamiléké students are honoured to write to your Excellency on the matter of the discrimination faced by students and teachers form the Western province.

This discrimination has presently reached levels never before seen in the history of our young Republic. Your Excellency permitting, we will clarify our position by illustrating it with examples taken from our universities.

I - Appointment of Administrative Authorities

Only one of the six university Rectors in Cameroon is Bamiléké.

There are no Bamiléké Assistant Rectors, General Secretaries, or Directors of Academic Affairs.

Of thirty heads of institutes (deans and directors) in Cameroon's six universities, only two (or 6 per cent) come from the West. Furthermore, by some coincidence, both are at the University of Dshang.

The discrimination is all the more striking if we examine each university separately.

Yaoundé I University

Out of approximately thirty high-ranking administrators in Yaoundé I University (from the position of rector to that of department head), there is only one Bamiléké, for a level of representation of 3 per cent.

Despite the fact that over 55 per cent of the teachers are from the West, the highest position occupied by a Bamiléké in the university is that of department head.

Yaoundé II University

Not one central administrator in this university hails from the Western province. Out of the five heads of institutes in the university, there is not a single Bamiléké. Only at the very bottom of the hierarchy are there two Bamiléké department heads.

As at Yaoundé I University, out of thirty administrative-level positions, two are held by people from the West, for a level of representation of 6 per cent, despite the fact that more than 50 per cent of the teaching staff is from the West.

Douala University

Douala is a cosmopolitan city, and more than half of its inhabitants come from the Western province. However, the position of the Bamiléké in that university is far from enviable.

There are no Bamiléké in top administrative positions.

As in the Yaoundé universities, the highest position held by a Bamiléké is department head (assistant management), despite the fact that here, as elsewhere, the majority of teachers and students are Bamiléké. Here as in Yaoundé, out of thirty administrators, two are Bamiléké and they are at the bottom of the hierarchy.

Ngaoundéré University

This university appears to have completely forgotten that there are any Bamiléké in the country. There are no Bamiléké on the administrative team.

University of Dshang

Here, the Bamiléké population is somewhat represented, perhaps to make up for their exclusion from the other universities. However, this justification does not stand up to serious analysis. Although two faculties of the university are in the hands of The Bamiléké, it is nonetheless true that the most important and only viable faculty is governed by a non-Bamiléké.

II - Harassment of All Kinds

Even when they hold important positions, the Bamiléké are targeted with all sorts of harassment and humiliations.

At Ngaoundéré University, an assistant professor was named assistant dean of a faculty that had no dean (merely because he was Bamiléké).

Also at Ngaoundéré, the Faculty of Legal and Political Science has no dean and no assistant dean, although there is a teacher capable of occupying the position (unfortunately, he is also a Bamiléké).

At Douala University, the Faculty of Legal and Political Science has no dean because the assistant dean, who has been acting as de facto dean for the last three years cannot be instated into the position since he is Bamiléké.

Again at Douala, a non-Bamiléké with no experience in administrative positions was appointed acting dean, simply because he is not a Bamiléké (this situation is both humiliating and vexing for his colleague at the Faculty of Legal and Political Science).

We could continue these examples endlessly in order to attract your attention to the highly frustrating situation experienced by Bamiléké students in today's Cameroon.

Bamiléké students face constant discrimination at all levels of university life: we are always presumed guilty. Whenever an incident takes place at the university, suspicion is immediately turned on the Bamiléké.

Nowadays, in order to score points with those in power, the university authorities feel obliged to take action against the Bamiléké.

Over 90 per cent of the students expelled from Cameroonian universities are from the Western province. Almost all teachers brought up before the disciplinary committee come from the West. Any pretext is seized to humiliate or ridicule teachers merely because they are Bamiléké.

Your Excellency, you complain that the Bamiléké do not support your policies. Under the circumstances we have described here, how could they support you? The young people we represent have the distinct impression that all your policies are directed against the Bamiléké.

You systematically grant precedence to minority groups to the detriment of the majority. The protection of the minority should not mean the dictatorship of the minority. The attempt to exclude the Bamiléké from the political sphere in our country can lead nowhere.

We are determined to defend our rights and our privileges. So far, we have kept a low profile, hoping the situation will lead you to modify your policy concerning us.

You yourself have declared that a few years ago, you were the best pupil in the school of democracy. How can you not comprehend that your policy means suicide for our country?

If this policy of exclusion and segregation of the Bamiléké is not abandoned, we will consider ourselves obliged to:

1 – Ensure that no Bamiléké or sympathizers vote for you or your party.

2 – Ensure that people from the West actively support any political movement that will take all the ethnic groups in the country into consideration.

We remind you that no country can develop and live in peace while it flouts the legitimate interests of the majority of the population.

Yours respectfully.

Copies:Prime Minister, Minister of Higher Education, LAAKAM, Western RDPC Officials (Rassemblement Démocratique du Peuple Camerounais (Democratic Union of the Cameroonian People), the party in power.

Source: The July 25, 1996 issue of the weekly newspaper, *Challenge Nouveau*.

Table 1: Books by Women Authors Published by CLE

Author	Title	Published	Genre
Lydie Dooh Bunya	Brise du jour (Day Breeze)	1977. 350 pages	Novel
Delphine Zanga Tsogo	Vies de femmes (Women's Lives)	1983. 122 pages	Novel
Virginie Belibi	Vers enivrants (Intoxicating Verse)	1987. 116 pages	Poetry
Rabiatou Njoya	La Dernière Aimée (The Last Sweetheart)	1980. 64 pages	Play
Damaris Mounlon	L'Infirmier et la santé Communautaire (Nurses and Community Health)	1979. 384 pages	Health & hygiene
Louise Eboule Ndoumbe	Guide de la Lecture (A Guide to Reading)	1988. 64 pages	Textbook
Georgina Tsala Clemenaon with Cameroonian teachers	*Lire et écrire ‡ la maternelle (Reading and Writing in Preschool) (student manual)	1994. 82 pages	Textbook
	*Lire et écrire a la maternelle (teacher's guide)	1994. 82 pages	Textbook

Source: Editions CLE. (Centre de Littérature Evangélique), Yaoundé.

Table 2: An Incomplete List of Cameroonian Women Authors Published by Companies Other Than CLE

Author	Title	Published	Genre
Thérèse Kuoh Moukouri	Rencontres essentielles (Essential Encounters)	Paris, Imprimerie Edgar, 1969	Novel
Philomène Bassek	La t.che de sang (A Spot of Blood)	L'Harmattan, 1990 (Coll. Encres noires)	Novel
Calixthe Beyala	C'est le soleil qui m'a br lée (Burned by the sun)	Stock, 1987	Novel
	Tu t'appeleras Tanga (And you shall be called Tanga)	Stock, 1988	Novel
	C'est le soleil qui m'a brlée (Only the Devil Knew)	J'ai lu, 1988	Novel
	Seul le diable le savait (Only the Devil Knew)	Le pré aux Clercs, 1990	Novel
	Le petit Prince de Belleville (The Little Prince of Belleville)	Albin Michel, 1992	Novel
	Maman a un amant (Mama has a lover)	Albin Michel, 1993	Novel
	Assézé l'Africaine (Asséze, an African Woman)	Albin Michel, 1994	Novel
	Lettre d'une Africaine ses sûurs occidentales (Letter from an African to her Western Sisters)	Spengler, 1995	Essay
	Les Honneurs Perdus (Lost Honours)	Albin Michel, 1996	Novel
Werewere Liking	Elle sera de jaspe et de Corail: journal d'une misovire (She shall be of Jasper and Coral. Diary of a Man-hater)	L'Harmattan, 1983	Novel
	L'amour cents vies (A Hundred Lives of Love)	PubliSud, 1988	Novel
	Une nouvelle terre: ritual d'investiture d'un nouveau village (suivi de) Du sommeil d'injustice: thé.tre rituel (Introduction by Marie-José Hourantier) (A New Land: Ritual for Inhabiting a New Village, followed by From the Sleep of Injustice: Ritual Theater)	Abidjan, Nouvelles Editions Africains	Plays
	Orphée – Dafric (suivi de Orphée d'Atrique, thé.tre rituel de Mandjock Manuma) (Orpheus Ovafricka, followed by Orpheus of Africa, a ritual play by Mandjock Manuma)	L'Harmattan, 1981	Plays
	Les mains veulent dire, suivi de La rougeole arc-en-ciel (thé.tre rituel) (What Hands Say, followed by Rainbow Measles, ritual plays)	Abidjan Nouvelles Editions Africains, 1986	Plays
	Un touareg s'est marié à une pygmee: épopée n'vet pour une Afrique presente (A Tuareg married a Pygmy: a N'vet Epic for Today's Africa)	Carniéres EDS Lansman (Belgium)	Play
Rabiatou Njoya	'La porteuse d'eau' 'The Water Bearer' in D. Aioa, R. Njoya, D. Miaffo and J. Kouakam	Douala, Africavenir, 1991, p. 13 - 21	Short story
Martine Kapko	La feuille d'ordonnance d'un cordonnier immigré Prescription for an Immigrant Cobbler	La Pensée Universelle, 1986	Novel
Marie Louise Kapche	'Les FantÛmes de PhilomÈne' (Philomène's Ghosts) in Quinze nouvelles d (Fifteen Short Stories by)	SEGHER, 1989	Short Story
Zanga Tsogo	L'oiseau en cage (The Caged Bird)	EDICEF, 1983	Youth
Marie Claire Daiti	Les Ecarlates (The Scarlet)	Yaoundé, Sopecam, 1992	Poetry

Table 2: continued

Marguerite Eko Ebongue	Comptines, Poésie, Chants (Rhymes, Poetry, Songs)	Yaoundé, CEPER, 1990	Poetry
Evelyne Mpoudi Ngolle	Sous la Cendre le Feu (Fire Under the Ashes)	L'Harmattan, 1990	Novel
Axelle Kabou	Et si l'Afrique refusait le développement (What if Africa Said No to Development)	L'Harmattan, 1991	Essay
Marie-Charlotte Mbarga Kouma	Les insatiables : La famille africaine (The Insatiable African Family)	Yaoundé, Sopecam Editions, 1984 coll Espaces Littéraires	Play
Marie Louise Eteki Otabela	Misère et grandeur de la démocratie au Cameroun (The Misery and Splendor of Democracy in Cameroon)	L'Harmattan, 1987	Essay
Paulette Beat Songue	Prostitution en Afrique : L'exemple de Yaoundé (Prostitution in Africa: The Yaoundé Example)	L'Harmattan, 1993	Sociol. Essay
	SIDA et Prostitution au Cameroun (AIDS and Prostitution in Cameroon)	L'Harmattan, 1986	

Sources: *Notre Librairie*, Issue 118, July – September 1994 and author's compilation

Table 3: Distribution of Students in Grandes Ecoles by School and Sex, 1986-1991

Grandes écoles and vocational training schools	1986/1987		1990/1991	
	male (%)	female(%)	male(%)§	female(%)
Ecole Normale Supérieure	78.4	21.6	76.7	23.3
Ecole Polytechnique	97.0	3.0	97.9	2.1
CUSS	80.9	19.1	85.0	15.0
ESSTIC	86.0	14.0	79.3	21.7
IRIC	80.6	19.4	82.1	17.9
ENAM	86.7	13.3	93.2	6.8
Ecole des Travaux Publics	98.9	1.1	98.9	1.1
Ecole des postes	92.4	7.6	77.6	22.4
INADER	93.5	6.5	88.7	11.3
ENSIAAC	96.3	3.7	97.3	2.7
ENSET	75.3	24.7	73.5	26.5
ESSEC	89.1	10.9	91.4	8.6
BTS	49.6	50.4	53.9	46.0
ASTI	75.5	24.5	87.9	12.1
Ecoles d'agriculture	74.2	25.8	86.3	13.7
Ecole des infirmiers	67.5	32.5	69.5	30.5
INJS	89.3	10.7	85.1	14.9

Source: school statistics from 1987 and 1991

Comments: Out of 17 schools, ten saw increases in the percentage of woman students. However, it should be noted that there has been a decline in the percentage of women in the medical schools. The proportion of women in science remains unchanged. Women's limited access to technical training is a factor of constraint. The female grassroots population is hardest to reach with appropriate technology. The number of women teachers in the scientific field has risen only slightly since 1985. An association of women scientists has been created and is working to make women and girls more aware of their role as contributors to development. (An excerpt from the National Report on the Evaluation of the Implementation of the Nairobi Prospective Action Strategies and the Abuja Declaration on Participatory Development, April 1994).

Abbreviations used in the table: CUSS = Centre Universitaire des Science de la Santé (University Centre for Medical Science), which became the Faculty of Medicine and Biomedical Science in 1993. ESSTIC = Ecole Supérieure des Sciences et Techniques de l'Information et de la Communication (Superior Institute of Information and Communication Science and Technology). IRIC = Institut des Relations Internationales du Cameroun (Cameroonian Institute of International Relations). ENAM = Ecole National de l'Administration et de la Magistrature (National School of Administration and Magistracy) ENSET = Ecole Normale Supérieure d'Enseignement Technique (Grande Ecole for the Training of Polytechnic Teachers) ESSEC = Ecole Supérieure des Sciences Economiques et Commerciales (Institute of Economic and Business Science). BTS = Brevet de Technicien Supérieur (Vocational Training Certificate) INJS = Institut National de la Jeunesse et des Sports (National Youth and Sports Institute) INADER = Institut National pour le Développement Rural (National Institute for Rural Development). ENSIAAC = Ecole Normale Supérieure des Industries Agro-Alimentaires du Cameroun ('grande école' for training in the farm-produce industry). ASTI = Advanced School of Translation and Interpretation.